研究生"十四五"规划精品系列教材

Quality Graduate Teaching Materials for the 14th Five-Year Plan of Xi'an Jiaotong University

新闻编译入门
Approach to News Transediting

主审 陈向京
主编 楚建伟
参编 赵晓英 吴 萍

图书在版编目(CIP)数据

新闻编译入门 / 楚建伟主编. -- 西安：西安交通大学出版社，2024.12. -- ISBN 978-7-5605-9372-2

Ⅰ.G210

中国国家版本馆CIP数据核字第2024V038J5号

新闻编译入门
XINWEN BIANYI RUMEN

主　　编	楚建伟
责任编辑	庞钧颖
责任校对	李　蕊
装帧设计	伍　胜

出版发行	西安交通大学出版社 （西安市兴庆南路1号 邮政编码710048）
网　　址	http://www.xjtupress.com
电　　话	（029）82668357 82667874（市场营销中心） （029）82668315（总编办）
传　　真	（029）82668280
印　　刷	西安五星印刷有限公司

开　　本	787mm×1092mm 1/16　印张　15.75　字数　344千字
版次印次	2024年12月第1版　2024年12月第1次印刷
书　　号	ISBN 978-7-5605-9372-2
定　　价	49.00元

如发现印装质量问题，请与本社市场营销中心联系。

订购热线：（029）82665248　（029）82667874

投稿热线：（029）82668531

版权所有　侵权必究

前　言

《新闻编译入门》是西安交通大学研究生"十四五"规划精品教材。本教材以教育部 2020 年发布的普通高等学校翻译专业教学指南为指导，以提高学生新闻翻译实践能力和跨文化交际能力为目标，着重培养学生对新闻传播价值的判断力和翻译职业素养，引导学生辨析和正确处理国际新闻报道中的意识形态，在翻译实践中增强对外传播意识，提高话语自信和讲好中国故事的能力。

本教材以目标为导向，以案例为抓手，按照"整体–部分–整体"的顺序解析新闻语篇的特点、编译原则和方法，通过案例分析和编译实践，帮助学习者充分理解和掌握新闻编译的原理和技巧，提高新闻编译的实践能力和对外传播意识，为将来从事新闻翻译、国际传播等工作打下良好的基础。教材共九章，包括三大部分：第一部分即第一章为导论，概述新闻编译的概念和特点；第二部分为"英汉新闻编译"，包括第二章至第五章；第六章至第九章为第三部分，即"汉英新闻编译"。第二部分和第三部分均涉及新闻语篇的基本知识、新闻各部分的编译要点以及不同题材新闻语篇的编译方法，内容循序渐进、逐步展开，并提供大量案例分析和相关练习。各章所选案例均来自国内外主流媒体网站发布的新闻报道，授课教师可根据教学进度和内容安排选择使用。

具体而言，本教材的编写特色体现在如下方面：

·案例丰富，突出实践。本教材以提高学生编译实践能力为目的，从新闻编译案例入手，将理论与实践紧密结合，使学生置身于真实的新闻编译实践场景，训练学生在编译实践中独立思考、科学删减、调整逻辑、打磨标题，掌握新闻编译方法。

·题材广泛，融入思政。选入本教材的新闻案例涉及政治、经济、科技、文化、教育、社会、体育等不同领域，题材广泛。编者在甄选编译素材时也考虑到思政元素的融入，在训练学生新闻编译能力的同时，培养学生的全球视野、家国情怀和社会责任感，帮助学生在新闻编译实践中增强话语自信，提高对外传播的意识和讲好中国故事的能力。

·选材新颖，分析详尽。本教材按照选新、选精、选典型的原则确定新闻编译素材，并提供了丰富的编译案例及详细的分析点评，以帮助学生更好地理解和掌握新闻编译的逻辑和方法，内容编排由浅入深、循序渐进，具有针对性、系统性和科学性。

本教材由新闻编译课程组精心编写而成，可作为高等院校新闻编译课的配套教材，也可满足翻译专业、新闻传播专业的教学需求，对新闻翻译和写作感兴趣的学生及广大英语学习者亦可参阅、使用本教材。在教材的编写过程中，我们获得了新闻业内专家、西安交通大学外国语学院的老师及其他高校专家、同行的鼎力支持和帮助，在此向各位专家、同行表示衷心感谢。我们在编写教材的过程中还参阅了大量相关文献及已发表的新闻稿件，在此也向所有相关人员致以深深谢意；教材中所选的新闻稿在体例、格式上都尽量保留了各新闻社或媒体的自身风格。此外，许多同学也为本教材的编写提供了宝贵的反馈意见，在此也向你们表示感谢。

本教材虽经反复讨论与打磨，但由于编者才疏学浅，加之时间仓促，书中不妥之处和谬误在所难免，恳请学界各位专家、学者及广大读者朋友提出宝贵的批评、修改意见和建议。

编 者

2024 年 8 月

目 录

第一部分 导 论

第一章 新闻编译概述 ·· 3
- 第一节 认识新闻编译 ·· 3
- 第二节 新闻编译的特点 ·· 8

第二部分 英汉新闻编译

第二章 英汉新闻编译概述 ·· 13
- 第一节 英汉新闻编译的选题 ·· 13
- 第二节 英语新闻报道的写作特点 ···································· 15
- 第三节 英汉新闻编译的原则 ·· 21
- 第四节 英语新闻报道的文体结构 ···································· 25
- 第五节 英汉新闻编译的步骤和方法 ·································· 42

第三章 英语新闻标题和导语的编译 ·································· 52
- 第一节 英语新闻标题的编译 ·· 52
- 第二节 英语新闻导语的编译 ·· 56

第四章 英语新闻正文的编译 ·· 72
- 第一节 英语新闻报道正文的文体特征 ································ 72
- 第二节 英语新闻报道正文的编译方法 ································ 73

第五章 不同题材的英语新闻编译 ···································· 87
- 第一节 灾难类新闻的编译 ·· 87
- 第二节 政治类新闻的编译 ·· 104
- 第三节 经济类新闻的编译 ·· 116
- 第四节 科技类新闻的编译 ·· 133
- 第五节 教育类新闻的编译 ·· 146
- 第六节 社会类新闻的编译 ·· 156

第三部分　汉英新闻编译

第六章　汉英新闻编译概述 ……………………………………………………… 169
 第一节　汉英新闻编译和对外新闻报道 ………………………………………… 169
 第二节　汉英新闻编译的选题和选材 …………………………………………… 172
 第三节　汉英新闻编译的原则 …………………………………………………… 177
 第四节　英语新闻稿的行文体例 ………………………………………………… 180

第七章　汉英新闻标题和导语的编译 …………………………………………… 185
 第一节　汉英新闻标题的编译原则 ……………………………………………… 185
 第二节　汉英新闻导语的编译原则 ……………………………………………… 186

第八章　汉语新闻正文的编译 …………………………………………………… 200
 第一节　汉英新闻正文对比 ……………………………………………………… 200
 第二节　汉语新闻正文的编译要点 ……………………………………………… 200

第九章　不同题材的汉语新闻编译 ……………………………………………… 212
 第一节　灾难类新闻的编译 ……………………………………………………… 212
 第二节　政治类新闻的编译 ……………………………………………………… 214
 第三节　政策类新闻的编译 ……………………………………………………… 220
 第四节　文化类新闻的编译 ……………………………………………………… 222
 第五节　社会类新闻的编译 ……………………………………………………… 225
 第六节　经济类新闻的编译 ……………………………………………………… 228
 第七节　科技类新闻的编译 ……………………………………………………… 232
 第八节　教育类新闻的编译 ……………………………………………………… 238
 第九节　体育类新闻的编译 ……………………………………………………… 241

参考文献 …………………………………………………………………………… 245

第一部分

导 论

第一章

新闻编译概述

第一节 认识新闻编译

阅读以下两组新闻稿及其编译稿，对比观察新闻稿与编译稿之间的不同。

◎新闻稿 1

UK faces puppy shortage as demand for lockdown companions soars[1]

Daniel Thomas MAY 22 2020

The UK is facing a puppy shortage as demand for new pets among lonely workers and harassed families forced to stay at home during the pandemic sends prices for the animals soaring.

Breeders report that demand for new dogs has risen sharply since the start of the lockdown, with prices being quoted at twice the level before the coronavirus outbreak and waiting lists for new puppies increasing fourfold.

With millions of people now working from home or on extended furlough from their careers, many families are reviving long-held dreams to have a pet to keep them company on socially distanced walks.

"There is unprecedented demand," said Bill Lambert, head of health and welfare at the Kennel Club, which operates the national register of pedigree dogs.

Inquiries through its puppy portal increased 140 per cent in April compared with last year, said Mr. Lambert, who is also a dog breeder. "Normally I get one or two inquiries a month but now it's four or five a day."

He said breeders had reported waiting lists for puppies increasing from 100 to 400 people. "Those waiting lists are all full now. People will have to wait as the initial supply has been taken up."

---

1 新闻稿来源：https://www.ft.com。

Dog buyers are being advised to seek out credible dog owners who treat breeding puppies as a hobby, rather than for commercial gain.

The Royal Society for the Prevention of Cruelty to Animals (RSPCA) reported a 600 per cent increase in visits to its dog fostering pages, and a rise of 30 per cent in its find-a-pet section.

Adam Levy, regional manager at pets charity Dogs Trust, said: "We know there is a shortage of pups in the UK — demand is just not met by UK breeders and rehomes."

Crossbreeds, such as cockapoos, which are seen as easier to look after, have been in particular demand, while among pure breeds there has been a sharp rise in popularity of French bulldogs.

Dog charities said the high demand had fuelled a darker side to the puppy trade. Mr. Lambert warned there was evidence of "profiteering" among sellers, although numbers were difficult to show given the "cottage industry" of dog breeding.

One buyer from Kent, who did not wish to be named, agreed to pay £1,000 for a dog before lockdown but was asked to stump up an extra £800 on pick-up day or lose out to another buyer. This was despite putting down a deposit two months earlier.

Mr. Lambert said buyers should seek out credible dog owners, who treat breeding puppies as a hobby, rather than for commercial gain. "We have heard that prices are being ramped up."

Owen Sharp, chief executive of Dogs Trust, said the number of people looking for dogs on its site had more than doubled. He raised concerns around puppy farming and smuggling, as buyers look outside registered breeders.

Mr. Levy noted that there had been a "tremendous amount of dogs brought into the UK", in particular from Romania. These have been able to travel during the lockdown because they are often brought in on commercial transport.

He added that a large number of pregnant dogs had been brought to the UK, which allows gangs to sell the pups when they arrive. "There is a lot of money to be made. These are often criminal gangs. It's a very lucrative business with few penalties."

Dog charities also worry that many unwanted dogs will be handed back when people need to return to work after the pandemic eases. Mr. Sharp said he had already "seen examples of people looking to return dogs because they're going back to work". He urged buyers to consider their long-term plans over home working, given their pets' needs. He warned that dogs could suffer from separation anxiety if they had grown used to lots of attention.

Peter Pritchard, chief executive of Pets at Home, which has seen strong demand for pet food and equipment, said: "People have had an awful lot more time. I have never seen as many dog walkers in my life." But, he stressed, buyers should remember that a "dog is not just for lockdown, it's for life".

编译稿

价格飙升供不应求，疫情"宅家"带动英国宠物狗市场

新冠疫情来袭，受封城令限制，英国人只能宅在家中，这让很多人更渴望养只狗狗来陪伴自己。眼下英国宠物狗供不应求，价格甚至翻了一番。

据英国《金融时报》22日报道，英国养犬协会的健康和福利负责人兰伯特表示，4月来协会咨询的人较去年同期上涨140%，排队等着领养幼犬的人从100人增至400人。而英国皇家防止虐待动物协会的工作人员也表示，协会养犬页面浏览量增加6倍。目前最受欢迎的是法国斗牛犬，其价格也随之飙升，供不应求，狗贩子从欧洲走私大量幼犬到英国售卖，以谋取利益。英国慈善机构警告称，由于人们只是寻找一时的心理安慰，疫情结束后，大量狗狗可能会被遗弃，希望人们在领养狗狗后要善待它们。

◎ **新闻稿2**

高校为新生提前匹配舍友，吃螺蛳粉、社恐有人陪了？[1]

中国青年报　2022-08-24　08:15　发表于北京

近日，"成都大学用算法推荐为新生匹配舍友"的消息，引发热议。

据@成都大学消息，8月23日，2022级新生开始网络预报到。在该校的互联网迎新系统中，新生可以填写在线问卷，由学校匹配兴趣爱好和生活习惯等相近的室友。在@成都大学发布的问卷截图中，包括"你是社牛还是社恐""你睡觉时是否打呼噜""你是否接受榴梿、螺蛳粉等异味食品"等问题。记者注意到，除了"精准推荐"室友，在迎新系统中，新生还可以自选床位。

据九派新闻消息，该校学生宿舍管理中心一工作人员称，这种"大数据选房"，是从2020年开始筹划的，今年起正式实行。选房系统会根据本班优先、同专业次之、同学院再次之的方式来推荐，精准推荐3名室友。

1　新闻稿来源：https://baijiahao.baidu.com。

对此，不少网友表示支持，还有网友为社恐新生担忧，社恐一定会被分在一起吗？问卷调查会决定宿舍分配吗？

成都大学宿管中心社区党建负责人王彩燕表示，在填写调查问卷后，系统生成的结果只是推荐、建议，具体要不要根据建议去选择，同学们可以视自身情况而定。

其实，不只是成都大学，此前，"上海交通大学可互选室友"的消息，也曾引发广泛关注。对此，有媒体评论称：互选室友的人性化管理举措，确实有亮点。不过，算法再先进，也不能保证选到的室友就一定能和自己志同道合，毕竟人的个性、品质是复杂的，人与人之间的相处和交流，更是一门学问。哪怕是精挑细选出来的室友，与之朝夕相处同样离不开尊重、理解、包容。说到底，不管在大学校园里遇到什么样的室友，都是一种难得的缘分，值得年轻的学子好好珍惜。你怎么看？

编译稿

Chinese university uses big data to recommend roommates to incoming freshmen

Chengdu University in the city of Chengdu, capital of southwest China's Sichuan Province, recently started to implement an innovative online system to help students who are going to study at the university soon to choose roommates and beds, the WeChat account of China Youth Daily reported on Wednesday.

The video grab shows the university's online pre-enrollment system. (Source: WeChat account of the Information Office of the People's Government of Chengdu)

After students fill in a questionnaire on the university's online pre-enrollment system, the university will recommend fellow peers who have the similar hobbies, interests, and living habits to them as their potential roommates.

Students are asked to answer questions including whether they are good at or afraid of socializing, whether they snore in their sleep, and whether they mind someone eating food with a strong smell, such as durian and river snail rice noodles, in their dormitory.

Besides recommending roommates, the system also allows students to select their beds.

The university began the planning for such a system capable of enabling students to choose roommates and select beds with the help of big data analysis in 2020, according to a staff member at the university's student dormitory management center.

With the online registration of freshmen starting on Aug. 23, the system was officially launched, the staff member said, adding that the system recommends three roommates to each student and that the recommendations are made according to an order of precedence as follows: classmates, students studying the same major, and students in the same faculty.

Nevertheless, the roommates recommended by the system are merely a suggestion, students can decide whether they want to follow the suggestion according to their own situation, said Wang Caiyan, an executive at the university's student dormitory management center.

编译其实就是编辑与翻译的有机结合，是编中有译、译中有编的活动，新闻编译是翻译人员对一篇或几篇原新闻稿进行加工而产生一篇新的稿件，从而进行二次传播。

在我国，新闻编译可以追溯到19世纪30年代。1833年8月1日普鲁士传教士郭士立（Karl Friedrich August Gützlaff）在中国广州创办了《东西洋考每月统记传》（*Eastern Western Monthly Magazine*），这是在中国内地出版的第一份中文近代报刊（月刊），内容主要是科学文化知识、宗教、伦理道德、新闻等。该报文字通俗，文风简短，尽可能与中国文化相吻合，每期刊登的新闻绝大部分是编者翻译加工外刊中的国际新闻，可被视为国际新闻外译中的开端。

1917年5月1日，《申报》驻京特派记者邵飘萍创办了新闻编译社，这是中国早期的民办通讯社，只有少数工作人员，这些工作人员主要编译外电，也自己采写一些当地新闻，比较有独立性，发布消息也较迅捷。

在革命战争年代，新闻编译也是一项重要的工作。1931年11月7日红中社在江西瑞金成立，这便是新华社的前身。中华人民共和国成立初期，新华社开始承担起收集和翻译国内外通讯社电讯的任务。此外，国家还设立了多个专门的翻译机构，如国际新闻局和中共中央编译局等，这些机构在对外宣传和国际交往中发挥了非常重要的作用。

改革开放以来，中国的新闻出版行业发展迅速，新闻编译领域也日益扩大。在互联网广泛普及的背景下，新闻媒体技术日新月异，促使新闻编译事业逐步迈向国际化与数字化的崭新阶段。

1989年，国际知名学者卡伦·斯戴汀（Karen Stetting）将英文中的translating（翻译）和editing（编辑）两个概念合二为一，提出了"transediting"（编译）的概念。《中国翻译词典》则将"编译"定义为译者把一个甚至几个文本的相关内容进行编辑加工，根据要求进行概述性的翻译的活动，编译者"集翻译与编辑于一身"。

法裔加拿大学者让－保罗·维奈（Jean-Paul Vinay）和让·达贝尔内（Jean Darbelnet）认为，当译语文化情境与原语情境不一致或是语义有差异时，往往要采用编译的形式，使译文在功能上对等。他们将这种翻译形式称为非直接的翻译，即译文并非照搬原文的结构与概念。

英国著名翻译家和翻译理论家彼得·纽马克（Peter Newmark）认为，编译属于交际翻译，是一种最自由的翻译形式，其目的是努力使译文对目的语读者所产生的效果与原文对源语读者所产生的效果相同。

我国著名学者刘其中教授曾在新华社和《中国日报社》等知名媒体工作，他这样定义新闻编译：新闻编译是通过翻译和编辑的手段，将用原语写成的新闻转化、加工为译语语言新闻的翻译方法。其实，从某种意义上来说，国际新闻的编译就是一种跨文化传播活动，对于增强跨文化交流和理解、推动国际合作、促进中外文明互鉴意义非凡。

本书所讲授的新闻编译主要包括英汉新闻编译和汉英新闻编译，前者是翻译工作人员将英语新闻编译为汉语新闻，为国内读者提供所需要的各种信息，以了解国际大事、经济发展、社会文化生活等；而后者则是翻译人员把在中国发生、与中国有关的新闻事件编译成英语新闻，供国外读者阅读，以了解中国的社会文化、经济生活等。

第二节　新闻编译的特点

一、新闻编译具有明确的目的性

新闻编译是对新闻的二次传播，要考虑受众的特点及需求。由于目标受众具有不同的社会文化背景，编译时要有选择性地针对特定的要求或环境传递信息，编译后的新闻信息与原文并不完全等值，而新闻报道的客观性要求编译人员尽可能还原事情的本来面貌，因此在编译中要避免被原文报道中的个人情感因素所干扰，避免原文报道中的主观因素在目标读者群中造成误会或产生歧义。

二、新闻编译具有新闻报道的客观性、准确性和时效性

新闻报道是一项对准确性和客观性要求极高的工作，新闻工作者必须在短时间内迅速、客观且尽可能准确地进行报道，将国内、国际发生的新闻事件传递给广大观众和读者。作为承担二次传播任务的新闻编译人员，也必须始终保持严肃、谨慎的态度。由于新闻发布的时间极其紧迫，新闻编译人员不可能做到对新闻报道进行细致入微的精雕细琢。但是，新闻报道的准确性要求新闻编译人员应该尽其所能核实消息的来源和真实性。"新"是新闻的属性，即我们经常提及的"时效性"。新闻一旦失去了时效性，就无法取得及时的社会效果，甚至完全失去了发表或播出的价值。

三、新闻编译稿具有与源语新闻大致相同的新闻文风

不同语言的新闻报道写作方式存在差异，因此，新闻编译人员必须要敏锐地捕捉这种区别，并且保证用译语语言编译出来的新闻与源语新闻的内容保持一致，同时具有与源语新闻大致相同的新闻文风。

四、新闻编译具有跨文化的传播属性

国际新闻编译从根本上来讲是一种跨文化传播行为，新闻编译由于身份特殊而被赋予了新闻学和翻译学方面的不同定义，从而使得新闻编译呈现出了多个学科融合的态势。新闻编译工作人员通过创造无障碍的信息沟通和传递方式，实现信息的跨文化国际传播。

第二部分

英汉新闻编译

第二章

英汉新闻编译概述

第一节 英汉新闻编译的选题

> 新闻编译人员需要对哪些新闻稿件进行编译？新闻编译的选题如何确定？请写出 3 条你感兴趣的国际新闻标题。
> (1) _____
> (2) _____
> (3) _____

英汉新闻编译要把英语新闻报道编译成汉语，因而需要考虑汉语受众的需求，同时新闻编译的选题与新闻的价值要素密切相关。

> 阅读以下新闻话题，并根据你的兴趣对这些话题进行排序。
> □ 日本核污染水排海
> □ 巴以冲突 / 乌克兰危机
> □ 冬季达沃斯论坛（世界经济论坛）
> □ 中美高层互访
> □ 美国总统大选
> □ 美国前总统特朗普竞选集会遇刺
> □ 疫情之后旅游市场回暖
> □ 意大利某市市长提出辞职
> □ "科目三"海外流行
> □ 华为遭受美国制裁
> □ 世界杯足球赛 / 奥运会 / 电竞
> □ "霉霉"成为史上最富有女音乐家
> □ 韩国首尔梨泰院踩踏事故

☐ OpenAI 创始人奥尔特曼秘密结婚
☐ 澳大利亚森林大火
☐ 法国一小镇超市遭持枪抢劫
☐ 波音飞机事故
☐ 马斯克宣布脑机接口公司完成首例人脑设备植入手术
☐ Open AI 推出文本转视频 AI 模型 Sora：可创建长达一分钟逼真视频

新闻的价值是指新闻事实本身所包含的满足社会需求的素质的总和，是新闻传播主体衡量和选择新闻事实的重要依据。新闻的价值要素包括重要性、显著性、时效性、接近性和趣味性。

● **重要性**指新闻事实所包含的社会意义，即新闻事实同新闻受传者的利害关系。事实越重要，其社会意义和新闻价值就越大。新闻的重要性与求近（利益接近）心理相关。

● **显著性**指新闻事实的知名度，或新闻事实的显要度。

● **时效性**指新闻事实越新，就越能满足受传者的需求，越能吸引受传者的注意力。新闻发生的时距越小，受传者的求知度就越大，新闻价值也就越大。

● **接近性**指新闻事实同接受该事实信息的受传者在地理上和心理上的接近程度。

● **趣味性**指新闻事实的有趣程度，即新闻事实是否能调动新闻受传者的共同兴趣，从而引起受传者的注意。趣味性越大，新闻价值越大。

根据新闻的五个价值要素查找新闻选题，写出五个国际新闻标题及其所对应的新闻价值要素。

序号	新闻标题	新闻价值要素
1		
2		
3		
4		
5		

第二节　英语新闻报道的写作特点

阅读下面这篇新闻稿，注意稿件在语言风格、词汇、语法、语篇结构等方面的特点。

◎新闻稿

Hit game boosts sales of related products[1]

By Zhu Wenqian | China Daily | Updated: 2024-08-26 07:02

　　Personal computers, Sony Play-Station 5 consoles and other derivative products are flying off the shelves in China, fueled by the overwhelming popularity of the newly launched Chinese-made video game *Black Myth: Wukong*.

　　The action role-playing game, developed by Chinese company Game Science and inspired by the 16th century classic novel *Journey to the West*, caught the fancy of gamers even before its launch on Tuesday, triggering a buying spree for advanced gaming consoles.

　　The sales of PS5 surged over 100 percent year-on-year between Aug. 13 and Aug. 19, according to Alibaba's e-commerce platform Tmall. During the same week, the sales of other electronic products such as laptops, keyboards and headphones for esports embraced robust year-on-year growth of over 80 percent, Tmall data showed.

　　Manufacturers of electronic products such as Sony, Ipason, Razer and Logitech saw their sales increase rapidly after the game was launched, the platform said.

　　Before *Black Myth: Wukong* hit the market, domestic coffee chain Luckin Coffee introduced an Americano variant inspired by the game, as well as free limited-edition 3D posters, cup holders and other accessories upon purchase of coffee combos.

　　While the special Americano was sold out at many Luckin stores, the company ran out of the 3D posters nationwide within seconds of their launch, almost crashing its online system.

　　"The buying frenzy demonstrated by male Chinese customers, who form the bulk of the country's video game consumer base, changed our perception about their purchasing power," said Yang Fei, chief growth officer of Luckin Coffee.

　　Black Myth: Wukong, which allows players to step into the shoes of one of the

---

1　新闻稿来源：https://www.chinadaily.com.cn。

heroes of the novel, Sun Wukong, also known as the Monkey King, and navigate his epic adventures westward, sold more than 10 million copies globally within three days of its launch.

It became one of the fastest-selling video games of all time, according to VG Insights, a market research platform for video games.

新闻报道旨在快速、准确、有效地传递信息，以满足不同受众的需求，新闻英语在语言总体风格上也呈现出准确性、客观性、简洁性、生动性、可读性等特点。新闻英语的语言简洁精练，常常用非常简练的语言表达丰富的内容。具体而言，英语新闻报道的写作特点主要体现在以下方面。

一、词汇特点

1. 使用新闻体词语

新闻体词语（journalistic words）指的是那些在新闻报道中常用的特定词语，它们包括专业术语、行业内的常用语以及具有特定新闻报道风格的词语。这些词语有助于传达新闻的时效性、准确性和客观性。例如：

- breaking news 通常用于突发新闻；
- exclusive interview 表示该新闻报道是独家专访；
- alleged 用于描述被指控但尚未证实的情况，如 alleged fraud 意为"涉嫌欺诈"；
- catastrophic 用于形容极其严重的灾难或事件，如 catastrophic earthquake（灾难性地震）；
- inflation 是经济新闻中常见的术语，意思是"通货膨胀"，如 inflation rate（通货膨胀率）。
- ceasefire 经常在政治或军事报道中使用，指暂时停战，如 ceasefire agreement（停火协议）。
- sanction 经常在国际关系报道中使用，指对国家或个人实施的惩罚性经济措施，如 economic sanctions（经济制裁）。
- nadir 常指两国关系的最低点。

此外，英语新闻报道中还有一些约定俗成的套语，如 according to sources concerned（据有关方面报道），cited as saying（援引……的话）。这些新闻体词语在新闻报道中的使用，不仅有助于传达具体、准确的信息，还能增强报道的专业性和可读性。

2. 使用"小词"

小词（midget words）即简短词，一般为单音节词。小词的广泛使用一是由于报纸篇幅有限，用小词可避免移行；二是由于小词的词义范畴很广，一般比较生动灵活。在新闻英语中，这类词也被称为 synonyms of all work（万能同义词），如 back（支持）、ban（禁止）等。以下新闻稿的标题就体现了小词的特点。

A UK faces puppy shortage as demand for lockdown companions soars

B Feline good: Asthmatic cat treated with acupuncture

3. 大量使用缩略语

为了节省时间和篇幅，英语新闻报道大量使用缩略词，例如上文练习例文中的 UK（United Kingdom 英国）、AIDS（Acquired Immune Deficiency Syndrome 艾滋病）等。下文再举几类例子。

A 组织机构类

UN—United Nations 联合国

NATO—North Atlantic Treaty Organization 北大西洋公约组织

WHO—World Health Organization 世界卫生组织

WB—World Bank 世界银行

IMF—International Monetary Fund 国际货币基金组织

FBI—Federal Bureau of Investigation 美国联邦调查局

NASA—National Aeronautics and Space Administration 美国国家航空航天局

B 经济金融类

GDP—Gross Domestic Product 国内生产总值

CPI—Consumer Price Index 居民消费价格指数

IPO—Initial Public Offering 首次公开募股

NASDAQ—National Association of Securities Dealers Automated Quotations 纳斯达克（美国全国证券交易商协会自动报价表）

biz—business 商业

C 科技互联网类

AI—Artificial Intelligence 人工智能

VR—Virtual Reality 虚拟现实

5G—5th Generation Mobile Communication Technology 第五代移动通信技术

IoT—Internet of Things 物联网

D 政策法律类

ACA—Affordable Care Act 平价医疗法案

BREXIT—British Exit 英国脱欧

E 军事安全类

ICBM—Intercontinental Ballistic Missile 洲际弹道导弹

WMD—Weapons of Mass Destruction 大规模杀伤性武器

NPT—Nuclear Non-Proliferation Treaty 核不扩散条约

4. 临时造词

为了表达需要和追求新奇，新闻报道常常使用"临时造词"或"生造词"，即临时创造或拼凑起来的词或词组，例如 Unfriend (un- + friend) 指在社交媒体上删除好友；Xiconomics (Xi Jinping + economics) 指习近平经济思想；Blog (web + log) 最初来源于 web log，后简化为 blog，指网络日志；Brexit (British + Exit) 指英国脱欧；chatbot (chat + robot) 指聊天机器人；Eurosummit (Euro + summit) 指欧元区国家的首脑会议；Gen Z (generation +Z) 意思是 Z 世代，具体指在 1995 至 2009 年之间出生的一代人。

二、语法特点

1. 多使用一般现在时

英语新闻报道中广泛使用一般现在时，无论是标题或是正文都常常采用现在时代替过去时，以营造真实感、现场感。当然，根据具体的新闻事件和新闻内容，新闻报道有时也采用过去时或现在完成时。另外，复合句中的主句与从句的时态也不一定呼应、一致，而是根据新闻事态的发展灵活变化，例如 said、told、reported、added 等动词过去时后面的 that 宾语从句有时会根据情况使用现在时。例如：

A Joe Biden's core Democratic support takes big hit after debate, exclusive poll shows

President Joe Biden's core support has been shaken by his stumbling performance in last week's debate, an exclusive USA TODAY/Suffolk University Poll finds, fueling a furor over whether he should continue his candidacy.

B Can you get the flu in the summer? Your guide to warm weather illnesses

Although flu season occurs during the colder months, seasonal influenza viruses are detected throughout the entire year in the U.S., according to the Centers for Disease Control and Prevention. The public health agency also notes that "timing and duration of flu activity has been less predictable" since the onset of the CDVID-19 pandemic.

2. 多使用扩展的简单句

受报道空间和篇幅所限，英语新闻报道在语言方面的一个重要特点是句型高度扩展，将丰富的信息压缩在有限的篇幅中，句子相对较长，结构较为松散，多使用同位语、介词短语、分词短语等扩展简单句，较多使用插入语代替从句，从而简化句子结构。例如：

Biden delivered his remarks after returning from the Camp David presidential retreat in Maryland, where he spent the weekend as his reelection campaign sought to limit the fallout of Biden's disastrous debate performance last Thursday.

3. 多使用高度浓缩的前置修饰语

新闻文体为了使句子结构紧凑严密，大量使用前置修饰语修饰名词，例如：

A China's historic lunar far side samples

B two suspected hate-motivated attacks

C Wimbledon's cherished strawberries and cream image

4. 多使用直接引语和间接引语

英语新闻报道中经常使用直接引语来提供消息来源，以增加报道的可信度、真实性，使读者有身临其境的感觉。新闻稿撰写人转述或概括新闻人物所说的话时则使用间接引语，以突出信息的重点。例如：

A Israeli Prime Minister Benjamin Netanyahu said Monday the country's military is nearing the "end of the stage of eliminating" Hamas' army in Gaza.（使用间接引语）

B "I returned yesterday from a visit to the Gaza Division. I saw very considerable achievements in the fighting being carried in Rafah. We are advancing to the end of the stage of eliminating the Hamas army; we will continue striking its remnants," Netanyahu said, speaking to a group of mainly Israeli and international military officials studying at the National Security College.（使用直接引语）

5. 交替使用主动语态和被动语态

英语新闻报道中，主动语态和被动语态都很常见，但在某些情况下，根据报道内容、报道的效果，尤其是在描述敏感事件、突出强调新闻事件本身而非行动者或者需要迅速抓住读者的注意力时，新闻报道者也常用被动语态代替主动语态。

A Images show large holes through the front windows and shattered glass covering the entrance to the synagogue.（使用主动语态）

B Police confirmed the incidents are being investigated as suspected hate crimes.（使用被动语态）

三、语篇结构特点

英语新闻报道有其独特的语篇结构，通常包括标题、导语和正文三个部分。标题概括新闻内容、揭示新闻主题。导语通常是新闻的开头部分，以简练而生动的文字介绍新闻事件中最核心的内容，引导读者继续阅读，常被看作是新闻稿件最精练、最重要的部分。正文是新闻报道的主体部分，呈现更多新闻事实和细节。新闻报道的语篇结构将在本章第四节里详细介绍。

分析此篇新闻稿的特点。

◎新闻稿

Feline good: Asthmatic cat treated with acupuncture[1]

Daily Mail

A cat that suffered asthma and a cough for three years has been cured, after her owner shunned traditional treatments and gave her pet a course of acupuncture.

South African alternative therapist Virginia Sanders turned to needle-based treatment to help her eleven-year-old Siamese cat Kiki. Kiki had been given cortisone injections for her asthma but Ms. Sanders was worried this might eventually damage the moggie's liver. She approached a holistic veterinarian who recommended the unconventional treatment. 'Kiki received acupuncture treatment, which will help her body to heal itself,' Ms. Sanders said. 'She has already received three treatments, and her condition has improved a lot. She still has a few "old person's" problems, like a stiff back.'

According to vet Dr. Barry Hindmarch, alternative treatments can be used on animals to relieve skin problems, chronic arthritis, kidney problems and cat AIDS. 'Infertile horses have been treated with homeopathic methods, and even livestock like cows with infections in their udders can be treated,' he added. Hindmarch says nature's gifts are used to supplement conventional medicine. 'The animal is being treated holistically,' he says. 'We look at its medical history, natural diet, surroundings, and we try to figure out a natural option. Animals also have emotional problems. They grieve, get anxious, some get traumatized, and then it makes a big difference treating them holistically.'

---

[1] 新闻稿来源：https://www.dailymail.co.uk。

'All conventional treatment methods are exhausted before we decide on a holistic method. With alternative medication we try to improve the animal's quality of living.'

(1) 语言总体风格：_____
(2) 词汇特点：_____
(3) 语法特点：_____
(4) 语篇结构特点：_____

第三节　英汉新闻编译的原则

中国的新闻编译工作者把国外的新闻编译成汉语，主要目的是让有价值的源语新闻能够在国内进行二次传播，满足国内读者获取相关新闻信息的需求，帮助国内读者了解世界、开阔视野，从而促进国际文化交流。新闻编译是一项复杂的工作，往往对编译工作者有较高的要求。在英汉新闻编译实践中，编译者应遵循以下原则：

● **新闻编译应确保新闻事实准确无误、客观真实。**"准确""真实"是新闻的生命，因此新闻编译首先要保证信息的准确。但由于不同文化之间的差异，新闻报道有时也会带有一定的政治、历史、文化、审美等价值观的倾向性。在新闻编译过程中，编译者需对原文中的内容作适当选择，从原作中选取最有价值的内容进行编译。

● **新闻编译应忠实于原文事实和风格，做到主题明确。**主题是新闻报道的灵魂。新闻编译应紧扣原作的主题思想，在译前编辑阶段就要确定该报道的主题，随后的编辑也要始终围绕主题进行。在编译阶段，编译者不仅要做到主题鲜明，还要深化主题。

● **新闻编译者应适当增补背景信息，提高译文可读性。**新闻报道往往包含特定的语境和背景信息，编译者往往要根据不同文化背景的受众，适当增补相应的背景信息，这样更易于目标读者理解。

● **新闻编译稿应通顺、流畅、精练、逻辑性强、结构合理。**不同语言的新闻报道方式存在差异，而且新闻稿的写作结构往往因文体不同而有所区别。因此，在英汉新闻编译过程中，编译者应根据需要适当调整新闻编译稿的结构，如增加导语、改变句式或重组句子结构，以满足目标读者的阅读习惯。

分析以下新闻稿及其编译稿，判断并说明编译稿是否符合上述编译原则。

◎新闻稿 1

Feline good: Asthmatic cat treated with acupuncture[1]

Daily Mail

A cat that suffered asthma and a cough for three years has been cured, after her owner shunned traditional treatments and gave her pet a course of acupuncture.

South African alternative therapist Virginia Sanders turned to needle-based treatment to help her eleven-year-old Siamese cat Kiki. Kiki had been given cortisone injections for her asthma but Ms. Sanders was worried this might eventually damage the moggie's liver. She approached a holistic veterinarian who recommended the unconventional treatment. 'Kiki received acupuncture treatment, which will help her body to heal itself,' Ms. Sanders said. 'She has already received three treatments, and her condition has improved a lot. She still has a few "old person's" problems, like a stiff back.'

According to vet Dr. Barry Hindmarch, alternative treatments can be used on animals to relieve skin problems, chronic arthritis, kidney problems and cat AIDS. 'Infertile horses have been treated with homeopathic methods, and even livestock like cows with infections in their udders can be treated,' he added. Hindmarch says nature's gifts are used to supplement conventional medicine. 'The animal is being treated holistically,' he says. 'We look at its medical history, natural diet, surroundings, and we try to figure out a natural option. Animals also have emotional problems. They grieve, get anxious, some get traumatized, and then it makes a big difference treating them holistically.

'All conventional treatment methods are exhausted before we decide on a holistic method. With alternative medication we try to improve the animal's quality of living.'

---

[1] 新闻稿来源：https://www.dailymail.co.uk。

编译稿

南非宠物猫接受针灸治疗　哮喘咳嗽三年终见好转

据英国《每日邮报》报道，南非一只暹罗猫患有哮喘病，咳嗽了三年之久，它的主人放弃传统哮喘治疗办法改用针灸治疗后，暹罗猫的哮喘病已经大大好转。

这只11岁大的暹罗猫Kiki最先被注射可的松来治哮喘，但它的主人维吉尼亚·桑德斯女士担心这会损坏它的肝脏。后来有兽医推荐用针灸方法来治疗猫的哮喘，于是Kiki接受了针灸治疗。三次针灸治疗之后，Kiki的状况改善了很多。

据悉，三十多年来，欧洲兽医学者翻译了不少中国典籍，将动物针灸普及。大约十年前，欧美等地的兽医开始广泛使用针灸为重病动物治疗，效果显著。

◎ 新闻稿2

S. Korea administrative robot defunct after apparent suicide[1]

A city council in South Korea said Wednesday their first administrative officer robot was defunct after throwing itself down some stairs, with local media mourning the country's first robot suicide.

South Korea's Gumi City Council announced the robot was found unresponsive after having apparently fallen down a two-meter (six-and-a-half foot) staircase last week.

Witnesses saw the robot officer "circling in one spot as if something was there" before the accident occurred, but the exact cause of the fall is still being investigated, a city council official told AFP.

"Pieces have been collected and will be analyzed by the company," the official said, adding that the robot had "helped with daily document deliveries, city promotion, and delivered information" to local residents.

"It was officially a part of the city hall, one of us," another official said. "It worked diligently."

Headlines in local media questioned the apparent robot suicide, saying "Why did the diligent civil officer do it?" or asking "was work too hard" for the robot?

1　新闻稿来源：https://techxplore.com。

Appointed in August 2023, the robot was one of the first to be used in this manner in the city.

Made by Bear Robotics, a Californian robot-waiter startup, the robot worked from 9 am to 6 pm and had its own civil service officer card.

Unlike other robots, which can typically only use one floor, the Gumi City Council robot could call an elevator and move floors on its own.

South Korea is one of the most enthusiastic users of robots globally.

It has the highest robot density in the world, with one industrial robot for every 10 employees, according to the International Federation of Robotics.

Gumi city council is currently not planning to adopt a second robot officer at this moment, it told AFP.

编译稿

工作太辛苦？韩国机器人官员"自杀"

美国科技媒体 Tech Xplore 6 月 28 日消息 据法新社 6 月 26 日报道，韩国一市政厅 26 日表示，他们的首个行政官机器人在自己摔下楼梯后失灵，当地媒体哀悼该国首个机器人"自杀"。

报道称，韩国龟尾市政厅宣布，上周，该机器人从两米高的楼梯上摔下来后，被发现没有反应。

一名市政委员会官员说，事故发生前，目击者看到机器人"在一个地方转圈，好像那里有什么东西"，但坠落的确切原因仍在调查中。

这名官员说："碎片已经收集完毕，公司将对它们进行分析。"他还说，该机器人"帮助完成每天的文件运送、城市宣传以及向当地居民传递信息的工作"。

另一名官员补充道："它是市政厅的正式一员，它工作很勤奋。"

当地媒体对机器人自杀事件提出了疑问，称："这名勤奋的公务员为什么要这么做？""工作对机器人来说是不是太辛苦了？"

该机器人于 2023 年 8 月被任命，是该市首批以这种方式使用的机器人之一。它从上午 9 点工作到下午 6 点，并有自己的公务员证。目前市政厅不打算招收第二名机器人官员。

第四节 英语新闻报道的文体结构

一、英语新闻的分类

英语新闻有不同的分类标准，一般可以根据新闻事件的性质、内容主题、传播媒介、发生地域、新闻体裁等进行分类（见表2.1）。

表2.1 英语新闻的分类标准

分类标准	新闻的类别
新闻事件的性质	硬新闻（hard news）：关注重大或紧急事件，如政治决策、自然灾害、重大犯罪、军事政变、武装冲突、科技突破等 软新闻（soft news）：关注生活方式、文化活动、娱乐、时尚或人物故事等
新闻的内容主题	政治新闻（political news） 经济新闻（economic news） 科技新闻（technological news） 军事新闻（military news） 体育新闻（sports news） 社会新闻（social news） 教育新闻（educational news） 娱乐新闻（recreational news）
新闻传播媒介	报纸新闻（newspaper coverage） 杂志新闻（magazine coverage） 广播新闻（radio news） 电视新闻（TV news） 网络新闻（Internet news） 图片新闻（picture news; photo news）
新闻事件发生地域	国际新闻（world news） 国内新闻（home news） 地方新闻（local news）
新闻体裁	消息报道（news reporting） 新闻特写（feature articles） 新闻评论（commentaries & columns）

基于不同的分类标准，英语新闻报道多种多样，但是就体裁而言主要包括新闻消息报道、新闻特写和新闻评论三类，这里主要介绍消息报道的文体结构。在英语新闻中，消息报道（News Reporting）或消息稿是以最简短的文字迅速、准确、明了地报道新闻事件，旨在提供事实和信息，具有时效性和客观性，是使用最广泛的

一种新闻体裁。

二、英语新闻消息稿的文体结构

消息稿最常用的结构包括倒金字塔结构、金字塔结构和沙漏式结构。

1. 倒金字塔结构

仔细阅读以下新闻稿，在段落对应的表格空白处标出"标题""导语"和"正文"，并分析每个段落提供了哪些与新闻事实相关的信息，写出关键词。

新闻稿	结构 + 关键词
More than 4,300 dead in Turkey and Syria after powerful quake[1]	
1　Istanbul, Turkey (CNN)—More than 4,300 people have died and rescuers are racing to pull survivors from beneath the rubble after a devastating earthquake ripped through Turkey and Syria, leaving destruction and debris on each side of the border.	
2　One of the strongest earthquakes to hit the region in a century shook residents from their beds at around 4 a.m. on Monday, sending tremors as far away as Lebanon and Israel.	
3　In Turkey, at least 2,921 people were killed and more than 15,800 others injured, according to Turkey's head of disaster services, Yunus Sezer.	
4　In neighboring Syria, at least 1,451 people have died. According to the Syrian state news agency SANA, 711 people have died across government-controlled areas, mostly in the regions of Aleppo, Hama, Latakia, and Tartus.	
5　The "White Helmets" group, officially known as the Syria Civil Defense, reported 740 deaths in opposition-controlled areas. Much of northwestern Syria, which borders Turkey, is controlled by anti-government forces amid a bloody civil war that began in 2011.	
6　The epicenter of the 7.8-magnitude quake was 23 kilometers (14.2 miles) east of Nurdagi, in Turkey's Gaziantep province, at a depth of 24.1 kilometers (14.9 miles), the United States Geological Survey (USGS) said.	
7　A series of aftershocks have reverberated throughout the day. The largest, a major quake that measured 7.5 in magnitude, hit in Turkey about nine hours after the initial quake, according to the USGS. That aftershock hit around 95 kilometers (59 miles) north of the original.	

1　新闻稿来源：https://edition.cnn.com。

新闻稿	结构+关键词
8　Video from the scene in Turkey showed day breaking over rows of collapsed buildings, some with apartments exposed to the elements as people huddled in the freezing cold beside them, waiting for help.	
9　A host of countries have sent rescue workers to help the stricken region, where a colossal effort to find and free trapped civilians is underway. A cold and wet weather system is moving through the region, further hampering that challenge.	
10　Monday's quake is believed to be the strongest to hit Turkey since 1939, when an earthquake of the same magnitude killed 30,000 people, according to the USGS. Earthquakes of this magnitude are rare, with fewer than five occurring each year on average, anywhere in the world. Seven quakes with magnitude 7.0 or greater have struck Turkey in the past 25 years—but Monday's is the most powerful.	

这篇新闻稿采用了消息稿最典型的倒金字塔结构，由标题、导语和正文三个部分组成（有些倒金字塔结构的新闻稿还包括结尾部分），具体分析如下：

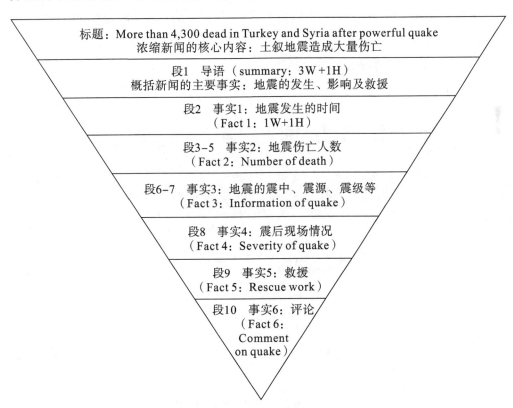

新闻正文按照新闻事实的重要性排列信息，叙述顺序为"最重要—重要—次重要——一般性"，形成了一个倒金字塔。

倒金字塔结构（Inverted Pyramid Structure）是指新闻报道按新闻事实重要性程度由高到低递减排列，逐步展开全文。最重要的新闻事实放在整个报道的开头，次要的新闻事实放在其后，最不重要的事实则放于报道的末尾。在报纸、广播、电视等各种媒体的新闻报道中，消息稿几乎都是倒金字塔结构，这种结构特别利于记者快速写作及后期编辑制作，可满足读者快速获取关键信息的需求，有助于提高信息传递效率，特别适合突发性新闻、硬新闻的报道。

"倒金字塔结构"的消息稿主要包括新闻标题、新闻导语、新闻正文和新闻结尾。

- 新闻标题（Headline）多使用短语，简洁明了，强调核心新闻事实。
- 新闻导语（Lead）通常是新闻报道的第一段或前两到三段，高度概括新闻的主要内容，往往包含新闻事件最重要的事实，如 who、when、where、what、why（即5W）和 how（1H）等新闻要素。当然新闻要素并非一定全部呈现在新闻导语里，导语中没有涉及的新闻要素将在正文中呈现。
- 新闻正文（Body）是新闻报道的主体部分，通常包含新闻事件的基本情况、过程、影响等相关细节及背景信息，新闻导语中没有出现的新闻要素都会在正文中出现。
- 新闻结尾（Ending）是新闻主体的自然延伸或总结，包括新闻事件的背景、其他相关的信息或对未来的影响等。

图1展示了倒金字塔结构的消息稿框架。

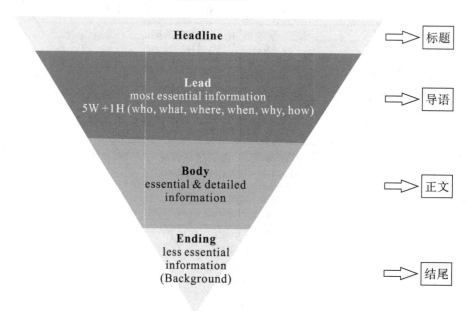

图1　倒金字塔结构的消息稿框架

以下新闻报道是一篇典型的倒金字塔结构的新闻报道，阅读并分析该新闻稿的结构。

Trump says he was shot in the ear at rally, with 1 spectator dead and 2 others injured[1]

By NPR Staff   July 13, 2024

Gunshots were fired Saturday at former President Donald Trump at his rally in Butler, Pa., police said.

One rally attendee is dead and two others are in critical condition, the Secret Service said. The suspected shooter is dead, a spokesperson added.

Trump was rushed off stage and the rally ended soon thereafter. Images from the scene showed blood on Trump's face. The Secret Service said Trump "is fine."

Here's what to know:

● Trump said on Truth Social that he was shot "with a bullet that pierced the upper part of [his] right ear."

● An eyewitness at the rally said he heard six to eight shots and saw a rally attendee just behind him who appeared to be very hurt.

● In a press briefing held in Rehoboth Beach, Del., Biden said he has tried to speak with Trump. He said he heard that Trump is doing well, and denounced all forms of violence in American politics.

● Historians say the attack marks one of the most serious acts of political violence involving leading political figures in recent memory.

NPR is providing live updates as the situation develops. Follow the coverage here.

_____

_____

_____

_____

1　新闻稿来源：https://alaskapublic.org。

2. 金字塔结构

消息稿除了采用倒金字塔结构之外，有时也会使用金字塔结构。"金字塔结构"（Pyramid Structure）也称为编年史结构（Chronological Structure）或时间顺序式结构，即按照新闻事件发生的时间顺序组织材料，叙述事件的发生、发展和结束，事件的开头就是消息的开头，事件的结尾就是消息的结尾。金字塔结构没有导语，通常包括开头（Beginning）、正文（Body）和结尾（Ending）三个部分。这种结构叙事条理清晰，现场感强，一开始就能抓住读者的注意力，并完整地呈现过程和背景，很适合报道故事性强、以情节取胜的新闻事件。金字塔结构消息稿的基本框架如图2所示：

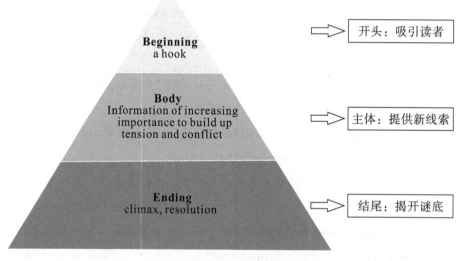

图2　金字塔结构的消息稿框架

以下新闻报道是金字塔结构消息稿的典型实例，阅读并分析该新闻稿的结构。

Mysterious streaks of light seen in the sky over California[1]

March 19, 2023（AP）–On Friday night, Jaime Hernandez was at the King Cong Brewing Company in Sacramento for a St. Patrick's Day celebration when some among the revelers noticed some mysterious streaks of light in the sky. Hernandez quickly began filming. It was over in about 40 seconds, he said Saturday.

"Mainly, we were in shock, but amazed that we got to witness it," Hernandez said in an email. "None of us had ever seen anything like it."

1　新闻稿来源：https://apnews.com。

The brewery owner posted Hernandez's video to Instagram, asking if anyone could solve the mystery.

Jonathan McDowell says he can. McDowell is an astronomer at the Harvard-Smithsonian Center for Astrophysics. McDowell said Saturday in an interview with The Associated Press that he's 99.9% confident the streaks of light were from burning space debris.

McDowell said that a Japanese communications package that relayed information from the International Space Station to a communications satellite and then back to Earth became obsolete in 2017 when the satellite was retired. The equipment, weighing 310 kilograms (683 pounds), was jettisoned from the space station in 2020 because it was taking up valuable space and would burn up completely upon reentry, McDowell added.

The flaming bits of wreckage created a "spectacular light show in the sky," McDowell said. He estimated the debris was about 40 miles high, going thousands of miles per hour.

The U.S. Space Force confirmed the re-entry path over California for the Inter-Orbit Communication System, and the timing is consistent with what people saw in the sky, he added. The Space Force could not immediately be reached Saturday with questions.

_____
_____
_____
_____

3. 沙漏式结构

沙漏式结构（Hourglass Structure）其实是倒金字塔结构和金字塔结构的结合，兼具两种新闻报道结构的特点，把新闻事件中最重要的信息点放在开篇和结尾两头，中间插入过渡部分，形成了两头大、中间小的结构，恰如一个沙漏，该结构也称双金字塔结构。在报道的开头或上半部分采用倒金字塔结构，通过导语点出最重要、最核心的新闻事实，充分吸引读者兴趣，下半部分再通过金字塔结构将故事娓娓道来，向读者展现事件全貌，事实具体完整、叙事清晰明了、情节引人入胜。沙漏式结构适用于既有新闻又有故事的新闻事件的报道，尤其适合报道一系列相继发生的事件。图3展示了沙漏式结构消息稿的具体框架：

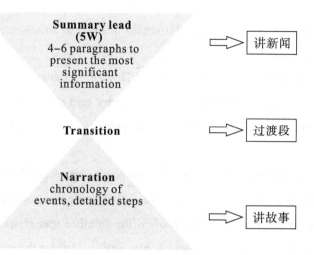

图 3　沙漏式结构的消息稿框架

以下新闻报道是沙漏式结构消息稿的典型实例，阅读并分析该新闻稿的结构。

Digital torchbearers for Hangzhou Asian Games exceed 100 mln[1]

(People's Daily Online) 14:26, September 20, 2023

On Sept.15, the digital torchbearer program for the Hangzhou Asian Games achieved a milestone moment as the total number of participants exceeded 100 million.

The extensive participation makes the digital torchbearer program for the Hangzhou Asian Games an online torch relay event that covers the widest range of regions, involves the most participants, and lasts the longest in the games' history.

The Hangzhou Asian Games will become the first event in Asian Games history to have a digital ignition ceremony at the opening ceremony.

In November 2022, the Hangzhou Asian Games Organizing Committee (HAGOC) launched the groundbreaking digital torchbearer program globally and invited people worldwide to become digital torchbearers. In June 2023, the Asian Games flame was lit at the Liangzhu ancient city in Hangzhou, marking the start of the world's first blockchain-based torch relay event.

Over the past three months, Internet users from over 130 countries and regions have become Asian Games digital torchbearers by participating in the online torch relay. The oldest participant is 98 years old, while the youngest is 12 years old. People

---

1　新闻稿来源：http://en.people.cn。

aged 20 to 39 years old account for 64 percent of the participants.

The online torch relay event has transcended the constraints of time and space, enabling Internet users worldwide to spread the Asian Games flame in the digital realm.

To create a digital representation for each of the users, the digital torchbearer team for the Hangzhou Asian Games used AI and other technologies for facial customization, motion capture, and costume design.

They conducted thousands of motion captures and created hundreds of thousands of design drafts, resulting in a total of 2 trillion possible appearances for the digital torchbearers, ensuring that each digital torchbearer is unique.

_____

_____

_____

4. 华尔街日报体结构

除了以上三种常见的消息稿文体结构，华尔街日报体（Wall Street Journal Structure）也是英语主流媒体中惯用的一种新闻写作方法，这种结构主要适用于非事件类题材的叙述。其基本特征是首先以一个具体的事例（小故事、小人物、小场景、小细节）开头，然后自然过渡进入新闻主体部分，接下来将所要传递的新闻大主题、大背景和盘托出，集中力量深化主题，结尾再呼应开头，回归开头的人物或故事，进行主题升华。这种写法从小处落笔、向大处扩展，感性而生动。

华尔街日报体在结构上一般由四部分组成：1）人性化的开头，即与新闻主题相关的人物故事。2）过渡，即从人物与新闻主题的交叉点切入，将真正的新闻内容推到读者眼前。3）展开，即集中而有层次地阐述新闻主题。4）回归人物故事，即重新将人物引入新闻，交代此人与新闻主题的深层联系。华尔街日报体也可总结为 DEE 结构：Description 描写、Explanation 解释、Evaluation 评价。这种结构有助于引导读者从个别到一般、从具体到抽象、从感性到理性地了解新闻事实。

华尔街日报体具有以下三个特点：

● **故事性**：华尔街日报体以故事开头，通过人物描绘、具体场景的刻画，使严肃、枯燥或刻板的硬新闻变得生动活泼、通俗有趣，增强了新闻的故事性、趣味性和可读性。

● **人文性**：华尔街日报体以小见大，从一个极具代表性的人物个案发散开，引入一个具有普遍意义的主题，最后再回到个体，在这个完整的叙事链条中强调人物故事、个案的命运，展现人与自然、人与社会、人与人之间各种关系的变化，具有很强的人文性，可引发读者对个人、社会和人生的思考。

● **接近性**：华尔街日报体从故事入手，以普通人的视角来写作，通过普通人的眼睛观察世界，使读者在心理上产生共鸣，解答读者心中的疑问，满足读者内心的期待，符合新闻报道中的"接近性原则"。

以下新闻报道采用了华尔街日报体，阅读并分析此篇新闻稿的结构。

Technology facilitates efficient spring farming in C China's Henan[1]

(People's Daily Online) 14:34, March 25, 2024

After breakfast, Ning Yong, a villager from Zhangwulou village in Wangmingkou township, Xiangcheng city in central China's Henan Province headed to his wheat fields and contacted the township's aerial spraying service team, asking the latter to send drones to spray herbicides, insecticides, and fungicides, and plant growth regulators on his wheat.

Ning, a major grain grower in the village, cultivates 650 mu (43.33 hectares) of farmland. Previously, he would hire over 10 workers to help irrigate his fields through flood irrigation and it took half a month to finish irrigating the fields.

"In those days, we didn't manage the fields well, resulting in low wheat yields. The best yield was only 500 kilograms per mu," Ning said.

In 2022, the township secured project funding to develop 15,400 mu of high-standard farmland. This involved constructing roads, drilling wells, digging ditches and channels, and laying pipelines.

Ning's 650 mu of land were transformed into high-standard farmland.

"The fields are equipped with sprinkler irrigation systems, which can be operated with a simple press of a button or swipe of a card," Ning said, while taking out a remote control from his pocket.

When he aimed the remote control at the well house, located several tens of meters away, the sprinkler irrigation system in the wheat field instantly turned on.

---

1 新闻稿来源：http://en.people.cn。

"Switching from flood irrigation to regular and controlled watering not only saves water but also effectively regulates soil moisture for optimal crop growth," explained Ning.

In recent years, Ning has invested in over 10 agricultural machines, streamlining the processes of plowing, planting, and harvesting.

The local agricultural technicians regularly visit the fields to provide guidance.

"They teach us the proper timing for watering, the appropriate use of pesticides, and the correct fertilization methods, guiding us in adopting scientific farming practices," said Ning.

"Thanks to the implementation of agricultural technologies, the wheat seedlings have thrived, resulting in yields of over 600 kilograms per mu. As a result, I can generate an annual net income ranging from 500,000 to 600,000 yuan ($69,000 to $83,000) from my fields," he said.

In less than half an hour, the aerial spraying service team arrived at the fields. "They can help finish spraying herbicides, insecticides, and fungicides, and plant growth regulators across the entire 650 mu of wheat before night," said Ning.

The 85 million mu of wheat in Henan has started to green up, and spring farmland management is underway. To provide effective support, the Henan Academy of Agricultural Sciences has initiated an agricultural technology service, which includes the establishment of 69 agricultural technology service teams.

More than 1,000 agricultural technicians are sent to the fields to evaluate seedling conditions, monitor soil moisture levels, implement pest and disease control measures, and prepare for potential extreme weather conditions.

_____

_____

_____

5. 对话式结构

对话式结构（Extended-Dialogue Structure）也是新闻报道的一种形式，即以新闻记者与采访对象的对话、对谈内容写成的新闻报道。对话式新闻将新闻以聊天对话的形式展现给读者，为读者提供沉浸式的对话场景，具有真实性、立体性和交互性的特点。

阅读以下三篇新闻稿，判断并说明它们分别采用了哪种新闻报道结构。

◎新闻稿 1

Philippines resumes talks with China on Chinese-funded transport projects[1]

August 15, 2022

MANILA, Philippines—The Department of Transportation (DOTr) and the Chinese ambassador to the country met in a formal meeting, said the agency on Sunday, officially restarting the negotiations on Chinese-funded transportation projects.

According to DOTr in a statement, Transport Secretary Jaime Bautista and Chinese Ambassador Huang Xilian discussed the resumption of negotiations on several projects during their first meeting at the Chinese Embassy in Makati last Thursday, August 11.

"The two officials discussed the resumption of talks for the major China-funded railway projects such as the PNR South Long Haul Project (North-South Commuter Railway), Subic-Clark Railway, and Mindanao Railway (Tagum-Davao-Digos)," said the DOTr.

Apart from these projects, the two also discussed maritime cooperation projects, specifically the hotline communication and legal affairs cooperation arrangements between the Philippine Coast Guard and the China Coast Guard.

They also discussed a possible collaboration on Maritime Traffic Safety, Ferry Safety, and the creation of a Memorandum of Understanding (MOU) on Maritime Search and Rescue, as well as the capacity building for maritime governance, safety supervision, and vessel safety inspection.

The DOTr said that the Chinese government's funding support for these projects will serve to strengthen bilateral relations and enhance the partnership between the Philippines and China.

---

1 新闻稿来源：https://asianews.network。

This came after the Chinese government withdrew the loan deals, following the end of former President Rodrigo Duterte's term, with his successor President Ferdinand "Bongbong" Marcos Jr. vowing to renegotiate these deals.

In all, the country under the Duterte administration had already borrowed from China a total of $1.1-billion.

◎ 新闻稿 2

Insects find their way onto Italian plates despite resistance[1]

July 9 2023

In a small room near the Alps in northern Italy, containers filled with millions of crickets are stacked on top of each other.

Jumping and chirping loudly—these crickets are about to become food.

The process is simple: they are frozen, boiled, dried, and then pulverised.

Here at the Italian Cricket Farm, the biggest insect farm in the country, about one million crickets are turned into food ingredients every day.

Ivan Albano, who runs the farm, opens a container to reveal a light brown flour that can be used in the production of pasta, bread, pancakes, energy bars—and even sports drinks.

Eating crickets, ants and worms has been common in parts of the world like Asia for thousands of years.

Now, after the EU approved the sale of insects for human consumption earlier this year, will there be a shift in attitudes across Europe?

Well, nowhere in Europe is there more resistance to eating insects than in Italy, according to data from the global public opinion company YouGov, and the objections come right from the top—the government has already taken steps to ban their use in pizza and pasta production.

"We will oppose, by any means and in any place, this madness that would impoverish our agriculture and our culture," Deputy Prime Minister Matteo Salvini wrote on Facebook.

But is that all about to change? Several Italian producers have been perfecting

---

1 新闻稿来源：https://www.bbc.com。

cricket pasta, pizza and snacks.

"What we do here is very sustainable," says Ivan. "To produce one kilo of cricket powder, we only use about 12 litres of water," he adds, pointing out that producing the same quantity of protein from cows requires thousands of litres of water.

Farming insects also requires just a fraction of the land used to produce meat. Given the pollution caused by the meat and dairy industry, more and more scientists believe insects could be key to tackling climate change.

At a restaurant near Turin, chef Simone Loddo has adapted his fresh pasta recipe, which dates back nearly 1,000 years—the dough is now 15% cricket powder.

It emanates a strong, nutty smell.

Some of the diners refuse to try the cricket tagliatelle, but those who do—including me—are surprised at how good it tastes.

Diners at the Turin restaurant that serves the insect pasta are trying cricket-based products out of curiosity.

Aside from the taste, cricket powder is a superfood packed with vitamins, fibre, minerals and amino acids. One plate contains higher sources of iron and magnesium, for example, than a regular sirloin steak.

But is this a realistic option for those who want to eat less meat? The main issue is the price.

"If you want to buy cricket-based food, it's going to cost you," says Ivan. "Cricket flour is a luxury product. It costs about € 60 (£52) per kilogram. If you take cricket pasta for example, one pack can cost up to € 8."

That's up to eight times more than regular pasta at the supermarket.

For now, insect food remains a niche option in Western societies, as farmers can sell poultry and beef at lower prices.

Cricket tagliatelle served with zucchini, zucchini cream, crispy bacon, parmesan and basil.

"The meat I produce is much cheaper than cricket flour, and it's very good quality," says Claudio Lauteri, who owns a farm near Rome that's been in his family for four generations.

But it's not just about price. It's about social acceptance.

Across Italy, the number of people living to the age of 100 and beyond is rising fast. Many point to the Mediterranean diet as the Holy Grail for a healthy lifestyle.

"Italians have been eating meat for centuries. With moderation, it's definitely healthy," says Claudio.

He believes that insect food could be a threat to Italian culinary tradition—which is something universally sacred in this country.

"These products are garbage," he says. "We are not used to them, they are not part of the Mediterranean diet. And they could be a threat for people: we don't know what eating insects can do to our bodies.

"I'm absolutely against these new food products. I refuse to eat them."

While insect farming is increasing in Europe, so too is hostility towards the idea.

The EU decision to approve insects for human consumption was described by a member of Italy's ruling far-right Brothers of Italy party as "bordering on madness".

Prime Minister Giorgia Meloni, who has referred to Italy as a "food superpower", created a Made in Italy ministry when she was elected, with the aim of safeguarding tradition.

"Insect products are arriving on supermarket shelves! Flour, larvae—good, delicious," she said in a tone of disgust in a video.

Amid concerns that insects might be associated with Italian cuisine, three government ministers announced four decrees aimed at a crackdown. "It's fundamental that these flours are not confused with food made in Italy," Francesco Lollobrigida, the agriculture minister, said.

Insect food is not just dividing opinions in Italy.

In Poland, it has become a hot topic ahead of an election this year. In March, politicians from the two main parties accused each other of introducing policies that would force citizens to eat insects—the leader of the main opposition party, Donald Tusk, labelled the government a "promoter of worm soup".

Meanwhile, Austria, Belgium and the Netherlands are more receptive to eating insects. In Austria, they eat dried insects for aperitivo, and Belgians are open to eating mealworms in energy shakes and bars, burgers and soups.

"Unfortunately there's still a lot of misinformation about eating insects," says Daniel Scognamiglio, who runs the restaurant that serves the cricket tagliatelle.

"I have received hate, I have been criticised. Food tradition is sacred for many people. They don't want to change their eating habits."

But he has identified a shift, and says more people—often out of curiosity—are ordering cricket-based products from his menu.

With the global population now exceeding eight billion, there are fears that the planet's resources could struggle to meet the food needs of so many people.

Agricultural production worldwide will have to increase by 70%, according to estimates by the UN's Food and Agricultural Organisation.

Shifting to eco-friendly proteins—such as insects—might become a necessity.

Until now, the possibilities for producing and commercialising insect food had been limited. With the EU's approval, the expectation is that as the sector grows, the prices will decrease significantly.

Ivan says he already has a lot of requests for his products from restaurants and supermarkets.

"The impact on the environment is almost zero. We are a piece of the puzzle that could save the planet."

◎新闻稿3

Our reporter finds community at a century-old Chinese teahouse in Chengdu[1]

By Ann Scott Tyson　　August 13, 2024| CSM

In the darkness before dawn, Yang Xingping opens the spigot of a huge, hissing tank, sending steaming hot water gushing into a big white thermos with a cork stopper. Two by two, he hoists full thermoses into a waiting cart.

"I've been here since 4:30 in the morning!" Mr. Yang exclaims. "I fill thousands!"

An intriguing tip has led me very early to Heming Tea House, nestled in Chengdu's lushly verdant People's Park. A longtime resident of this balmy southwestern Chinese city told me that "old-timers" arrive before six, when tea costs three yuan, or 42 cents.

I imagined Chengdu's version of the small-town coffee shop or diner, filled with regulars debating local affairs. The open-air, century-old teahouse was an ideal spot for an observer. Along with the three-yuan tea, it seemed worth rising at five for.

---

1 新闻稿来源：https://www.csmonitor.com。

Heming provided all that—and, unexpectedly, much more.

A symphony of birdsong greets daybreak visitors entering the park en route to the teahouse. A lone cat crosses a stone path and darts into the underbrush. A man in a sleeveless undershirt strolls solo, his arms swinging loosely. From over a moat and under a tall gate, the heavy wooden teahouse appears with its black-tiled roof and upturned eaves, along with the sound of Mr. Yang's clanging thermoses.

Customers take morning tea at the 100-year-old, lakeside Heming Tea House in Chengdu, China, as a boatman clears weeds from the lake.

"Find a seat!" he shouts, with an urgency that seems out of place in the nearly-empty teahouse. I pick out what appears to be a good table—one that fits neatly into a corner protruding over the lake that surrounds the building.

Mr. Yang disappears, and returns moments later holding a small, bowl-like white cup containing a packet of jasmine tea leaves favored by Chengdu residents. He explains that the three-yuan tea normally comes with "restricted hours"—from 6:30-9:30 a.m., after which the penny-pinching tea drinkers must depart.

But "you come from afar," he says, setting down a full thermos. "You can stay and drink it all day and into the night, if you like."

Not long afterward, a retired Chengdu worker with a buzz cut and plaid shirt arrives at a nearby table. He rinses his cup, tossing the water into the lake with a splash. After steeping his tea, he uses the lid to stir and cool it. "I come here whenever I have time," he says, holding the lid to strain the leaves and sipping tea off the rim.

Following his example, I steep my tea, and wait. Birdsong draws my gaze upward to the forest-like canopy. A golden carp jumps in the water below my teahouse perch, creating ripples on the lake. I take a sip, and time slows down.

Little by little, more people arrive. At seven, a retired manager called Mr. Wang occupies his usual corner spot. "This is my custom. It's the morning habit of Chengdu people," he says, nodding at the men seated beside him. "These are all my friends."

The sound of conversation rises. A peddler, Dai Da, sells newspapers—food for discussion. A villager from just outside Chengdu, Mr. Dai has served as a soldier, labored on the railways, and is proud, in his 80s, to remain a jack-of-all-trades.

Then the out-of-towners arrive. Suddenly, we're all chatting—small talk giving way, in good time, to weighty topics of the world, life, and dreams deferred.

> From the adjacent table is Ms. Wu, a shop owner from Wuhan, visiting with her daughter, who just finished China's rigorous university entrance exams. Ms. Wu plans to go back to her childhood home in a rural village, grow flowers and vegetables, and care for her parents, who still farm. "Our neighbors also farm and we share, so we have everything we need," she says.
>
> Before I know it, hours have passed. Planning to merely observe, I'd been drawn in. People came to the tea house with their cares and left unburdened, no longer strangers.
>
> Then, across the patio I spot a woman holding the hand of a young girl in pigtails searching for a seat. Admittedly with a twinge of reluctance, I catch up to them and pass on the best seat in the house, made better by the giving.

第五节　英汉新闻编译的步骤和方法

一、英汉新闻编译的步骤

英汉新闻编译就是编译者把一条或几条英语新闻或新闻资料改编加工成汉语新闻，以满足受众的需要。新闻编译是一个译中有编、编中有译的过程，通常情况下，编译都是采用先编辑后翻译的顺序。一般来说，新闻编译有四个步骤：

- 通读并理解原文；
- 提炼核心信息，分析、筛选原文中有价值的新闻事实并进行编辑；
- 翻译编辑过的新闻稿；
- 通读译文，修改润色。

编辑与翻译没有绝对的先后顺序，有时根据实际需要，编译者也会采用先翻译后编辑的顺序，许多编译初学者或编译实习人员多采用后一种做法。

例如，2024年1月29日美国消费者新闻与商业频道（CNBC）报道了一篇新闻，1月30日中新网对这条消息进行了编译报道。下文将以此篇新闻稿的编译为例，对英汉新闻编译的步骤进行具体讲解。

◎ 新闻稿

Elon Musk's Neuralink implants brain tech in human patient for the first time[1]

UPDATED TUE, JAN 30 2024 9:23 AM EST CNBC

Elon Musk's neurotech startup Neuralink implanted its device in a human for the first time on Sunday, and the patient is "recovering well," the billionaire said in a post on X, formerly known as Twitter, on Monday.

The company is developing a brain implant that aims to help patients with severe paralysis control external technologies using only neural signals. Neuralink began recruiting patients for its first in-human clinical trial in the fall after it received approval from the U.S. Food and Drug Administration to conduct the study back in May, according to a blog post.

Musk said Monday that Neuralink's first product is called Telepathy, according to an X post.

If the technology functions properly, patients with severe degenerative diseases like ALS could someday use the implant to communicate or access social media by moving cursors and typing with their minds.

"Imagine if Stephen Hawking could communicate faster than a speed typist or auctioneer," Musk wrote. "That is the goal."

The in-human clinical trial marks just one step on Neuralink's path toward commercialization. Medical device companies must go through several rounds of intense data safety collection and testing before securing final approval from the FDA.

Neuralink did not disclose how many human patients will participate in its initial in-human trial. The company did not immediately respond to CNBC's request for comment about the recent procedure.

As part of the emerging brain-computer interface, or BCI, industry, Neuralink is perhaps the best-known company in the space thanks to the high profile of Musk, who is also the CEO of Tesla and SpaceX. A BCI is a system that deciphers brain signals and translates them into commands for external technologies, and several companies like Synchron, Precision Neuroscience, Paradromics and Blackrock Neurotech have also created systems with these capabilities.

---

1 新闻稿来源：https://www.cnbc.com。

> Paradromics is aiming to launch its first trial with human patients in the first half of this year. Precision Neuroscience carried out its first in-human clinical study last year. A patient who received Synchron's BCI used it to post from CEO Tom Oxley's Twitter account back in 2021.
>
> It is not clear which company will be the first to reach the market.

1. 通读并理解原文

这里所谓的理解原文主要是指理解新闻事件的核心事实、新闻报道的内容与新闻稿的文体结构。就本篇新闻稿来说，编译前可先进行如下分析：

- **新闻事件的核心事实**：马斯克的 Neuralink 公司完成了首例人类大脑设备植入手术。
- **新闻报道的内容**：Neuralink 公司所做研发工作的目的和目标；招募患者进行人体临床试验的计划以及该计划对产品商业化的意义；脑机接口的工作原理；其他公司在该领域的研究进展等。
- **新闻稿的文体结构**：倒金字塔结构。

2. 提炼并编辑核心信息

本篇新闻稿共包括十个段落，具体来说各段主要内容为：

1	Elon Musk's neurotech startup Neuralink implanted its device in a human for the first time on Sunday, and the patient is "recovering well," the billionaire said in a post on X, formerly known as Twitter, on Monday.	导语，概括新闻事件的核心事实
2	The company is developing a brain implant that aims to help patients with severe paralysis control external technologies using only neural signals. Neuralink began recruiting patients for its first in-human clinical trial in the fall after it received approval from the U.S. Food and Drug Administration to conduct the study back in May, according to a blog post.	公司研发目标及人体临床试验计划
3	Musk said Monday that Neuralink's first product is called Telepathy, according to an X post.	引语：公司研发产品的名称
4	If the technology functions properly, patients with severe degenerative diseases like ALS could someday use the implant to communicate or access social media by moving cursors and typing with their minds.	研发产品的应用前景
5	"Imagine if Stephen Hawking could communicate faster than a speed typist or auctioneer," Musk wrote. "That is the goal."	引语：公司研发的目标

6	The in-human clinical trial marks just one step on Neuralink's path toward commercialization. Medical device companies must go through several rounds of intense data safety collection and testing before securing final approval from the FDA.	人体临床试验对于该研究的意义
7	Neuralink did not disclose how many human patients will participate in its initial in-human trial. The company did not immediately respond to CNBC's request for comment about the recent procedure.	有关公司研发的补充信息
8	As part of the emerging brain-computer interface, or BCI, industry, Neuralink is perhaps the best-known company in the space thanks to the high profile of Musk, who is also the CEO of Teslaand SpaceX. A BCI is a system that deciphers brain signals and translates them into commands for external technologies, and several companies like Synchron, Precision Neuroscience, Paradromics and Blackrock Neurotech have also created systems with these capabilities.	Neuralink公司知名度和脑机接口的工作原理及其他公司在该领域的研发情况
9	Paradromics is aiming to launch its first trial with human patients in the first half of this year. Precision Neuroscience carried out its first in-human clinical study last year. A patient who received Synchron's BCI used it to post from CEO Tom Oxley's Twitter account back in 2021.	Paradromics公司的研发情况
10	It is not clear which company will be the first to reach the market.	对各公司研发产品上市

阅读原新闻稿可知马斯克的Neuralink公司在脑机接口方面取得了重大进展，由于马斯克在中国具有一定知名度，此篇新闻稿很有可能引起国内读者的兴趣，原文所采用的倒金字塔结构突出了该新闻的核心和重点，符合此类新闻的特点，编译时可以保留此结构。就新闻报道的内容而言，该公司的研发产品、研发目标、产品应用前景、人体临床试验的意义和产品工作原理（第二、三、四、五、六、八段）都是读者所关心的内容，可以合并呈现。最后三段中并没有涉及特别实质性的内容，大部分国内读者不太熟悉国外相关研发公司，也不需要了解特别详细的信息，所以此部分可以在编译稿中省略。就内容顺序来说，先介绍所研发产品的相关内容和信息，再补充其他相关的信息，符合中文读者的思维习惯和阅读方式，所以编译者可根据这个思路对新闻稿进行编辑，包括繁简优化、语言表达、逻辑顺序调整等。

3. 翻译编辑过的新闻稿

筛选过新闻材料并进行编辑之后，编译者就可以着手进行翻译了。其实，编与译并非完全分开，而是糅合在一起进行的。编译稿初稿内容如下：

编译稿1

埃隆·马斯克的Neuralink首次将大脑技术植入人类患者体内

中新网1月30日报道,埃隆·马斯克的神经技术初创公司Neuralink于周日首次将其设备植入人体,这位亿万富翁周一在X(前身为推特)上发帖称,患者"恢复良好"。

该公司正在开发一种大脑植入物,其第一款产品名为Telepathy,旨在帮助严重瘫痪患者仅使用神经信号控制外部技术。根据一篇博客文章,Neuralink在5月份获得美国食品和药物管理局批准进行这项研究后,于秋季开始招募患者进行首次人体临床试验。

如果这项技术正常运行,患有严重退行性疾病(如ALS)的患者有朝一日可以使用植入物通过移动光标和用意念打字来交流或访问社交媒体。马斯克写道:"想象一下,如果斯蒂芬·霍金能比一个快速打字员或拍卖师更快地交流。""这就是目标。"

这项人体临床试验只是Neuralink走向商业化道路上的一步。医疗器械公司必须经过几轮密集的数据安全收集和测试,才能获得美国食品药品监督管理局的最终批准。

作为新兴脑机接口行业的一部分,Neuralink可能是该领域最知名的公司。脑机接口是一种破译大脑信号并将其转换为外部技术命令的系统,Synchron等几家公司也在进行这方面的研究。

4. 通读译文,修改润色

完成了编译初稿后,编译者还需要通读译文,对标题、导语、正文的语言表达、逻辑顺序等进行修改和润色。

阅读以下修改后的编译文,比较两篇编译文,说明二者的不同。

编译稿1	编译稿2	两稿区别
埃隆·马斯克的Neuralink首次将大脑技术植入人类患者体内 中新网1月30日报道,埃隆·马斯克的神经技术初创公司Neuralink于周日首次将其设备植入人体,这位亿万富翁周一在X(前身为推特)上发	"恢复良好"!马斯克称已完成首例人类大脑设备植入手术 中新网1月30日电 据综合报道,当地时间29日,马斯克在社交媒体上表示,其脑机接口公司Neuralink已完成首例人类大脑设备植入手术,接入	

编译稿 1	编译稿 2	两稿区别
帖称，患者"恢复良好"。 　　该公司正在开发一种大脑植入物，其第一款产品名为 Telepathy，旨在帮助严重瘫痪患者仅使用神经信号控制外部技术。根据一篇博客文章，Neuralink 在 5 月份获得美国食品和药物管理局批准进行这项研究后，于秋季开始招募患者进行首次人体临床试验。 　　如果这项技术正常运行，患有严重退行性疾病（如 ALS）的患者有朝一日可以使用植入物通过移动光标和用意念打字来交流或访问社交媒体。马斯克写道："想象一下，如果斯蒂芬·霍金能比一个快速打字员或拍卖师更快地交流。""这就是目标。" 　　这项人体临床试验只是 Neuralink 走向商业化道路上的一步。医疗器械公司必须经过几轮密集的数据安全收集和测试，才能获得美国食品药品监督管理局的最终批准。 　　作为新兴脑机接口行业的一部分，Neuralink 可能是该领域最知名的公司。脑机接口是一种破译大脑信号并将其转换为外部技术命令的系统，Synchron 等几家公司也在进行这方面的研究。	者"恢复良好"。 　　马斯克还表示，Neuralink 公司的首款产品被命名为 Telepathy（心灵感应）。对于产品的前景，他写道，"只需要思考，就可以控制手机或电脑，并通过它们控制几乎任何设备。首批使用者将是失去肢体功能的人。想象一下，如果霍金能比一位快速打字员或拍卖员更快地交流。这就是目标。" 　　美国消费者新闻与商业频道（CNBC）称，Neuralink 公司正在开发一种大脑植入物，旨在帮助严重瘫痪患者仅使用神经信号控制外部技术。 　　Neuralink 公司于 2023 年 5 月获美国食品药品监督管理局（FDA）批准，可在人体上开展临床研究，之后开始招募试验参与者。 　　CNBC 称，此次人体临床试验是 Neuralink 公司商业化道路上的一步，医疗器械公司还须经过多轮密集的数据安全收集和测试，才能获得 FDA 的最终批准。	

二、英汉新闻编译的方法

在将英语新闻稿编译成汉语新闻稿的过程中，编译者需根据新闻传播的目的，从原文中筛选出有价值的内容以及目标读者感兴趣的内容，按照目的语新闻报道的要求、新闻报道的结构模式以及读者的阅读习惯进行篇章结构与逻辑顺序的调整和加工，即编译者综合采用增、减、并、改、述等多种手法对原英语新闻稿件进行加工，从而得到一篇新的新闻稿，然后再翻译至目标语言。经过编译的新闻稿件往往更符合译入语读者的阅读心理和阅读习惯，可读性更强，同时能够满足不同传播媒介的传播需求。具体来说，这五个常用的编译方法是：

● 增：增补辅助理解信息，即增补原文未介绍的关键性背景、事件背景、术语阐释等。

● 减：删减信息，即删减重复、非必要、无关联、无意义的信息或背景。

● 并：合并同类项，即将一篇或多篇新闻稿中密切关联的内容进行合并与整理。

● 改：调整与重构，即根据内容与重要新闻点的关联和逻辑关系，对源语新闻的段落顺序和段落内的语序进行重新调整。

● 述：概括与转述。概括指对新闻中非关键性细节内容进行归纳总结和提炼；转述指在不影响原意的前提下转述原文中的某些说法或直接引语。

阅读以下新闻稿及其编译稿，分析编译稿中主要使用了哪些编译技巧。

◎例文 1

新闻稿	编译稿	编译技巧
Blockchain to 'save food industry $31 billion,' new research says[1] CNBC NEWS-NOV 27 2019-7:27 AM EST Blockchain will facilitate $31 billion in "food fraud savings" by the year 2024, according to new data from Juniper Research. According to the research, which was released earlier this week, blockchain, along with "internet of things" trackers and sensors, would help to drive down costs for retailers. This would be achieved through the streamlining of supply chains, efficient food recall processes and "simpler regulatory compliance." The research is contained within the "Blockchain: Key Vertical Opportunities, Trends & Challenges 2019—2030" report. Blockchain refers to a tamper-proof, distributed digital ledger that records transactions. The European Commission has described the internet of things as merging "physical and virtual worlds, creating smart	研究：区块链将避免食品行业造假 降低经济损失 美国全国广播公司财经频道 11 月 27 日报道，英国市场调研机构朱尼普研究公司发表的最新研究显示，区块链技术可以帮助食品行业减少"食品造假"现象，截至 2024 年，有望挽回损失高达 310 亿美元。 如今，很多消费者对食品产地和生产过程越来越了解，但信任感仍旧是个大问题，尤其是针对供应链环节。2013 年欧洲发生了将马肉充当牛肉的食品丑闻，在牛肉食品中掺入马肉和其他未申报的肉	

---

[1] 新闻稿来源：https://www.cnbc.com。

新闻稿	编译稿	编译技巧
environments." In a statement Monday, Juniper Research said that the internet of things and blockchain would add "significant value" to those involved in the supply chain, namely, farmers, retailers and the consumer. Today, many consumers are increasingly aware of where their food comes from and how it is produced. Nevertheless, trust is still a big issue, especially when it comes to supply chains. In 2013, for example, the food industry in Europe was rocked when horse meat was found to be present in food products that did not list it as an ingredient. "Today, transparency and efficiency in the food supply chain are limited by opaque data forcing each company to rely on intermediaries and paper-based records," Morgane Kimmich, the research author, said in a statement. "Blockchain and the IOT (internet of things) provide an immutable, shared platform for all actors in the supply chain to track and trace assets; saving time, resources and reducing fraud," Kimmich added. The applications of blockchain technology are wide ranging. Major utility Iberdrola, for instance, has used it to "guarantee" that the energy it sends to its customers comes from 100 percent renewable sources. In an announcement in January, the firm said that it had undertaken an "experiment" with the financial entity Kutxabank. Using blockchain, Kutxabank was able to track the origin of energy supplies, in real time, "from the generation asset to the point of consumption."	类，如猪肉。这使欧洲食品行业受到了影响。 朱尼普研究公司在题为《区块链：2019—2030年的关键垂直机遇、趋势和挑战》的报告中指出，区块链和物联网技术追踪器和传感器的运用有助于降低零售商成本。这将通过精简供应链、提高食品召回流程效率和"简化监管规范"来实现。物联网和区块链对供应链参与者（包括农民、零售商和消费者）大有裨益。 研究作者摩根·金米奇(Morgane Kimmich)表示："如今，食品供应链的透明度和效率受到数据不透明的限制，迫使每家公司依赖中间商和纸质记录。而物联网和区块链可以为供应链的所有参与者提供不可篡改的共享平台，从而更好地跟踪资产，有效节省时间和资源，减少食品造假现象。" 区块链是指一种防篡改的分布式数字账本，可以记录交易。欧盟委员会将物联网技术描述为"物理和虚拟世界的融合，创造智能环境"。如今，区块链技术的应用非常广泛，包括能源供应和金融领域等。	

◎例文2

新闻稿	编译稿	编译技巧
Olympics: Recyclable cardboard bed, customizable mattress for 2020 athletes[1] KYODO NEWS　Sep 25, 2019　20:00 　　TOKYO-Recyclable cardboard beds and customizable mattresses for athletes to sleep on during the 2020 Tokyo Olympics and Paralympics were unveiled this week, as organizers aim to provide comfort at the athletes village while fulfilling environmental sustainability goals. 　　The bed frames, made of high-resistance cardboard, can support up to about 200 kilograms, the organizers said. They come with three-part polyethylene mattresses that can be mixed and matched to suit each athlete's preferred firmness for the upper, middle and lower body, according to Japanese bedding maker Airweave Inc. 　　After the games, the beds and mattresses will be recycled into other paper and plastic products. 　　The lightweight beds will enable athletes to easily rearrange the room layout as they like, the organizers said. For extremely tall athletes, 20-centimeter extensions can be attached to the 210 cm by 90 cm bed frames. 　　"Sleep determines (the athlete's) performance the following day," said Airweave President and CEO Motokuni Takaoka. The company is considering how to provide personalized advice to athletes on adjusting the mattresses. 　　Airweave will supply 18,000 beds for the Olympics and 8,000 beds during the Paralympics next year. The 21 residential buildings in the athletes	**秉持环保理念 2020 东京奥运会为运动员提供纸板床** 【环球网综合报道】据日本共同社9月25日报道，2020年东京奥运会和残奥会组委会公布了可循环利用的纸板床与定制床垫，举办方想要在保证运动员睡眠质量的同时实现环保目标。 　　东京奥组委表示，这种由硬纸板做成的床长2.1米，宽0.9米，高0.4米，可以承载200千克的重量。对于那些身高较高的运动员，长度为2.1米的床还可以额外增加20厘米。 　　日本床上用品生产商爱维福表示，床垫使用的是聚乙烯材料，分为肩、腰、腿三个部分，运动员可以根据身体不同部位的软硬度需求进行调节。奥组委同时表示，轻质的床体让运动员可以更加随意地安排自己的房间布局。 　　爱维福在2020年东京奥运会和残奥会期间将为奥运村提供2.6万张这样的床。奥运会结束后，纸板床和床垫将会得到回收，用来制造塑料产品和纸质产品。	

---

[1] 新闻稿来源：https://english.kyodonews.net。

新闻稿	编译稿	编译技巧
village, currently under construction in Tokyo's Harumi waterfront area, are expected to be completed in December this year.		

第三章

英语新闻标题和导语的编译

新闻标题和导语在新闻报道中扮演着重要且相似的角色。从功能上来说，二者都是为了引发读者的兴趣并引导他们进一步阅读，以深入了解新闻事件。从结构上看，新闻标题和导语都遵循简洁明了、客观中立的原则。在实际应用中，标题位于新闻报道的最上方，导语紧随其后，二者共同作用，确保第一时间抓住读者的心。鉴于新闻标题和导语关系紧密、结构和功能相似，本章将新闻标题和导语放在一起进行讲解，以便学习者能够更好地理解二者在新闻报道中的重要作用和相互关系。

第一节 英语新闻标题的编译

一、英语新闻标题的作用

俗话说："看书看皮，看报看题。""题好一半文"这句话充分说明了标题的重要性，新闻报道更是如此。具有全球影响力的自媒体网站 Upworthy 的联合创始人彼得·科奇利（Peter Koechley）曾多次表示，一个精心设计的标题比任何承诺都更能吸引读者。新闻可以没有导语，但是不可以没有标题。撰写英语新闻标题通常需遵循三条基本原则：准确具体、鲜明简洁、生动活泼。

阅读以下新闻标题，思考新闻标题的作用：

A Palestinian Factions Sign Beijing Declaration on Ending Division and Strengthening Palestinian National Unity

B Temporary tattoo-like 'artificial throat' could help mute people 'speak'

C Chinese courier runs into Paris Olympics, a first in history

D Trump wounded at rally in assassination attempt; gunman killed (USA Today)

E After banning ChatGPT, Italy now plans to ban English language with fines

F House passes bill that could lead to TikTok ban

G South Korea administrative robot defunct after apparent suicide

H Greece train crash: 29 dead, 85 injured as two trains collide in Larissa

I China's Chang'e-6 moon mission returns to Earth with historic far side samples

以上新闻标题高度概括和浓缩了新闻稿的主要内容，其作用主要有以下四点：

- 吸引读者兴趣，引导读者阅读；
- 概括新闻事实，突出新闻价值；
- 评价新闻事件，揭示新闻本质；
- 提供新闻资讯，满足读者需求。

新闻标题是新闻转化为故事的关键部分，从长远来看，它们在故事的记录和复述中发挥了巨大作用。

二、英语新闻标题的特点

1. 英语新闻标题的词汇特点

▶ **常使用"小词"和简短词**

由于报刊的空间限制，新闻标题一般为单行，因此新闻标题常常使用包含字母较少、词义宽泛、生动灵活的小词，或者其他简短词，如 dorm（=dormitory）、biz（=business）、lab（=laboratory）、gym（=gymnasium）等。

英语中常用以下小词代替括号中相同意义的词：

- aim (goal, object, target, intention, etc.)
- ban (restraint, restriction, prohibition, etc.)
- bid (try, offer, attempt, proposal, endeavor, etc.)
- chief (oversee, supervisor, governor, director, commander, etc.)
- cut (fall, decrease, decline, deletion, shorten, abbreviation, etc.)
- deal (bargain, transaction, agreement, negotiation, etc.)
- echo (response, reflection, repercussion, reverberation, etc.)

▶ **常使用"时髦词"**

所谓"时髦词"指的是新出现的词，这些词用来表达新概念、新事物、新现象、新思想、新风尚等，如 ChatGPT、AI、bitcoin、meta、VR、e-sports、Gen Z 等。

▶ **常使用缩略词和数字**

一般来说，英语新闻标题中的缩略语仅用于人名、地名、政府机构名、公司名等专有名称，以及头衔、月份、星期名等。

阅读以下新闻标题，观察下划线部分的特点。

(1) March Madness <u>kicks off</u> with First Four games and teams looking to do some bracket busting

(2) How bad are <u>flu</u>, <u>COVID-19</u> and <u>RSV</u>? These charts show you

(3) Geely to produce <u>7nm</u> auto chips from <u>Q3</u>

(4) India announces 6-week general elections starting April 19 with Modi's BJP topping surveys

(5) After banning ChatGPT, Italy now plans to ban English language with fines

(6) Elon Musk sues OpenAI and CEO Sam Altman, claiming betrayal of its goal to benefit humanity

2. 英语新闻标题的语法特点

英语新闻标题具有以下语法特点：
- **时态**：常使用一般现在时态。
- **结构**：常使用非谓语动词构成的短语。
- **语态**：常使用主动语态。
- **标点**：常使用逗号、冒号、破折号、引号。
- **省略**：常省略冠词、连词、介词、系（助）动词、关系代词。

阅读以下新闻标题，观察标题的语法特点

(1) Biden drops reelection bid, endorses Harris

(2) NASA Plans to Crash the International Space Station Into the Ocean in 2031

(3) Homegrown ARJ21 completes ultra high-altitude flight

(4) Elon Musk elected to the National Academy of Engineering

(5) Xiaomi to set up smartphone production base in Argentina soon

(6) Tesla included into Chinese government purchase list

(7) UK opposition party set to win by a landslide

(8) Brain scan of dying man suggests life may really flash before our eyes

(9) Chinese acrobat wows audience at NBA halftime show

(10) Remembering Jerry West, 'Logo' of NBA

三、英语新闻标题编译的原则和方法

编译英语新闻标题时需做到精练准确，要概括、揭示新闻内容，体现出最新、最重要或最精彩的新闻点，吸引读者关注。另外还要注意，标题的语言风格平实，要言之有物；必要时标题中要体现信源，尤其是在信息仅来自单一信源的情况下；要避免语病、短语搭配不当等问题；要尽量保留原标题的修辞特点。编译英语新闻标题，常常采用以下几种方法：

- 直译或基本直译；
- 意译；
- 直译加注释。

对比以下新闻标题及其译文，说明标题编译中采用的方法。

(1) Biden drops reelection bid, endorses Harris
　　拜登放弃连任竞选 全力支持哈里斯

(2) NASA Plans to Crash the International Space Station Into the Ocean in 2031
　　外媒：国际空间站将于 2031 年坠入太平洋

(3) Homegrown ARJ21 completes ultra high-altitude flight
　　国产 ARJ21 飞机完成首次高海拔地区飞行 / 国产 ARJ21 飞机开通首条高原航线

(4) Elon Musk elected to the National Academy of Engineering
　　马斯克入选美国国家工程院院士

(5) Xiaomi to set up smartphone production base in Argentina soon
　　外媒关注：小米将在阿根廷投资设厂

(6) Tesla included into Chinese government purchase list
　　特斯拉进入江苏省政府用车采购目录

(7) UK opposition party set to win by a landslide
　　英国反对党将以压倒性优势获胜

(8) Brain scan of dying man suggests life may really flash before our eyes
　　人临终前真有最后一次"人生闪回"？

(9) Chinese acrobat wows audience at NBA halftime show
　　中国杂技演员在 NBA 中场表演中惊艳全场 / 中国大妈表演杂技燃爆 NBA 现场

(10) Remembering Jerry West, 'Logo' of NBA
　　纪念杰里·韦斯特，NBA 的"标志"人物

编译以下新闻标题。

(1) US man gets genetically-modified pig heart in world-first transplant

(2) US: China is still the ultimate prize that Western banks can't resist

(3) Will Smith would face little more than a slap if charged

(4) What Will China's Metaverse Look Like?

(5) Peace is the 'only goal' that China hopes for, FM says

(6) Overseas grads facing tougher job market

(7) Amazon announces huge rocket deal to launch its satellite internet constellation

(8) Michael Jordan donates $10M to Make-A-Wish for 60th birthday

(9) Japan's 1st piloted flying taxi test held ahead of 2025 World Expo

(10) TikTok to open two new data centers in Europe amid rising security concerns

第二节 英语新闻导语的编译

一、英语新闻导语概述

1. 什么是新闻导语

新闻导语就是新闻或消息的开头部分，一般情况下是新闻的第一段或前两到三段，以极其简洁的文字，呈现最核心、最具新闻价值、最重要或最精彩的新闻事实，提纲挈领，牵引全文，吸引读者继续阅读下文。导语必须包含实质性内容，切忌空泛无物。

2. 新闻导语包含的新闻要素

美国密苏里大学新闻学院的布莱恩·S. 布鲁克斯 (Brian S. Brooks) 等几位教授曾对新闻导语进行了这样的定义："The lead is a simple, clear statement consisting of the first paragraph or two of a story. In this paragraph, you have to answer six basic questions: who, what, when, where, why and how."。新闻导语中必须回答六个基本问题，即何人、何事、何时、何地、为何以及如何，就是常说的"5W + 1H"。可见，新闻导语是对整条新闻内容的高度概括和浓缩。新闻导语必须言简意赅、突出重点，但由于实际工作中时间紧迫、对新闻事实的了解受限，因而导语并不一定包含新闻的全部六个要素，有时为了增加新闻的可读性，导语中只包含最核心的要素，其他新闻要素留在正文中逐步呈现给读者。

阅读以下新闻导语，指出导语中所包含的新闻要素。

(1) Ukraine has claimed it killed the commander of Russia's Black Sea Fleet, in one of Kyiv's boldest attacks yet on the occupied peninsula of Crimea.

(2) Extreme weather disruptions and supply chain snags forced Japanese snack brand Calbee, Asia's biggest potato chip maker, to hike prices three times last year and rethink how it sources its most important ingredient.

(3) At least 12 people were killed and 14 injured in Odisha, India, after 61,000 lightning strikes occurred in nearly two hours. The India Meteorology Department (IMD) has warned of extreme weather conditions in the state until September 7, with heavy rainfall expected. The lightning strikes were attributed to the collision of cold and warm air masses, which created favorable conditions for such events. The affected families will receive an ex gratia payment of INR 4 lakh each.

---

3. 英语新闻导语的特征

新闻导语简明扼要地概括新闻事实，确定新闻的基调，吸引读者继续阅读，被认为是新闻报道的精髓。新闻导语主要包括以下特征：

- 开门见山，点明新闻核心；
- 言简意赅，勾画新闻轮廓；
- 内容充实，避免过多细节；
- 引人入胜，激起读者兴趣；
- 形式多样，表现不拘一格。

阅读以下新闻导语，分析它们的特征，并对其进行编译。

(1) A former cosmetic surgery patient is suing a doctor and a Tulsa clinic following 22 nose surgeries that his lawyer said made his face appear "grotesque." (ABC News 6/5/2013)

_____

_____

(2) Lionel Messi failed to score as Inter Miami drew 0-0 with Nashville SC in Major League Soccer, ending the club's nine-game winning run in all competitions. (Fox News 8/30/2023)

_____

_____

(3) As millions bake under a relentless heat wave in the South and Southwest US—and as temperatures soar around the Northern Hemisphere—NASA scientists warned Thursday that we haven't even seen the worst of El Niño and next year will likely be even warmer for the planet. (CNN 7/20/2023)

_____

_____

(4) The European Union is launching an antisubsidy investigation into China's electric-vehicle makers, opening a new front in the battle for leadership of the global clean-technology industry. (WSJ 9/14/2023)

_____

_____

(5) Following the 2023 Federal Budget announcement and the Migration Review report release, Australia's migration system is set to undergo a dramatic overhaul, with several changes in visa policies and procedures taking effect on 1 July. (SBS 2/3/2023)

_____

_____

二、英语新闻导语的编译原则

在编译英语新闻导语时，应遵循以下原则。

● **体现核心新闻要素**：编译后的导语也要体现核心新闻要素，导语中若有新闻发生的时间，媒体源报道的时间可以省略。

● **确保翻译信息准确**：编译导语时先通读全文，保证新闻事实的准确性。
● **调整新闻叙事逻辑**：编译导语时应注意英汉新闻叙事逻辑的差异，并作出适当调整。
● **符合目标读者阅读习惯**：编译导语时应根据中文读者的阅读习惯对外媒中一些表述进行适当调整。

阅读以下新闻导语，比较其译文的不同版本，勾选你认为较好的版本并说明理由。

(1) A former cosmetic surgery patient is suing a doctor and a Tulsa clinic following 22 nose surgeries that his lawyer said made his face appear "grotesque." （ABC News 6/5/2013）

（　）译文1：美国广播公司6月5日报道，美国一名男子近日起诉一名医生，原因是该医生为他实施的鼻孔整容手术失败，导致其在随后又被迫接受22次手术，并且鼻子最终被彻底切除，令其面目怪异。

（　）译文2：随着医疗技术的发展，越来越多的人选择用整容变美，但这种行为也可能引发风险。据美国广播公司6月5日报道，美国一名男子经历22次面部整容后鼻子被迫切除，成为一名"无鼻人"。

理由：_____
_____

(2) Lionel Messi failed to score as Inter Miami drew 0-0 with Nashville SC in Major League Soccer, ending the club's nine-game winning run in all competitions. (Fox News 8/30/2023)

（　）译文1：在美国职业足球大联盟联赛中，国际迈阿密0-0战平纳什维尔SC，莱昂内尔·梅西未能进球，结束了俱乐部在所有比赛中的九连胜。

（　）译文2：美国职业足球大联盟联赛中，梅西所在的迈阿密国际队0-0战平同属东部球队的纳什维尔队。自加盟迈阿密国际俱乐部之后，梅西持续进球的势头被打断，俱乐部各项赛事的9连胜也就此终结。

理由：_____
_____

(3) As millions bake under a relentless heat wave in the South and Southwest US—and as temperatures soar around the Northern Hemisphere—NASA scientists warned Thursday that we haven't even seen the worst of El Niño and next year will likely be even warmer for the planet. （CNN 7/20/2023）

（　）译文1：据美国有线电视新闻网7月20日报道，随着美国南部和西南部数百万人在无情的热浪中烘烤，以及北半球气温飙升，美国国家航空航天局的科学家周四警告说，我们甚至还没有看到最严重的厄尔尼诺现象，明年地球可能会更加温暖。

（　）译文2：美国科学家警告称，尽管2023年已经很炎热，但2024年可能会更热。美国有线电视新闻网7月20日报道，美国国家海洋暨大气总署首席科学家卡普尼克表示，2023年有近50%的概率成为历年来最温暖的一年，但另一个不太好的消息是：明年也就是2024年有可能会更热。

理由：_____

_____

(4) The European Union is launching an antisubsidy investigation into China's electric-vehicle makers, opening a new front in the battle for leadership of the global clean-technology industry. （WSJ　9/14/2023）

（　）译文1：据《华尔街日报》9月14日报道，欧盟正在对中国电动汽车制造商展开反补贴调查，为争夺全球清洁技术行业的领导地位开辟了一条新战线。

（　）译文2：美国《华尔街日报》9月14日报道，欧盟正对中国电动汽车制造商展开反补贴调查。此举为争夺全球清洁技术产业的领导地位开辟了一条新战线。

理由：_____

_____

(5) Following the 2023 Federal Budget announcement and the Migration Review report release, Australia's migration system is set to undergo a dramatic overhaul, with several changes in visa policies and procedures taking effect on 1 July. (SBS 2/3/2023)

（　）译文1：澳大利亚特别广播服务公司3月2日报道，根据澳大利亚教育部官网消息，从2023年7月1日起，在澳大利亚教育机构毕业的具有合格高等教育资格的国际学生将获得延期2年的毕业后工作权利。

（　）译文2：据澳大利亚特别广播服务公司3月2日报道，继2023年联邦预算公告和移民审查报告发布后，澳大利亚的移民制度将进行重大调整，签证政策及程序中的几项变化将于7月1日生效。

理由：_____

_____

(6) Mysterious streaks of light were seen in the sky in the Sacramento area Friday night, shocking St. Patrick's Day revelers who then posted videos on social media of the surprising sight. （AP News 3/19/2023）

（　）译文1：美联社3月19日消息，周五晚上，萨克拉门托地区的天空中出现了神秘的光带，震惊了圣帕特里克节的狂欢者，他们随后在社交媒体上发布了这一令人惊讶的景象的视频。

（　）译文2：美联社3月19日消息，一串拖着长尾巴的神秘光点日前划过美国加利福尼亚州中部夜空，有关视频和图像在社交媒体上获大量点击。专家推测，这极可能是日本太空垃圾燃烧所致。

理由：_____

编译案例

◎新闻稿1

Two polar bears kill Canadian worker in rare attack[1]

Aug. 14, 2024

Two polar bears killed a worker at a remote Arctic radar station in Canada's northern Nunavut territory, prompting an investigation into the rare fatal attack.

The employee, who has not been named, was working for Nasittuq Corporation—a logistics company which operates radar defence sites on behalf of the Canadian government.

Other workers responded to the scene and killed one of the bears, the company said in a statement.

"We are working closely with local authorities and regulatory agencies to conduct a thorough investigation into the circumstances surrounding this incident," the company said.

"The safety and well-being of our employees is our highest priority, and we are deeply committed to ensuring a safe working environment."

The attack took place last week on Brevoort Island, southeast of Baffin Island.

---

1 新闻稿来源：https://www.bbc.com。

The site is one of dozens of North Warning System outposts in northern Canada, according to CBS News, the BBC's partner in the US.

The network, which spans 3,100 miles (5,000km), exists to detect aircraft or missiles entering the region.

Polar bear attacks on humans are extremely rare, but this is at least the second recorded deadly incident involving a polar bear attack since 2023.

Last year, a woman and her 1-year-old son were killed by a polar bear in an Alaskan village.

There are about 17,000 polar bears living in the country—making up around two-thirds of the global population of the species, according to the Canadian government.

The species is in decline, and scientists attribute it to the loss of sea ice caused by global warming—leading to shrinking of their hunting and breeding grounds.

Elsewhere, a three-year-old girl in the US state of Montana was dragged out of her tent at a private campground by a black bear on Sunday.

Wildlife officials have set traps, and euthanised one bear believed to have been involved in the attack.

Black bears are much smaller than polar bears but can still be very dangerous to humans.

In 2023, a woman in California was fatally attacked and eaten inside her home, marking the first death by a black bear in the state's history.

编译稿（标题+导语）

加拿大雷达站遭北极熊偷袭

据英国广播公司（BBC）14日报道，加拿大北部努纳武特地区的一处北极雷达站8日发生北极熊袭击致人死亡事件。

案例分析

编译的标题虽然很短，但呈现出了事件的核心信息，包括事件发生地点、涉事单位、事件发生原因。译文标题的主语与原文不同，选择雷达站作为主语替代了原主语北极熊（polar bears），表明编译者的关注点是事件中的人（worker）。

编译的导语基本与原文对应，包含了新闻中最核心的要素，一些细节如熊的数量、袭击之后的情况等没有呈现在导语中，以吸引读者继续阅读正文报道。

◎新闻稿2

What Asia's top potato chip maker learned from a huge supply shortage[1]

Published 8:08 PM EDT, Fri August 4, 2023

Hong Kong（CNN）— What happens when Asia's biggest potato chip maker runs out of potatoes? Japanese snack brand Calbee had to learn the hard way.

Extreme weather disruptions and supply chain snags forced the company to hike prices three times last year and rethink how it sources its most important ingredient.

"That is our headache," Calbee CEO Makoto Ehara told CNN in an interview.

The issue is critical to the company as it embarks on an ambitious $1 billion turnaround and overseas expansion plan that will see it plow deeper into the world's top two economies.

The humble potato is serious business for the 74-year-old snack maker. The Tokyo-based firm uses hundreds of thousands of tons of the vegetable annually to make chips in a variety of flavors, from pizza to soy sauce.

These products rake in hundreds of millions of dollars in sales a year for the company, which posted a profit of 22.2 billion yen ($156 million) in the last fiscal year.

In Asia Pacific, Calbee sells more chips than anyone else besides Pepsi (PEP) Co, its longtime partner that owns about 20% of the company via a subsidiary. Pepsi (PEP) controls about 24% of the region's potato chip market, while Calbee has about 12%, according to data from Euromonitor International.

Both have been hit over the past two years by ruptures in commodity supplies that led to a record surge in food prices in 2022, affecting virtually everything from tomatoes to rice to peaches.

Experts have called it the worst food crisis in modern history and warned of continued instability ahead, even as the high prices have largely receded.

Supply chain nightmare

Calbee faced a major crisis when it was confronted with a shortage of potatoes from the summer of 2021 to the fall of 2022.

It came against a global backdrop of historically high food prices, as producers grappled with pandemic-related supply chain issues, a historic drought in Brazil and increased global use of vegetable oils, sugar and cereals.

---

1 新闻稿来源：https://www.cnn.com。

Then the war in Ukraine broke out in February 2022, cutting off access to a critical global grain and vegetable oil exporter.

The crisis contributed to another record jump for food prices last year, with a benchmark index compiled by the United Nations' Food and Agriculture Organization (FAO) reaching its highest annual level since 2005.

Calbee typically sources as much as 90% of its potatoes in Japan, with 80% of that supply coming from Hokkaido, a northern island.

But the area was ravaged by drought in 2021, and the firm's domestic potato supply fell by 8% and 14% in the 2021 and 2022 fiscal years, respectively.

Calbee tried to make up for the shortfall by importing more from the United States, which normally accounts for the remaining 10% of its potato supply. But it didn't have much luck.

A global shortage of shipping containers caused delays and higher prices.

To make matters worse, in late 2021, floods in the US Pacific Northwest stopped ports from operating as usual, making it harder for Calbee to get both potatoes and potato flakes: small, white chunks of dried mashed potatoes used to make Jagarico, its popular line of crispy biscuit sticks.

As a result, the company had to suspend sales promotions and new product launches, while accepting higher procurement and shipping costs. The challenges contributed to a 7% decline in operating profit in the financial year that ended in March 2022.

编译稿（标题 + 导语）

日本最大薯片制造商闹"土豆荒"，已3次提高相关零食价格

【环球时报综合报道】由于本土土豆短缺，从去年开始日本最大薯片制造商卡乐比公司已3次提高以土豆为原料的零食价格，个别种类甚至暴涨数倍。卡乐比首席执行官江原信4日在接受美国有线电视新闻网（CNN）采访时称，土豆短缺问题"令人头疼"。

案例分析

编译的标题与原标题的结构有很大不同，原标题采用了what引导的问题结构，强调了土豆供应短缺造成的影响，而编译的标题采用前后两段式，点

出了事件主体、原因和结果。此外，编译者还将原标题中的 Asia's top potato chip maker 处理为"日本最大薯片制造商"，为读者提供了一定的背景信息。

编译的导语综合了原文前三段的内容，第一段相当于一个引子，引起读者兴趣。第二段说明了事件发生的原因，第三段通过引述该公司 CEO 的话，说明目前情况严峻。

◎ 新闻稿 3

2024 will probably be hotter than this year because of El Niño, NASA scientists say[1]

CNN—As millions bake under a relentless heat wave in the South and Southwest US—and as temperatures soar around the Northern Hemisphere—NASA scientists warned Thursday that we haven't even seen the worst of El Niño and next year will likely be even warmer for the planet.

Climate change, caused by burning fossil fuels, is unequivocally warming the Earth's temperature, NASA scientists said.

And El Niño, the natural climate pattern in the tropical Pacific that brings warmer-than-average sea-surface temperatures and influences weather, has only just started in recent months and therefore is not having a huge impact yet on the extreme heat people around the globe are experiencing this summer, said Gavin Schmidt, a climatologist and director of the NASA Goddard Institute for Space Studies.

"It's really only just emerged, and so what we're seeing is not really due to that El Niño," Schmidt told reporters. "What we're seeing is the overall warmth pretty much everywhere—particularly in the oceans. ... The reason why we think that's going to continue is because we continue to put greenhouse gases into the atmosphere. Until we stop doing that, temperatures will keep on rising."

Last month was the hottest June on record for the planet, the EU's Copernicus Climate Change Service reported earlier this month. Several days in July were the planet's warmest in modern records kept by two climate agencies in the US and Europe.

All of that heat is adding up, and Schmidt said he believes there is a 50-50 chance that 2023 will be the warmest year on record.

---

1 新闻稿来源：https://www.cnn.com。

But, he added, it is likely that a sweltering 2024 will exceed it, precisely because of El Niño's influence.

"We anticipate that 2024 is going to be an even warmer year because we're going to be starting off with that El Niño event," Schmidt said. "That will peak towards the end of this year, and how big that is is going to have a big impact on the following year's statistics."

Scientists also discussed the devastating impact climate change is having on the Earth's oceans, as North Atlantic Ocean temperatures have soared this summer.

"The oceans are running a fever," said Carlos Del Castillo, chief of NASA's Ocean Ecology Laboratory. "This issue with ocean temperature is not a problem that stays in the ocean—it affects everything else." Castillo noted hotter ocean temperatures can make hurricanes stronger and make ocean levels rice due to glacial melt.

Schmidt noted that rising temperatures are in line with what scientists have predicted as humans burn more fossil fuels and pump more greenhouse gas emissions into the atmosphere.

"Even the things that are unprecedented are not surprising," Schmidt said.

编译稿（标题＋导语）

美国科学家警告2024年可能会更热

美国科学家警告称，尽管2023年已经很炎热，但2024年可能会更热。

美国有线电视新闻网7月20日报道，美国国家航空航天局科学家施密特表示，2023年有近50%的概率成为历来最温暖的一年，但另一个不太好的消息是：2024年有可能会更热。

案例分析

编译的标题将原标题前后两个部分的顺序进行了调换，更符合中文的表达习惯。考虑到有些读者可能不熟悉NASA，所以编译者在编译标题时作了模糊处理，将NASA翻译成美国科学家，更易于读者接受。

编译的导语对应原文中的第一段，不同的是导语采用了两段式结构，第一段极为概括，以2023年作为参照说明2024年炎热的程度，以吸引读者。第二段采用导语常规的写作模式，进一步补充相关新闻要素，如who、what、when等。

阅读以下两篇新闻稿并编译新闻的标题和导语。

◎新闻稿1

Short of IT workers at home, Israeli startups recruit elsewhere[1]

JUNE 26, 2017, Reuters

TEL AVIV (Reuters)—When Alexey Chalimov founded software design firm Eastern Peak in Israel four years ago he knew he would not find the developers he needed at home.

He went to Ukraine and hired 120 people to develop mobile apps and web platforms for international clients and smaller Israeli startups.

"I worked for years in the Israeli market and I knew what the costs were in Israel and I knew there was a shortage of workers," he told Reuters.

Driven by startups, Israel's technology industry is the fastest growing part of the economy. It accounts for 14 percent of economic output and 50 percent of exports.

But a shortage of workers means its position at the cutting edge of global technology is at risk, with consequences for the economy and employment.

The government's Innovation Authority forecasts a shortage of 10,000 engineers and programmers over the next decade in a market that employs 140,000. Israel has dropped six spots in three years to 17th in the World Economic Forum's ranking of the ease of finding skilled technology employees.

The shortage is particularly painful for Israel's 5,000 startups which compete for talent with development centers of technology giants such as Google, Intel, Microsoft and Apple. They offer big incentives that a startup cannot afford.

Israel will lose its edge if the shortage isn't tackled, said Noa Acker, head of policy at the societal challenges division at the Innovation Authority.

"Salaries will be very high and the industry will shrink to only very high level R&D while much of the work will be exported," she said.

The main reason for the shortfall is a sharp drop in the number of computer science, maths and statistics graduates, down from a peak of 3,000 in 2005 to a low of 1,600 in 2008.

---

1 新闻稿来源：https://www.reuters.com。

This is partly due to problems in secondary and primary schools where lack of funding means some classrooms do not have computers and advanced maths teachers are in short supply.

"Why do we still have classes where there are no computers?" said Yifat Turbiner, a researcher in entrepreneurship and innovation at Ben-Gurion University.

"If more budgets aren't allocated to generate a technological state of mind ... from elementary school, I believe all industries will suffer, not just high-tech."

Another reason for the shortage of computer science graduates is that after the dotcom bubble burst in 2000 many Israeli high tech workers lost their jobs, Acker said.

This meant that students lost interest in tech careers and university applications declined.

The Education Ministry has announced plans to boost studies of maths and science, especially in high-schools outside the cities where advanced classes are not always available. But Turbiner said initiatives are also needed for a higher standard of maths at a younger age including training more teachers.

The government also has long-term initiatives to integrate ultra-Orthodox Jews and Arabs—two fast-growing segments of the population with low labor participation—into the industry.

Ultra-Orthodox Jews make up about 11 percent of the population and many prioritize religious studies over science and maths.

Military technology expertise gained by soldiers during their service has been behind several successful Israeli firms including the country's biggest tech company, Check Point Software Technologies.

The government is also running "boot camps" of up to 18 months to train tech workers without technology degrees.

While the government takes steps to stimulate organic growth of workers at home, it is also making changes to visas for a quick fix of importing foreign workers.

The government is preparing 500 visas for students from abroad who studied science and engineering at Israeli universities so they can stay to work at tech firms for a year. It is also working on easing bureaucratic hurdles to unlimited "expert visas."

In the meantime, many Israeli startups are looking abroad.

Ukraine is the top destination with about 100 Israeli development centers. A strong tradition of maths and computer science teaching that is present in many countries in Soviet Union countries means Ukraine has more than 20,000 IT graduates each year.

The 1990s arrival of a million immigrants from Soviet countries, many of them scientists who went to work for technology companies, has also created strong ties.

Israeli companies have also recruited workers in other eastern European countries such as Poland and Bulgaria.

Wix.com, which helps small businesses build websites and is one of Israel's hottest tech companies, employs 120 workers in two development centers in Ukraine and another 80 at a site in Lithuania.

"They are in the same time zone, they have a good level of English and all are Russian speakers. Some of our people here are former Russians," said Boaz Inbal, general manager of Wix's development centers. "We have direct flights to both countries. It's easy for us to collaborate and communicate."

Salaries for software developers in Ukraine are about 40 percent lower than in Israel, said Andrey Link, an executive vice president at Ukrainian software engineering firm Infopulse.

But he said: "The key argument in our favor is not the cost but availability. To find 2-3 people (in Israel) is not a problem, but if they need...an R&D center for 100 people, it is very difficult in Israel."

标题：_____

导语：_____

_____

◎新闻稿2

China's Chang'e-6 moon mission returns to Earth with historic far side samples[1]

Updated 3:34 AM EDT, Tue June 25, 2024, CNN

Hong Kong (CNN)—China's Chang'e-6 lunar module returned to Earth Tuesday, successfully completing its historic mission to collect the first ever samples from the far side of the moon in a major step forward for the country's ambitious space program.

The reentry module "successfully landed" in a designated zone in China's northern Inner Mongolia region just after 2 p.m. local time, according to state broadcaster CCTV. A livestream carried by CCTV showed the module touching down via parachute to a round of applause in the mission control room.

"The Chang'e-6 lunar exploration mission has been a complete success," said Zhang Kejian, head of the China National Space Administration (CNSA), from the control room.

A search team located the module minutes after its landing, according to CCTV. The livestream showed a worker carrying out checks on the module, which lay on grassland beside a Chinese flag.

In a congratulatory message Tuesday, Chinese leader Xi Jinping hailed the mission as "another landmark achievement in building a strong country in space, and science and technology."

Beijing plans to send astronauts to the moon by 2030 and build a research base at the lunar south pole—a region believed to contain water ice, where the US also hopes to establish a base.

The Chang'e-6 probe is expected to have returned to Earth with up to 2 kilograms of moon dust and rocks from the lunar far side, which will be analyzed by researchers in China before being opened for access by international scientists, according to the CNSA.

---

1 新闻稿来源：https://edition.cnn.com。

Results from the analysis of the samples could help scientists peer back into the evolution of the moon, the Earth and the solar system—while also aiding China's aim to utilize resources on the moon to further its exploration there, experts say.

标题：_____
导语：_____
_____

第四章
英语新闻正文的编译

第一节　英语新闻报道正文的文体特征

　　如前文所述，英语新闻报道语篇结构严密紧凑，通常包括新闻标题、导语和正文三个部分，有些新闻报道也包含结尾。新闻报道通常要回答六个基本问题（要素），即我们常说的"5W"和"1H"。这六个要素并非在导语中全部呈现，有时事件发生的原因、引起的相关反应及其他背景信息将在导语后的正文中加以说明。

　　新闻导语之后就是正文部分。正文部分主要解释导语，补充导语中没有涉及的新闻要素、新闻事实和背景信息，起到深化导语的作用。简单来说，新闻正文的功能就是完成导语没有完成的任务。

　　英语新闻报道的正文往往具有以下特征：

　　● **使用长句**：英语新闻的正文大量使用长句，有时长句中包含多个从句和非谓语形式，呈现的信息量大且紧凑，也有助于表达复杂的逻辑关系或思想观念。

　　● **段落简短**：英语新闻报道通常段落较短，这主要是考虑读者的阅读体验。简短的段落会减少读者的阅读心理负担，增加文章的可读性。

　　● **引述较多**：新闻英语报道常常使用引述，包括直接引述和间接引述，即我们常说的"直接引语"和"间接引语"，引述的内容可以是一段完整的话或其中一部分，或是其中某一句话。"直接引语"可增强客观性和真实性，提高生动性、现场感和可信度；"间接引语"有助于突出重点、传递更多信息、提高文章的可读性。

　　● **词汇专业**：英语新闻报道多使用专有名词，如 the Pentagon 指代美国国防部，Downing Street 指代英国政府。另外，涉及时政、财经、科技、军事、社会、文化、体育等不同领域的新闻报道常常包含大量的专业术语，如经济领域的 quantitative easing（量化宽松）、capital gain（资本收益）、CPI（居民消费价格指数）、PPI（生产者价格指数）；社会文化领域的 helicopter parents（过度关注孩子的家长）、boomerang generation（回巢族）；军事领域的 medium-range missile（中程导弹）、

military intelligence（军事情报）等。

● **常见新词**：英语新闻报道中新词层出不穷，如 Black Lives Matter（简称 BLM），是非裔男子乔洛·弗洛伊德（George Floyd）遭美国白人警察暴力执法惨死后民众抗议中的口号，意思是"黑人的命也是命"。再如，随着社交媒体的兴起，越来越多的年轻人成为某个明星或品牌的狂热粉丝，于是出现了 stan 这个词语，意为"死忠粉"。现在 stan 已经成为流行文化符号，与音乐、电影、体育等多个领域密不可分。英语短语 touch-screen generation（触屏一代）则指伴随新潮电子触屏设备（如智能手机或平板电脑）成长起来的年轻一代。

英语和汉语新闻稿在篇幅、段落、句子方面有着明显的区别（见表 4.1）：

表 4.1 英语新闻稿和汉语新闻稿的区别

对比范畴	英语新闻稿	汉语新闻稿
篇幅	大	小
段落	短	长
句子	长	短
分句	多	少
信息量	与同篇幅汉语新闻稿大体相当	与同篇幅英语新闻稿大体相当

鉴于英语和汉语新闻报道各自存在明显的特点，在英汉新闻编译过程中，编译者应使编译文符合汉语新闻写作的习惯以及汉语读者的思维和阅读习惯。

第二节 英语新闻报道正文的编译方法

新闻正文是对导语的全面阐释，即要说明新闻事件的起因、经过和结果，因而新闻正文的编译须紧扣主题，与标题和导语的主旨保持一致，同时，编译稿的文体风格也要符合原新闻稿的风格，该严肃的严肃，该活泼的活泼。新闻编译过程中一定要确保编译文准确、恰当、流畅。

第二章简单介绍了英汉新闻编译的方法，这里将从词汇、句子和语篇三个方面，对英语新闻报道正文的编译方法进行整理和归纳（见表 4.2）：

表 4.2 英语新闻报道正文的编译方法

类别	项目	编译方法	具体操作
词汇	普通词语	查找、核对	翻译成体现新闻文体特色的词语
句子	长句	化整为零，化长为短	翻译成汉语新闻中常见的短句子

续表

类别	项目	编译方法	具体操作
语篇	内容	增补	增补辅助理解信息，即原文未介绍的关键性背景、事件背景、术语阐释
		删减	删减重复性、非必要、无关联的背景信息及无意义的直接引语
	结构	合并同类项	合并一篇或多篇新闻稿中关联密切的内容并进行整理
		调整与重构	根据内容与重要新闻点的关联和逻辑关系，对源语新闻的段落顺序及段落内的语序进行重新调整
	语言	概括与转述	概括新闻中非关键的细节内容，并进行归纳总结和提炼转述，在不影响原文意思的前提下转述直接引语或原文中的某些说法

在编译英语新闻报道正文的过程中，编译人员还应考虑原文的内容、结构和风格三个方面的因素：

- **内容**：是否选择原文的主要内容作为编译稿的主要内容。
- **结构**：是否对原文进行大幅度的调整，例如调整原文的文体或结构方式等。
- **风格**：是否采用原文的写作文体和风格。

编译案例

◎新闻稿 1

AI Now Beats Humans at Basic Tasks-new benchmarks are needed, says major report[1]

By Nicola Jones

Artificial intelligence (AI) systems, such as the chatbot ChatGPT, have become so advanced that they now very nearly match or exceed human performance in tasks including reading comprehension, image classification and competition-level mathematics, according to a new report (see 'Speedy advances'). Rapid progress in the development of these systems also means that many common benchmarks and tests for assessing them are quickly becoming obsolete.

These are just a few of the top-line findings from the Artificial Intelligence Index Report 2024, which was published on 15 April by the Institute for Human-Centered

---

1 新闻稿来源：https://www.nature.com。

Artificial Intelligence at Stanford University in California. The report charts the meteoric progress in machine-learning systems over the past decade.

In particular, the report says, new ways of assessing AI—for example, evaluating their performance on complex tasks, such as abstraction and reasoning—are more and more necessary. "A decade ago, benchmarks would serve the community for 5–10 years" whereas now they often become irrelevant in just a few years, says Nestor Maslej, a social scientist at Stanford and editor-in-chief of the AI Index. "The pace of gain has been startlingly rapid."

Stanford's annual AI Index, first published in 2017, is compiled by a group of academic and industry specialists to assess the field's technical capabilities, costs, ethics and more—with an eye towards informing researchers, policymakers and the public. This year's report, which is more than 400 pages long and was copy-edited and tightened with the aid of AI tools, notes that AI-related regulation in the United States is sharply rising. But the lack of standardized assessments for responsible use of AI makes it difficult to compare systems in terms of the risks that they pose.

The rising use of AI in science is also highlighted in this year's edition: for the first time, it dedicates an entire chapter to science applications, highlighting projects including Graph Networks for Materials Exploration (GNoME), a project from Google DeepMind that aims to help chemists discover materials, and GraphCast, another DeepMind tool, which does rapid weather forecasting.

编译稿

人工智能在多项任务中击败人类

2024 年 04 月 17 日 06:50 中国科学报

4 月 15 日，美国斯坦福大学人工智能研究所发布《2024 年人工智能指数报告》，描绘了过去 10 年机器学习系统的飞速发展。

报告显示，聊天机器人 ChatGPT 等人工智能（AI）系统在阅读理解、图像分类和竞赛级数学等任务上的表现，已接近甚至超过人类。AI 系统的快速发展意味着，许多用于评估它们的通用基准和测试很快就会过时。

报告特别指出，推出评估 AI 的新方法越来越有必要，如评估其在抽象和推理等复杂任务上的表现。斯坦福大学社会科学家 Nestor Maslej 表示，10 年前，基准可以为社会服务 5 至 10 年，而现在，它们往往在短短几年内就变得无关紧要了。"增长的速度快得惊人。"

斯坦福大学的年度人工智能指数于 2017 年首次发布。该指数由学术和行业专家编制，旨在评估 AI 领域的技术能力、成本、道德等，从而为研究人员、政策制定者和公众提供信息。今年这份长达 400 多页的报告指出，美国对与 AI 相关的监管正在升级。但是，由于缺乏对负责任地使用 AI 的标准化评估，因此很难就系统构成的风险对它们进行比较。

新报告还首次用整个章节专门介绍 AI 的科学应用，包括谷歌 DeepMind 的一个旨在帮助化学家发现新材料的图形网络材料探索（GNoME）项目，以及 DeepMind 的另一个工具 GraphCast，它可以进行快速天气预报。

当前的 AI 热潮建立在神经网络和机器学习算法之上，这可以追溯到 2010 年代早期。此后，这一领域迅速发展壮大。

案例分析

原新闻稿采用倒金字塔结构，开头先点题——人工智能系统在多项任务中接近甚至超过人类，以此引出美国斯坦福大学新发布的《2024 年人工智能指数报告》；然后指出评估 AI 的新方法的必要性、发布人工智能指数报告的背景以及新报告的亮点。

经对比可以看出，编译稿在内容、结构和风格上都与原文保持高度一致，唯一不同之处在于编译稿把原新闻稿中的前两段顺序进行了微调，先说指数报告的发布，再说人工智能系统发展的现状，符合中文读者的阅读习惯。另外，编译稿末尾加了一句背景介绍，以帮助读者更好地理解新闻稿的内容。编译稿的标题只保留了前半部分，简洁明了，也符合中文新闻的报道习惯。

◎ 新闻稿 2

IOC and Deloitte Expand Partnership to Transform Sports Tech[1]

By Amber Jackson August 13, 2024

Deloitte will become Games Technology Integration Partner for the Olympic Games, partnering with the IOC to continue transforming technology within sports.

As the Paris 2024 Olympic Games drew to a close over the weekend, the International

---

1 新闻稿来源：https://technologymagazine.com。

Olympic Committee (IOC) announced it would be continuing its partnership with Deloitte.

The expanded partnership sees the professional services company becoming Games Technology Integration Partner for the Olympic Games, the Paralympic Games and the Youth Olympic Games until 2032. This includes the Olympic Winter Games Milano-Cortina 2026, until the Olympic Games Brisbane 2032.

Deloitte will help advance the IOC's vision of establishing a new integrated technology infrastructure to enhance and secure technology operations for future Olympic and Paralympic Games.

"This is an exciting moment for Deloitte as we build on the incredible work we have already begun with the IOC around digital transformation, knowledge management infrastructure, as well as programmes supporting athletes and sustainability initiatives," comments John Skowron, Vice Chairman of the Olympic and Paralympic Games at Deloitte.

"The expansion of our partnership is a tremendous opportunity for Deloitte to share our vast global management consulting experience and technology capabilities to help transform the Games Technology infrastructure."

Driving operational excellence

The Olympic Games continues to represent innovation and excellence as it strives to set new standards across a range of sports.

Within this, Deloitte is committed to being at the forefront of technological advancement to ensure that future Games are robust, efficient and sustainable. Likewise, it aims to use its IT infrastructure to not only drive operational excellence, but to enhance the performance of Olympic athletes and make the viewing experience unforgettable.

The company's technology strategy is driven by the want to push boundaries and inspire the world through the power of sport.

Since 2022, Deloitte has worked with the IOC as part of its digital transformation journey. Its expertise and approach to innovation has helped the IOC navigate the technology landscape as it continues to change with increased agility.

"Together with Deloitte, we are excited to explore new possibilities and drive forward the future of technology in sport," says Ilario Corna, IOC Chief Information and Technology Officer.

"Our shared vision of excellence and innovation will ensure that the Olympic Games remain a symbol of human potential and achievement. We look forward to continuing this journey, setting new benchmarks, and inspiring future generations through our commitment to technological advancement and excellence in the world of sport."

Enhancing the Olympic Games with AI

Deloitte is also working across the Olympic Movement to enhance athlete employability and accelerate sustainability initiatives.

A large portion of these offerings involves AI, as Deloitte aims to guide the IOC into a future where the disruptive technology is able to enhance human potential at the Olympic Games. The expanded partnership between both organisations aims to bring vast digital consulting experience and help facilitate the development of the Olympic AI Agenda, the IOC's strategy to incorporate AI successfully across multiple areas of the Games.

Deloitte's John Tweardy states: "This is an incredible opportunity for Deloitte to bring together the depth and breadth of our entire organisation to support the transformation and modernisation of the platforms that will drive forward the next generation of scalable technology solutions to optimise the Olympic Games experience."

Deloitte is working with the IOC to not only drive AI transformation for the Olympic Games, but also to imagine how the technology can improve referee insights, sports equipment maintenance and athlete performance.

It is also seeking to develop new ways in which sports can be democratised. The Sports Innovation Hub by Deloitte in Madrid, Spain is central to this effort, designed to bring together a wide range of capabilities to support cities and organisations with state-of-the-art technology solutions to enhance and protect sport's biggest moments.

John adds: "With Deloitte's experience in sport, data-driven marketing, cybersecurity, tax and technologies such as AI, we will join the IOC and other partners to create a 'one team' model that we believe can have a positive and lasting impact on the IOC, Organising Committees, and the fan experience."

编译稿

国际奥委会扩大与德勤的全球合作伙伴关系

据技术杂志网站8月13日消息，当地时间8月10日，国际奥林匹克委员会（IOC）宣布和德勤（Deloitte）扩大其全球合作伙伴关系。从2026年米兰-科尔蒂纳冬奥会到2032年布里斯班冬奥会，德勤将担任奥运会、残奥会和青年奥运会的奥运会技术集成合作伙伴。德勤将帮助国际奥委会推进愿景，即建立新的综合技术基础设施和奥运会平台，以加强和保障奥运会和残奥会未来的技术运营。

早在2022年，国际奥委会就和德勤共同宣布建立长达10年涉及5届奥运会的全球合作伙伴关系，以从根本上改变未来奥运会和残奥会的体验方式以及奥运会向世界展示的方式。

2026年至2032年期间，德勤将负责设计、构建、实施、运营和保障技术集成、应用开发和网络安全服务。德勤将引领奥运会科技变革，持续提升奥运会运营效能和效率。此外，德勤还将支持国际奥委会实施《奥林匹克2020议程》中有关优化奥运会举办的建议，通过开发可为每届奥运会和残奥会定制技术。这种定制将有助于减少为每届奥运会重新创建应用程序的需求，并在未来嵌入持续的知识共享和改进。

案例分析

对比英、汉两篇新闻稿可以发现，编译稿在内容和结构上有比较大的调整。原新闻稿主题是国际奥委会与德勤的战略合作，通过使用小标题详细描述了一些合作细节，包括合作中的角色、相关举措和实现的目标等。通过引用合作双方相关负责人的话表达了双方对合作的愿望、信心及对未来的愿景。

编译者考虑到广大目标读者对信息的一般需求，对内容细节和直接引语作了幅度较大的删减处理，以综合概括为主，提供最核心的信息。另外编译稿在结构上也有较大调整，采用了三段式结构：第一段以导语开头，根据新闻报道的需要增加了事件发生的具体时间，直接点明双方扩大合作伙伴关系这个核心新闻事实，指出双方合作将实现的目标。第二段接着说明合作的背景，以及合作将带来的结果或效果。第三段结尾部分具体说明了德勤在合作中承担的角色、将要带来的变化和合作的意义。这篇编译稿将最重要的信息提炼出来并呈现给读者，满足了普通读者对信息的需求。

在工作实践中，很多时候编译者需要将两篇或两篇以上的英语新闻稿编译成一篇汉语新闻稿。在进行这项工作时，编译者通常需要遵循以下步骤：

- **了解新闻稿内容**：仔细阅读每篇英语新闻稿的内容，充分了解每篇新闻稿涉及的背景、主要人物、地点和时间等信息。
- **提取重要信息和数据**：从每篇新闻稿中提取最重要的信息和数据，包括标题、导语、主体部分的主要观点和结论。

● **整合所提取的信息**：将各篇新闻稿中提取的信息进行整合，按照逻辑顺序排列。如果两篇新闻稿涉及同一主题但角度不同，可以根据编译目的分别介绍其各自的观点并补充细节。在实际操作中，通常以影响力大的某一主流媒体的报道内容为主，而将其他媒体报道中的信息作为补充。

● **确定编译稿的结构**：根据新闻事件的发生，结合编译的目的确定编译稿采用的叙事结构，如倒金字塔、金字塔或沙漏结构等。

● **完成编译稿的内容**：按照已确定的新闻稿的报道框架，将筛选的新闻事件的主要信息按逻辑进行排列，完成编译稿，必要时根据读者的阅读习惯可适当增补背景信息或解释性的语句，在语言表达上也可适当作其他调整，确保编译稿信息的准确性、完整性和流畅性，便于读者更好地理解新闻事件。

● **通读并修改润色全文**：完成编译稿后，仔细阅读全文并进行校对和修改，重点核查信息是否准确、结构是否合理、逻辑是否清晰、语句是否有语法错误和拼写错误等。

编译案例

◎ 新闻稿

Japan Plans Autonomous Vehicle Lane on Shin-Tomei Expressway[1]

Mar 31, 2023 18:52 (JST)

Tokyo, (Jiji Press)—The Japanese government plans to set up a lane for autonomous vehicles on part of the Shin-Tomei Expressway（东名高速公路）, which connects the greater Tokyo and Nagoya areas, it was learned Friday.

The plan was presented at a meeting of the government's council for achieving Prime Minister Fumio Kishida's "digital garden city state" initiative, held at the prime minister's office the same day.

Under the plan, autonomous trucks will be allowed to drive in the special lane, running over 100 kilometers, from as early as fiscal 2024.

Kishida instructed industry minister Yasutoshi Nishimura to consider specific measures to achieve the plan.

The government will also engage in efforts for automation in the logistics sector by creating dedicated drone flight routes.

---

1 新闻稿来源：https://jen.jiji.com。

b

Japan to designate lane for self-driving cars and route for drones[1]

Friday, March 31, 14:43（Kyodo News）

Tokyo—The Japanese government has unveiled a plan to set up a dedicated lane for self-driving vehicles on a highway and establish a flight route for drones for delivery use. The move is part of an initiative to expand digital technologies nationwide.

Prime Minister Kishida Fumio and relevant ministers gathered at the Prime Minister's Office on Friday to discuss the initiative.

Kishida said work to complete the projects will start in the fiscal year that begins in April 2024. They are part of infrastructure development for creating a digitalized society.

He told Industry Minister Nishimura Yasutoshi to flesh out the plan.

Nishimura said his ministry will consider setting up a dedicated lane for self-driving trucks on a 100-kilometer section of the Shin-Tomei Expressway, which connects Kanagawa Prefecture, near Tokyo, with Aichi Prefecture in central Japan.

Nishimura also said his ministry officials will discuss designating a new flight course of more than 150 kilometers over Saitama Prefecture, north of Tokyo, as a route for drones to make deliveries and to maintain power lines.

Kishida expressed his determination to press ahead with the infrastructure development and land planning required for digitalization.

He instructed ministers in the meeting to continue working to achieve digitalization across the country to revitalize rural areas.

编译稿

日计划2024年度在东名高速设自动驾驶车道

据日本时事通讯社3月31日报道，日本政府计划于2024年在东名（东京–名古屋）高速公路的部分区间设置自动驾驶专用车道。

该计划是经济产业省在31日召开的会议上提出的，会议在首相官邸召开，讨论如何实现首相岸田文雄提出的"数字田园都市国家构想"倡议。按照该计划，最早于2024财年可允许自动驾驶卡车驶入自动驾驶车道，时速100公里以上。

岸田文雄指示产业大臣西村康稔负责推进该计划的实施。报道称，日本政府还

---

1 新闻稿来源：https://newsonjapan.com。

将在物流自动化方面加大投入，设置专用无人机飞行航线用于物资运输。

另据共同社 31 日消息，作为"全国范围普及利用数字技术倡议"的一部分，日本政府公布计划将在东名高速公路上设置自动驾驶车道，并开辟运输物流无人机专用飞行航线。

首相岸田文雄指出，该计划将于 2024 年 4 月新财年开始的时候实施，这将是完善基础设施建设、创建数字社会宏大目标的一个组成部分。会上他还表达了他坚决推进基础设施建设、实现国内数字化、振兴乡村地区的决心。

根据首相的指示，产业大臣西村康稔负责该计划的落实。他表示他将与经产省其他官员商讨自动驾驶车道和专用飞行航线等相关议题。

案例分析

将两篇或两篇以上的英语新闻稿编译成一篇汉语新闻稿的时候，最重要的操作是将两篇新闻稿中最核心的信息进行整合，合并同类信息、补充新的信息，然后合成一篇完整、独立、要素齐全的编译稿。

以上面这篇编译稿为例，它采纳了原新闻稿的结构，导语中明确了日本政府将设置自动驾驶车道的计划，然后在正文中提供更多该计划的细节。该编译稿分别从两篇新闻稿件中抽取出各自的核心信息进行编排，同时还明确指出了信息源（日本时事通讯社和共同社），这一点在编译多篇新闻稿时需特别注意。此篇编译稿包含了新闻中的 what、when、where、who 和 how 等基本要素。

将以下英语新闻稿编译成汉语新闻稿。
◎新闻稿

Chinese social media sensation Xiaohongshu wins major foreign VC backing[1]

Eleanor Olcott in Beijing　JULY 11 2024

Xiaohongshu, China's fastest-growing social media platform, has gained the backing of venture capital firm DST Global in a rare example of foreign investors putting money into a tech sector.

---

1 新闻稿来源：https://www-ft-com.ezphost.dur.ac.uk。

The photo and video-sharing platform, wildly popular with female city dwellers, arranged stake sales of existing shares in recent weeks to current and new investors that valued the company at $17bn, according to three people with knowledge of the matter.

DST, founded by Moscow-born Israeli tech entrepreneur Yuri Milner and a past investor in Facebook, took part in the round along with Hong Kong-based HongShan, formerly Sequoia China, which added to its existing stake. Chinese private equity firms Hillhouse Investment, Boyu Capital and Citic Capital also invested. The size of DST's investment could not be ascertained.

The vote of confidence comes after Xiaohongshu, which translates as "little red book" and is also backed by VC firm GSR Ventures and Singaporean state-backed investor Temasek, turned profitable in 2023. It made $500mn in net profit last year on revenues of $3.7bn, the *Financial Times* reported previously. By contrast, it made a $200mn loss on revenues of about $2bn in 2022.

Xiaohongshu also has the backing of Chinese internet giants Tencent and Alibaba. Support from both parties means it is unlikely to be an acquisition target for either group, given their effective veto over a sale to a rival, according to people familiar with the matter.

Investors are betting that Xiaohongshu is one of a small group of Chinese tech unicorns that can look forward to a blockbuster initial public offering (IPO) after delivering strong growth.

Xiaohongshu reached 312mn monthly active users in 2023, a 20% increase from the previous year, making it the fastest-growing large social media platform in China last year, based on a *Financial Times* calculation.

"Xiaohongshu hit a $20bn valuation during the peak of VC tech investment. But unlike many other start-ups that are forced to do successive down rounds or close down, it is growing into its valuation," said one VC in Shanghai. Investor confidence in Xiaohongshu has been boosted by its strong financial performance and revived hopes for overseas listings of large tech companies.

Xiaohongshu is a go-to manual for international Chinese travellers in search of restaurant and shopping tips. The company has been expanding its overseas business development team to scour markets popular with Chinese tourists and bring more advertisers to the platform, according to a person with knowledge of the matter.

Xiaohongshu has also become important to retailers looking to grow their audiences and it has been offering to promote artificial intelligence start-ups on its platform in exchange for equity, the FT reported previously.

将以下两篇英语新闻稿编译成一篇汉语新闻稿，编译前请画出拟保留的原新闻稿的信息。

◎新闻稿

a

China Digital Currency Expands to Hangzhou and Chongqing[1]

April 4, 2022

China will expand the trial of its sovereign digital currency to a number of Chinese cities including Chongqing, Tianjin, Hangzhou and Guangzhou, as the central bank works on incentives for banks, technology firms and local authorities to take part in its e-CNY.

The decision was made at a People's Bank of China (PBOC) meeting on March 31, according to a statement published by the central bank on Saturday. It is the PBOC's first-ever symposium on digital currency, where the central bank's governor Yi Gang spoke, in a sign of escalated support for the digital yuan.

The programme will cover Fuzhou and Xiamen in Fujian province, and five cities in Zhejiang province that will host the 2022 Asian Games, namely Ningbo, Wenzhou, Shaoxing, Jinhua and Huzhou.

China's e-CNY experiment, which generally involved giving cash reward to consumers to spur usage and asking merchants to accept e-CNY payments, have demonstrated the initial feasibility of the digital sovereign currency, but additional research and exploration are needed in security, compliance and potential impact on the existing banking system, the central bank said.

"Policies must be designed to stimulate creativity and enthusiasm among the banks, technology firms and the local government in the development, promotion and

---

1 新闻稿来源：https://finance.yahoo.com。

proliferation of the digital yuan," the central bank said. "In the process of promotion, competition should be encouraged."

China's active roll-out of its sovereign digital currency has moved ahead of other major central banks like the US Federal Reserve and the Bank of Japan, raising suspicion as to the Chinese government's intent. Robert Greene, a former senior adviser to the US Treasury, published an article last July saying one potential function of the e-CNY may be to skirt US financial sanctions.

To be sure, the Chinese central bank's summary of the symposium didn't mention cross-border use of the digital currency, mostly focusing the discussion on domestic usage. The e-CNY is a digital form of the Chinese central bank's fiat money, which is not freely convertible outside China.

China's digital yuan experiments have already taken place in Beijing, Shenzhen, Shanghai, Suzhou, Xiong'an, Chengdu, Hainan, Changsha, Xi'an, Qingdao and Dalian. According to the latest data from the central bank, the e-CNY had 261 million users at the end of 2021, nearly double the user number in October.

Hong Kong plans to soon roll out a pilot scheme for the use of the digital yuan for shopping and dining, making the special administration region the first offshore city to use the e-CNY outside the mainland, Eddie Yue Wai-man, CEO of the Hong Kong Monetary Authority (HKMA) said in February.

For Chinese consumers, the e-CNY offers an alternative option in cashless payment, an area dominated by Alipay and WeChat Pay, which also support e-CNY as part of their functions. Alipay is offered by Ant Group, the fintech affiliate of this newspaper's owner South China Morning Post.

The expansion of the roll-out coincides with a hiring spree at the central bank's Digital Currency Research Institute (DCRI) for hundreds of data and infrastructure engineers. The institute's head Mu Changchun delivered a report last Wednesday to the Chinese People's Political Consultative Conference (CPPCC), the country's top political advisory body, about the progress of e-CNY, according to a report by Xinhua news agency.

China Expands Digital Yuan Trials to More Cities[1]

April 29, 2022 Bloomberg News

(Bloomberg)—China will expand its digital yuan trial to more areas from the current 11 cities and regions, according to the central bank.

The market's response toward the use of the digital yuan in pilot cities and Winter Olympic venues has been good, and user and transaction scales have both been "growing steadily," the People's Bank of China said Saturday following a meeting chaired by Governor Yi Gang.

In the next step to promote the use of digital yuan, the central bank said it will work on privacy protection and crime prevention, and conduct "deep research" of the impact on the country's financial system.

Trials have taken place in Shenzhen, Suzhou, Xiong'an, Chengdu, Shanghai, Hainan, Changsha, Xi'an, Qingdao, Dalian and the closed loop of the 2022 Winter Olympic Games.

China will add Tianjin, Chongqing, Guangzhou, Fuzhou, Xiamen, Hangzhou, Ningbo, Wenzhou, Huzhou, Shaoxing and Jinhua to the list of trial cities. Beijing and Zhangjiakou, the co-host cities of Winter Olympics and Winter Paralympic Games, will continue to use the digital yuan after trials inside venues of the Games end.

---

1 新闻稿来源：https://www.bnnbloomberg.ca。

第五章
不同题材的英语新闻编译

第一节 灾难类新闻的编译

一、灾难类新闻的概念

灾难类新闻报道的主要是那些突然发生、具有强烈破坏性和影响力、会造成重大人员伤亡和财产损失的事件，这些事件往往能够给受众带来巨大的冲击力。灾难类新闻主题包括但不限于自然灾害（如地震、火灾、洪水、台风等）和社会安全事件（如恐怖袭击、重大刑事案件、突发群体性事件、重大疫情、食品安全事件等）。自然灾害往往具有突发性和破坏性，社会安全事件通常涉及公共安全和社会稳定，这些事件的发生能够迅速吸引公众的关注，成为社会舆论的热点和焦点，也是媒体报道特别关注的内容。

灾难类新闻的报道主要包括以下几个要素：
- 灾难事件的发生；
- 灾难波及的范围；
- 灾难造成的影响（人员伤亡、财产损失等）；
- 灾难发生的原因；
- 灾难发生的进程；
- 灾难引起的各方反应（国际社会、国内相关部门等）；
- 灾难引起的社会救助；
- 救援及善后工作的开展；
- 相关信息辟谣；
- 对灾难事件的反思，包括存在的问题以及应对、预防及自救措施；
- 相关历史背景。

以上这些要素不一定会全部呈现在一篇灾难类新闻报道中，但对此类稿件的新闻编译非常重要，将这些内容交代清楚可以帮助公众了解事件真相、化解负面舆情。

二、灾难类新闻稿的结构

一般来说，灾难类新闻稿通常采用倒金字塔结构，下文将以 2024 年 1 月 1 日日本发生强烈地震这条新闻为例，对灾难类新闻稿的结构进行详细说明。

◎新闻稿

Powerful Quake Rocks Japan, Nearly 100,000 Residents Ordered to Evacuate[1]

By Reuters Jan. 1, 2024, at 2:26 a.m

1　TOKYO (Reuters)—A powerful earthquake struck central Japan on Monday, killing at least one person, destroying buildings, knocking out power to tens of thousands of homes and prompting residents in some coastal areas to flee to higher ground.

2　The quake with a preliminary magnitude of 7.6 triggered waves of about 1 metre along Japan's west coast and neighbouring South Korea.

3　The Japan Meteorological Agency (JMA) initially issued a major tsunami warning—its first since the March 2011 earthquake and tsunami that struck northeast Japan killing nearly 20,000 people—for Ishikawa prefecture. It later downgraded that and eventually cut it to an advisory.

4　It was the strongest quake in the region in more than four decades, according to the U.S. Geological Survey.

5　Houses were destroyed, fires broke out and army personnel were dispatched to help with rescue operations, government spokesperson Yoshimasa Hayashi told reporters.

6　An elderly man was pronounced dead after a building fell down in Shika Town in Ishikawa, broadcaster NTV reported citing local police.

7　Local media footage from the prefecture showed a building collapsing in a plume of dust in the city of Suzu and a huge crack in a road in Wajima where panicked-looking parents clutched their children.

8　One witness on social media platform X posted footage of the Keta Grand Shrine near the coast in Hakui rocking in the quake as a crowd of visitors watched. "It's swaying," she exclaims. "This is scary!"

---

1 新闻稿来源：https://www.usnews.com。

9 Millions of Japanese traditionally visit shrines and temples on Jan. 1 to mark the start of the new year.

10 In nearby Kanazawa, a popular tourist destination, images showed the remnants of a shattered stone gate strewn at the entrance of another shrine as anxious worshippers looked on.

11 The tremor was also felt in the mountains of neighbouring Nagano prefecture.

12 "The snow from the electric wire (came) down, and also from the roof it fell down and all the cars are shaking, and so everybody was panicked," Jonny Wu, a tourist visiting Nagano for a skiing holiday, told Reuters.

13 More strong quakes in the region, where seismic activity has been simmering for more than three years, could occur over coming days, JMA official Toshihiro Shimoyama said.

14 Russia and North Korea also issued tsunami warnings for some areas.

15 The Japanese government said that as of Monday night it had ordered more than 97,000 people in nine prefectures on the western coast of Japan's main island Honshu to evacuate. They were set to spend the night in sports halls and school gymnasiums, commonly used as evacuation centres in emergencies.

16 Kanazawa resident Ayako Daikai said she had evacuated to a nearby elementary school with her husband and two children soon after the earthquake hit. Classrooms, stairwells, hallways and the gymnasium were all packed with evacuees, she said.

17 "We haven't decided when to return home yet," she told Reuters when contacted by telephone.

NUCLEAR PLANTS

18 Japanese Prime Minister Fumio Kishida told reporters late on Monday that he had instructed search and rescue teams to do everything possible to save lives, even though access to quake-hit areas was difficult due to blocked roads.

19 The Imperial Household Agency said that following the disaster it would cancel Emperor Naruhito and Empress Masako's slated New Year appearance on Tuesday.

20 The quake comes at a sensitive time for Japan's nuclear industry, which has faced fierce opposition from some locals since the 2011 earthquake and tsunami that triggered nuclear meltdowns in Fukushima. Whole towns were devastated in the disaster.

21 Japan last week lifted an operational ban imposed on the world's biggest nuclear plant, Kashiwazaki-Kariwa, which has been offline since the 2011 tsunami.

22 The Nuclear Regulation Authority said no irregularities have been confirmed at nuclear plants along the Sea of Japan, including five active reactors at Kansai Electric Power's Ohi and Takahama plants in Fukui Prefecture.

23 Hokuriku's Shika plant in Ishikawa, the closest nuclear power station to the epicentre, had already halted its two reactors before the quake for regular inspections and saw no impact from the quake, the agency said.

'TSUNAMI! EVACUATE!'

24 Following the quake, a bright yellow message reading "Tsunami! Evacuate!" flashed across television screens advising residents in specific areas of the coast to immediately evacuate.

25 There were reports of at least 30 collapsed buildings in Wajima, a town of around 30,000 known for its lacquerware, and fire engulfed several buildings.

26 The quake also jolted buildings in the capital Tokyo, some 500 km from Wajima on the opposite coast.

27 Almost 32,000 households were still without power in Ishikawa prefecture late on Monday, according to utilities provider Hokuriku Electric Power, with temperatures set to drop to near freezing overnight in some areas.

28 Tohoku Electric Power said 700 households remained without power in neighbouring Niigata prefecture.

29 West Japan Railway reported late on Monday that a combined 1,400 passengers remained stuck on four halted bullet train services between Kanazawa and Toyama cities.

30 One of Ishikawa's airports was forced to shut due to cracks that had opened up in the runway, transport authorities said.

31 Japanese airline ANA turned back planes headed to airports in Toyama and Ishikawa, while Japan Airlines cancelled most services to the Niigata and Ishikawa regions.

阅读新闻稿并分析其结构，请对应灾难类新闻的要素填入相应的段落编号。

段落编号	1-2							
要素	灾难发生	范围	影响	原因/背景	进程	引起反应	救援/善后	反思

这篇新闻稿是典型的倒金字塔结构，由标题、导语和正文三个部分组成。标题采用两段式结构，前面部分 Powerful Quake Rocks Japan 说明灾难的发生，后面部分 Nearly 100,000 Residents Ordered to Evacuate 说明灾难造成的影响。导语（第一、二段）概述地震发生的基本情况，包含了地震发生的时间、地点、震级、造成的影响等新闻的基本要素。正文（第三段至结尾）详细说明了地震的相关情况，包括地震发生所影响的范围、发生的背景、引起的反应、政府采取的救援措施及对地震发生的反思等。

编译稿

日本 7.6 级地震致近 10 万人被疏散 超 3 万户家庭停电

1　据路透社 1 月 1 日消息，本周一下午，日本中北部的石川县能登地区发生了 7.6 级大地震。截至当地时间 1 月 2 日上午 5 时，日本石川县警察本部宣布，此次地震共造成该县 6 人死亡，数万户家庭停电，建筑物倒塌、近 10 万居民被迫撤离。当地电力、交通系统均受到较大影响。

2　美国地质调查局称，这是日本该地区 40 多年来发生的最强烈的地震。日本气象厅官员表示，未来 3 天到一周内该地区可能发生更强烈的地震。

3　据报道，这次地震引发了日本西海岸和邻国韩国约 1 米高的海浪，日本几乎整个西海岸都发布了海啸警报。俄罗斯和朝鲜也对部分地区发布了海啸预警。日本气象厅（JMA）最初对石川县发布了"重大海啸警报"，这是自 2011 年 3 月日本东北部发生 9.1 级地震以来的第一次。不过，该机构随后将本次海啸警报降为"海啸预警"。

4　日本政府官员表示，截至周一晚间，政府紧急疏散了本州西海岸 9 个县的 9.7 万多居民，并下令搜救队尽一切可能挽救生命，然而，由于道路封锁，救援工作面临挑战。

5　地震发生后，原定于周二举行的德仁天皇和雅子皇后的新年活动也被迫取消。

6 此次地震也影响了日本的核电产业,自 2011 年地震和海啸引发福岛核反应堆熔毁以来,日本核电站一直处于停运状态,上周日本刚刚解除了世界上最大的核电站之一的柏崎刈羽核电站的运行禁令。尽管靠近震中以及日本海沿岸的多个核电站未发现异常,但电力供应依然紧张,石川县约 3.2 万户家庭断电,邻近的新潟县有 700 户家庭断电。交通方面,铁路和航空服务也受到影响,石川县的一个机场被迫关闭,其他航线部分航班取消,高速列车停运,部分旅客被困。

阅读此篇新闻稿的编译稿,请对应灾难类新闻的要素填入相应的段落编号,并对比两稿的结构顺序及内容排列之不同(原新闻稿段落编号已填入)。

原稿段落	1,2	2,10,11,26	2-8,14,25-30	13	无	3,14,15,19,24,31	4,18	20
要素	灾难发生	范围	影响	原因/背景	进程	引起反应	救援/善后	反思
译稿段落								

灾难类新闻的报道与媒体的社会角色和责任息息相关,媒体通过新闻报道唤起社会关注和反思,以避免类似事件发生。新闻编译者也要采用适当的编译方法,不仅要传递信息,还要注意信息的传递效果。

三、灾难类新闻稿的编译原则

灾难类新闻报道不仅要传递相关信息,还应正确引导社会舆论。编译此类稿件时,编译者应遵循以下原则:

● **准确客观**:编译时必须确保与灾难发生的相关信息准确,能客观反映灾难的真实情况,为受众提供真实有效的信息,不可添枝加叶或凭空想象。

● **人性关怀**:编译时应关注灾难救援,注重报道内容的人性化,突出受灾群体的生活和情感状态,以引发读者的共鸣和关注。

● **引导舆论**:编译时需考虑受众的反应及可能产生的舆情,编译稿应正确引导舆论,内容表述应客观理性,在使受众了解真相的同时避免恐慌情绪的产生,以唤起社会的广泛关注,并对造成灾难的原因进行反思。

四、灾难类新闻稿的编译步骤

灾难类新闻稿的编译通常包括以下步骤:

● **梳理新闻要点**:阅读原文并分析新闻事件的主要事实,弄清新闻稿的文体结构。

- **确定编译结构**：灾难类新闻稿通常采用倒金字塔结构，编译稿多半也采用相同的结构，将梳理的新闻事件按照重要性由高到低进行排列。
- **编译导语和正文**：导语应简洁明了、概括最重要的新闻事实；新闻正文需清晰传达灾难新闻的关键要素。
- **调整和优化**：在完成初稿后，还需要对编译稿进行反复校对和修改，以确保新闻事实的准确性和表达的流畅性。
- **拟定新闻标题**：新闻标题的拟定要基于对原文的充分理解，标题应凸显最重要的信息，同时要能够吸引读者。

编译案例

◎新闻稿1

Helicopter carrying Iranian President Raisi crashes, prompting massive search operation[1]

Updated 10:46 PM EDT, Sun May 19, 2024

（CNN）—Rescuers are searching in the dark for a helicopter that crashed while carrying Iranian President Ebrahim Raisi in northern Iran on Sunday, according to Iranian officials. Raisi's condition and that of Iranian Foreign Minister Hossein Amir Abdollahian, who was also on board, remain unknown as overnight temperatures drop in the mountainous area.

The aircraft came down in the early afternoon in Iran's East Azerbaijan province, sparking a massive search effort, including military drones and dozens of rescue teams, state media reported.

Officials have said they were able to make contact with some of the passengers aboard the helicopter and Turkish drone has located a heat source. But despite hours of searching, emergency crews have not been able to reach the crash site amid reported fog and extreme cold.

A regional commander for the Islamic Revolutionary Guard Corps announced late on Sunday night that they had detected the exact location of the crash after receiving a signal from the helicopter and the mobile phone of one of the crew, IRNA reported.

"Military forces are heading to the location and hope to have some good news," the commander reportedly said.

The incident comes at a sensitive time domestically for Tehran and seven months

---

[1] 新闻稿来源：https://edition.cnn.com。

into Israel's war against Hamas in Gaza that has sent tensions soaring throughout the Middle East and brought a decades long shadow war between Israel and Iran out into the open. Last month Iran launched an unprecedented drone and missile attack on Israel — its first ever direct attack on the country — in response to a deadly apparent Israeli airstrike on Iran's consulate in Damascus.

Iran's hardline leadership has faced significant challenges in recent years, convulsed by youth-led demonstrations against clerical rule and grim economic conditions. Iranian authorities have launched a widening crackdown on dissent since nationwide protests broke out over the 2022 death of Mahsa Amini in the custody of Iran's notorious morality police.

Raisi's official Instagram account and state television have urged Iranians to pray for the president and his entourage.

Iranian Supreme Leader Ayatollah Khamenei, the country's top leader, echoed in the call in a video statement, saying, "Everyone should pray for the health of this group of servants ... People of Iran, do not worry. There will be no disruption in the work of the country."

Poor weather complicates search for helicopter

The accident occurred as Raisi and Amir Abdollahian were returning from a ceremony for an opening of a dam on Iran's border with Azerbaijan, IRNA reported. Seven other people were also in the helicopter, according to the IRGC-run media outlet Sepah, including a local imam, the provincial governor, security staff and the helicopter's crew.

Two other helicopters in the same convoy of dignitaries arrived at their destinations safely, officials said.

Iranian authorities have identified a 2-kilometer radius for the crash site and believe the accident was "not severe" after speaking with two people who were traveling on the downed helicopter, Iranian Vice President for Executive Affairs Mohsen Mansouri told Iranian semi-official FARS news.

"Three helicopters were on this route, but the helicopter carrying the President lost contact with the other two. They began searching and established contact with one of the helicopter's occupants and the flight crew, indicating the incident was not severe. The Red Crescent, FRAJA, Army, and IRGC rescue teams have arrived and divided tasks," he said.

The crash site is believed to be somewhere in the Dizmar Forest area between the villages of Ozi and Pir Davood, according to IRNA, which reported that residents in the northern Varzeqan region said they heard noises from the area.

Poor weather and low visibility are complicating rescue efforts in the rural area. Iranian Minister of Health, Bahram Eynollahi, has warned that the crash site is very foggy, making it difficult for rescuers to search. "We have set up treatment facilities. We are now in the area and all rescue forces are busy searching," Eynollahi said on state TV Sunday. "We have deployed all medical facilities, including emergency medicine, surgery and ambulance."

A deployment of helicopters in the area has already failed due to the weather, Iranian military officials said.

"The helicopters of the 6th combat base of Tabriz Air Force arrived in the Varzeqan area according to the order to carry out relief operations," the Commander of Iran's 6th Air Force Base said. "These helicopters, along with the rescue team, were sent to the helicopter accident area of the president's convoy from the early hours. Unfortunately, the operation failed due to unfavorable weather conditions."

Iraq and Azerbaijan have offered assistance to Iran in the ongoing search operation. In response to requests from Iranian authorities, the European Union said it was activating its satellite mapping service, and Turkey said it would send a night-vision search and rescue helicopter, plus 32 mountaineer search and rescue personnel.

Russia has also pledged to send two planes with 50 professional mountain rescuers to help reach the crash site on Monday, IRNA reported.

US President Joe Biden has been briefed on the incident, according to the White House.

编译稿

伊朗总统所乘直升机发生"硬着陆",大规模搜救仍在进行

据美国有线电视新闻网(CNN)19日报道,当地时间19日下午,一架载有伊朗总统莱希、外长以及其他随行人员的直升机在东阿塞拜疆省瓦尔扎甘地区发生事故,引发大规模搜救行动。

伊朗国家媒体当天表示,军方出动无人机和数十个救援小组正在事故发生地区积极搜寻,由于当地山区夜间气温骤降,搜救困难重重。伊朗官员表示,尽管通过卫星信号和机上手机信号定位到坠机大致位置,但大雾和极寒天气使救援进展缓慢。莱希和同机的伊朗外长情况仍然不明。

据伊朗伊斯兰共和国通讯社报道,此次坠机事故发生在莱希结束在伊朗与阿塞

拜疆边境的水坝开工仪式返回途中，伊朗塔斯尼姆通讯社称，同行的三架直升机中仅载有总统的直升机失联，另外两架直升机已安全抵达目的地。

目前包括伊朗最高领袖哈梅内伊在内的伊朗高层呼吁全国祈祷。多个国家表示将向伊朗提供援助，包括伊拉克、阿塞拜疆、俄罗斯和欧盟。据白宫消息，美国总统拜登也已获悉此事件。

当地时间20日凌晨，伊朗外交部就总统莱希乘坐的直升机发生事故一事发表声明，感谢多国政府和国际组织向伊朗政府和人民表达的人道主义情感和声援，以及为搜救行动提供的帮助和援助。

案例分析

这篇新闻稿描述的是一起空难事件，原新闻稿采用了倒金字塔结构，导语先介绍了核心新闻事实，即直升机坠毁，然后说明事件发生的背景、发生后政府相关部门的紧急搜救（包括一些细节）、与事件相关的国际政治背景分析、国际社会的反应和援助等。新闻稿采用了小标题形式，结构清晰、重点突出，有助于读者快速获取相关信息。

对比原新闻稿，编译稿省略了哪些信息，结构上是否有所调整？编译者为什么要这样处理？

_____
_____
_____

◎ 新闻稿2

July Fourth violence nationwide kills at least 33, Chicago 'in state of grief,' mayor says[1]

BY JOHN RABY Updated 7:14 AM GMT+8, July 6, 2024

Shootings and other violence during the extended Fourth of July weekend have left at least 33 people dead, including 11 in Chicago, and injured dozens more nationwide, authorities said.

---

1 新闻稿来源：https://apnews.com。

The Fourth of July historically is one of the nation's deadliest days of the year. A flurry of shootings around the holiday a year ago left more than a dozen people dead and over 60 wounded. And a year before that, seven people died in a mass shooting at a Fourth of July parade near Chicago.

Violence and mass shootings often increase in the summer months, with more people gathering for social events, teens out of school and hotter temperatures.

Chicago 'in state of grief'

In Chicago alone, 11 people had been killed and 55 wounded in shootings as of Friday morning during the extended July Fourth weekend, the *Chicago Sun-Times* reported. The violence included a mass shooting on Thursday that killed two women and an 8-year-old boy.

The recent violence "has left our city in a state of grief," Mayor Brandon Johnson said.

A community rally was planned for Friday evening, and the city will beef up police presence over the weekend, Johnson said in a statement.

"We are devastated by the recent violence that has left our city in a state of grief and we extend our heartfelt condolences to the families and communities impacted by these recent events," Johnson said.

Eight people were wounded in Chicago's Little Italy neighborhood shortly after midnight Friday. About 90 minutes later, a shooting in the city's Austin neighborhood injured six. Police said preliminary findings suggest the separate shootings involved an exchange of gunfire between two people who then fled.

Recent violence at a popular Lake Michigan beach in Chicago prompted officials to close it early each night through the holiday weekend as a precaution. The 31st Street Beach has been the scene of recent stabbings and shootings.

Southern California violence

In Huntington Beach, California, two people were killed and three others injured in an Independence Day attack less than two hours after a fireworks show ended, police said. Authorities arrested a suspect after responding to reports of an assault with a deadly weapon Thursday night.

15-year-old boy arrested in Niles, Ohio, shooting, 10-year-old girl dies in Cleveland

In the northeastern Ohio community of Niles, Police Chief Jay Holland said a

15-year-old male was in custody after a 23-year-old man was fatally shot Thursday night at a Fourth of July party at a residence.

A 10-year-old girl, identified as Gracie Griffin, was fatally shot in a Cleveland neighborhood, police said. It is not yet known what sparked the shooting or if she was targeted.

Fatal drive-by shooting in Philadelphia

A 19-year-old man was killed and six others were wounded in a drive-by shooting in Philadelphia on Thursday night.

The wounded, which included four juveniles, were being treated at hospitals for various injuries that were not considered life-threatening. It is not known yet what prompted the shooting.

Boston-area shootings leave 1 dead, 5 wounded

Three shootings occurred in the Boston area following the city's Fourth of July celebrations, leaving one man dead. The fatal shooting occurred about 1:30 a.m. Friday in a park near Boston's South End neighborhood. At about the same time, three other people were wounded in the city's Jamaica Plain neighborhood. A third shooting at a gas station later left a victim with life-threatening injuries.

A 17-year-old male suffered a stomach wound in another shooting Thursday night in a condominium parking lot in East Bridgewater, Massachusetts.

Connecticut woman fatally shot in car

In Connecticut, a woman was found shot in her car early Friday and was pronounced dead at a hospital. Police identified her as Shamyria Williams, 23, of Hartford. Relatives told reporters they believed she had just left a Fourth of July party.

Six teens shot at home in Albany, New York

Police in Albany, New York, said six males ranging in age from 16 to 19 were being treated at a hospital for injuries that were not considered life-threatening after a shooting at a large gathering.

Police responded to reports of a shooting at a home around 12:15 a.m. Friday. None of the victims were found at the scene but police said they located evidence consistent with gunfire in the yard behind the residence and in the street.

One teenager who had been shot flagged down officers along a street a short time later, police said.

Five teens shot during party in suburban Detroit

Five teens were wounded when shots were fired into a crowd following a fight at a party early Friday morning in Pontiac, about 30 miles (48.2 kilometers) northwest of Detroit.

Three of the victims are 14 years old. The other two are 15 years old. All are males. Authorities said they were taken to hospitals with wounds not considered to be life-threatening.

Tampa nightclub shooting wounds 4

Four people were wounded in a shooting early Friday outside a Tampa adult nightclub after an altercation between the club's security guard and two men, police said.

The two men drove their car to the front of the Pink Pussycat Lounge and one of them shot the security guard with a handgun, police said. The security guard underwent surgery at a hospital and was in stable condition. Three other men suffered unspecified minor injuries. Police said both suspects were arrested and charged with several crimes.

编译稿

独立日暴力事件席卷美国，芝加哥陷入悲痛

美联社 7 月 6 日报道，今年美国"独立日"假期各类暴力事件已导致至少 33 人死亡，数十人受伤。报道称，"独立日"是美国一年中死亡人数最多的日子之一。2023 年"独立日"前后发生的一系列枪击事件共造成十多人死亡，超过 60 人受伤。2022 年 7 月，芝加哥北郊海兰帕克市"独立日"游行现场发生枪击事件，造成 7 人死亡、30 多人受伤。

独立日，原本是美国人民欢聚一堂、共庆自由的时刻。然而，随着民众出行的增加和庆祝活动的密集，枪支暴力事件也随之攀升，给原本喜庆的节日氛围笼罩上了一层不安的阴影。

根据《芝加哥太阳报》，截至周五上午仅在芝加哥就有 11 人死于枪击、55 人受伤。其他地区也发生多起暴力事件：南加州 2 人死亡；俄亥俄州一 10 岁小女孩死亡；费城 1 人死亡、6 人受伤；波士顿 1 人死亡、5 人受伤；纽约 6 个青少年受伤；底特律 5 个青少年在聚会时受伤……

近日美联社也进一步指出，暴力和大规模枪击事件经常在夏季激增，尤其是在

7月初前后，这是"美国历史上一年中最致命的日子之一"。据美国"枪支暴力档案"数据显示，在过去的10年里，美国"独立日"发生了58起至少4人死伤的大规模枪击事件。但是近日美国"枪支暴力档案"网站发布的最新数据进一步指出，2024年美国已经发生262起大规模枪击事件，因枪支暴力而死亡的人数达8,642人，受伤人数超1.6万人。

> **案例分析**
>
> 这篇新闻报道的是有关美国独立日假期多地发生的枪击暴力事件，以芝加哥为事件核心，辐射到美国国内多个城市和地区，以引起人们对枪支暴力事件的关注和思考。这是一篇典型的灾难类新闻，采用倒金字塔结构，先说核心事实，再分析事件原因、背景及后续社会的反应。原新闻稿采用小标题形式，信息明确醒目，起到了引导读者阅读的作用。
>
> 原新闻稿标题中的数字直指新闻核心，说明了此次暴力事件的严重性，编译稿虽未照搬原新闻稿的标题，但措辞上也体现了事件的严重性。同时，编译稿采用了与原新闻稿相同的结构，但在内容上进行了高度概括。

◎新闻稿3

At least 14 killed after billboard collapses in Mumbai during thunderstorm[1]

By Reuters Updated 6:46 AM EDT, Tue May 14, 2024

At least 14 people have died and dozens were injured after a huge billboard fell on them during a thunderstorm in India's financial capital Mumbai, according to local authorities.

The billboard collapsed on some houses and a petrol station next to a busy road in the eastern suburb of Ghatkopar following gusty winds and rain late on Monday.

Scores were trapped following the incident with rescue operations continuing till early on Tuesday. The thunderstorm brought traffic to a standstill in parts of the city and disrupted operations at its airport, one of the country's busiest.

Mumbai's municipal corporation said at least 74 people were taken to hospital with injuries following the accident and 31 have been discharged.

---

1 新闻稿来源：https://edition.cnn.com。

News channels and posts on social media showed the towering billboard billowing in the wind for a while before it gave way and crashed to the ground.

The local weather department had predicted that moderate spells of rain, accompanied by gusty winds reaching 40–50 kilometers per hour (25–30 miles per hour) were likely to occur in parts of Mumbai district on Monday.

There were temporary flight disruptions at the Mumbai airport, with 15 flight diversions and operations suspended for a little over an hour, ANI news agency, in which Reuters has a minority stake, reported.

Mumbai, like several Indian cities, is prone to severe flooding and rain-related accidents during the monsoon season, which usually lasts from June until September every year.

编译稿

印度孟买巨型广告牌倒塌，已致 14 人死亡，市政人员：该广告牌是非法的

据路透社 14 日报道，印度孟买当地时间 13 日发生的 30 米高铁制广告牌倒塌事件，目前已造成 14 人死亡、74 人受伤。

据报道，孟买市当天遭遇狂风和暴雨。在该市加特科帕尔区，一个约为 10 层楼高的铁制广告牌倒塌，其金属框架砸毁了附近加油站几辆汽车的车顶，造成车辆和人员被困，当地警方表示，救援行动仍在进行中。

孟买市政服务专员称，倒塌的广告牌没有许可证，是非法安装的。当地政府已下令对此次事件进行调查。

2018 年印度也曾发生过一起广告牌倒塌事故。2018 年 10 月 5 日，在印度浦那市，一个 40 英尺（约合 12.2 米）高的广告牌框架突然倒塌，造成 4 人死亡，5 人重伤。此外有至少 6 辆人力车、1 辆轿车和 3 辆两轮车被压坏。

案例分析

新闻稿报道了发生在印度孟买由自然因素酿成的惨痛事故，这是一篇典型的灾难类新闻报道，采用了倒金字塔结构，内容包括事故的具体情况、发生的原因、造成的影响和救援情况等。

编译稿的受众群体是国内读者，因此其主要目的是提供新闻信息、引起广大受众的注意，以避免此类事件发生。所以编译稿比较简洁，只呈现客观新闻事实。

在各种应急突发事件中，重大自然灾害因其受灾面广、造成的损失大，受到全社会的关注。因此，重大自然灾害也是新闻媒体机构报道的重点，除了文字描述，图片和视频也是突发事件报道常用的手段，可提高新闻的直观性和现场感。

将以下英语新闻稿编译成汉语新闻稿。

Death toll from Moscow concert hall attack rises to 133 as Putin addresses the nation[1]

UPDATED MARCH 23, 2024 9:28 PM ET By Rebecca Rosman

The death toll from a mass shooting at a concert hall on the outskirts of Moscow Friday evening has risen to at least 133 people. At least another 145 others were reported injured.

The governor of the Moscow region said rescuers ended their search for victims late Saturday evening.

In his first televised address to the nation since the attacks took place, Russian President Vladimir Putin said Saturday afternoon that the Kremlin had arrested all four assailants directly involved in the shooting as well as seven others with suspected ties to the attack.

"All the perpetrators, organizers and those who ordered this crime will be justly and inevitably punished," Putin said.

"We will identify and punish everyone who stands behind the terrorists who prepared this atrocity, this strike against Russia, against our people."

Russia's interior minister said Saturday that all four suspected attackers are foreign citizens.

A U.S. official confirmed to NPR that the U.S. believes an Islamic State affiliate group known as Islamic State Khorasan Province, or ISIS-K, was responsible for the attack. The group, based in eastern Afghanistan, claimed responsibility for the attack on its Telegram channel late Friday.

U.S. intelligence officials also said they had warned the Kremlin earlier this month about a possible attack based on intelligence information.

"The U.S. Government had information about a planned terrorist attack in Moscow—potentially targeting large gatherings, to include concerts," Adrienne Watson, a spokesperson for the National Security Council, said in a statement on Friday.

---

1 新闻稿来源：https://www.npr.org。

Watson said the intelligence prompted the U.S. Embassy to issue a security advisory to Americans living in Russia, and share the information with Russian authorities in accordance with its longstanding "duty to warn" policy.

In his remarks on Saturday, Putin made no mention of ISIS-K, instead accusing Ukrainian authorities of trying to help the four assailants escape via Ukraine.

"They tried to hide and moved towards Ukraine, where according to preliminary data, a window was prepared for them on the Ukrainian side to cross the state border," Putin said.

Russian investigators said the assailants were detained in the western Bryansk region, not far from the border with Ukraine. Ukrainian officials have denied any involvement, with Ukraine's foreign ministry accusing Russian authorities of using the deadly assault to try to rally support for the Kremlin's war in Ukraine.

"ISIS bears sole responsibility for this attack," Watson, the NSC spokeswoman, said in a statement on Saturday. "There was no Ukrainian involvement whatsoever."

The attack began late Friday after camouflaged gunmen carrying automatic assault rifles burst into the Crocus City Hall—a large shopping and entertainment center on the western outskirts of Moscow. Concertgoers had gathered at the venue to see the veteran Russian rock band Piknik.

Harrowing video footage shows the men firing at bystanders as they attempted to hide or rush for the emergency exits. Some witnesses reported seeing the assailants pour a liquid on the concert hall's seating and curtains before setting it on fire. Additional footage released by Russian authorities shows the charred seating and debris from inside the venue.

NPR's Charles Maynes spoke to some of those who were inside the venue during the attack.

"The smoke kept coming and coming," said Alexei, a stagehand who told NPR's Charles Maynes he fled his third floor office to escape. He would only give his first name because of security forces present around the site.

"I'm still in a dream," he added, staring at the facade of the now-gutted concert hall.

Another venue employee, Josef, who refused to give a last name for similar reasons, said he was also still reeling from Friday night's events.

> "You can imagine any terrorist, you can imagine anything. But to come through this main entrance. To kill the glass and to kill the people behind. I mean ... no words. No words."
>
> Putin declared Sunday a national day of mourning in Russia.
>
> People across the country, meanwhile, have made spontaneous memorials with flowers, toys and candles to honor the victims. The local health ministry also said that more than 2,700 people donated blood in the Moscow region on Saturday to support the injured.

第二节 政治类新闻的编译

一、政治类新闻的概念

政治类新闻是国家政治生活中新近或正在发生的事实的报道。政治类新闻主要涉及政党、社会集团、社会势力在处理国家生活和国际关系方面的方针、政策和活动。政治类新闻关乎国家政策、政府决策以及国际关系等重大事件，往往对国家和社会的未来发展产生深远影响，因此具有极高的新闻价值。政治类新闻在人们生活中扮演着至关重要的角色，它是公众获取信息、参政议政及监督政府的关键渠道，因此，政治类新闻始终是人们关注的新闻热点。政治类新闻涉及的内容非常广泛，包括但不限于以下方面：

- 领导人互访等外事活动；
- 国际组织或地区性组织的活动；
- 国家领导人或政党选举（包括国家首脑和领导人变更、新政府组成等）；
- 国家和政府间政治性磋商、谈判或会议；
- 国家政党、政府国事大会；
- 政府的改革及政策措施发布；
- 战争或地区性冲突；
- 政要遇刺或遭暗杀；
- 政变、暴乱、骚乱；
- 恐怖袭击事件；
- 反政府集会、示威游行或其他政治行动。

总之，政治类新闻不仅是信息传播的渠道，更是政党政府与公众互动、提升形象、加强监督以及促进社会融合的重要工具。

一般来说，政治类新闻报道通常包括政治新闻事件参与的主体、事件过程、涉及的主要内容、结果、影响和意义。

政治类新闻不仅具有一般新闻报道的典型特征，即时效性、重要性、真实性、显著性、接近性、公开性等，而且往往包含一定的倾向性，即媒体在报道或评述新闻事实时所表现出的特定立场和思想倾向，引导读者对信息的接收和理解。这种倾向有时表现得直接而明显，有时则表现得含蓄而隐晦，但在新闻传播过程中，新闻的倾向性总是客观存在的，因此，公众在阅读政治类新闻时，应保持警惕，提高自辨意识，尽量从多个渠道获取信息，以便更全面地了解事件的真相，并努力识别媒体的立场和倾向，以避免产生偏见和误解。

二、政治类新闻稿的结构

基于新闻事件本身的性质、特点以及新闻事件的情况等，政治类新闻报道往往采用倒金字塔结构（尤其是对于突发性的政治类新闻）。当然，对于具体的新闻事件的描述有时也会采用金字塔结构，而有些连续性的新闻报道也采用沙漏式结构。

阅读以下新闻稿及其编译稿，说明新闻稿和编译稿各有什么特点。

◎新闻稿

Trump says he had 'a very good phone call' with Zelensky, discussed Russia-Ukraine war[1]

Updated 8:03 PM EDT, Fri July 19, 2024, CNN

(CNN)—Former President Donald Trump said he "had a very good phone call" with Ukrainian President Volodymyr Zelensky on Friday.

The call between the two leaders, who have had a complicated relationship, marks their first conversation since Trump left the White House and comes the day after he formally accepted the Republican Party's nomination for president. It also comes amid concerns in Europe about what Trump's policy toward the Russia-Ukraine war would be if he were to win the presidential election in November.

"President Zelenskyy of Ukraine and I had a very good phone call earlier today. He congratulated me on a very successful Republican National Convention and

---

[1] 新闻稿来源：https://edition.cnn.com。

becoming the Republican nominee for President of the United States," Trump said in a post on Truth Social. "He condemned the heinous assassination attempt last Saturday and remarked about the American people coming together in the spirit of Unity during these times."

Trump continued, "I appreciate President Zelenskyy for reaching out because I, as your next President of the United States, will bring peace to the world and end the war that has cost so many lives and devastated countless innocent families. Both sides will be able to come together and negotiate a deal that ends the violence and paves a path forward to prosperity."

In a post on X describing the call, Zelensky said he congratulated Trump on his nomination and condemned the "shocking assassination attempt in Pennsylvania."

"I wished him strength and absolute safety in the future," he said. "I noted the vital bipartisan and bicameral American support for protecting our nation's freedom and independence."

Zelensky concluded, "We agreed with President Trump to discuss at a personal meeting what steps can make peace fair and truly lasting."

Since Russia's invasion of Ukraine in 2022, Trump has repeatedly said he could settle the Ukraine war in a day, but it remains unclear how he would pursue peace.

In last month's CNN presidential debate, Trump said that Putin's terms for an agreement—which would include Ukraine ceding the four territories currently occupied by Russia—are "not acceptable."

But the former president and his allies have also criticized US military aid to Kyiv.

Trump has long been critical of NATO defense spending. In February, the former president said he would encourage Russia to do "whatever the hell they want" to any NATO member country that doesn't meet spending guidelines on defense, alarming many leaders in Washington and Europe.

Trump and Zelensky also have their own history. Nearly five years ago, Trump repeatedly pushed for Zelensky to investigate his political rival Joe Biden and his son, Hunter, on a call ahead of the 2020 election. That "perfect phone call," in Trump's words, led to his first impeachment.

European diplomats have been preparing for Trump's potential return to the

White House, CNN previously reported, working to set up guard rails for NATO and trying to ensure lasting support for Ukraine in its war with Russia.

Last week, when Zelensky was in the US, he said that "everyone is waiting for November," including Putin. He also said that Biden and Trump are "very different" but both support democracy, which is why he claimed: "I think Putin will hate both of them."

编译稿

特朗普与泽连斯基通话，称将"结束乌克兰危机"

据美国有线电视新闻网（CNN）报道，美国前总统特朗普表示，当地时间7月19日，他与乌克兰总统泽连斯基通电话，双方讨论了俄乌局势。

报道称，这是特朗普离开白宫后，与泽连斯基的首次通话。特朗普在社交媒体发帖，称这次谈话"非常好"，泽连斯基祝贺他成为美国共和党总统候选人，并谴责"暗杀企图"。特朗普还称，他将"结束乌克兰危机"，"（俄乌）双方将能够走到一起，通过谈判达成一项协议"。

另据《基辅独立报》报道，泽连斯基在社交媒体上证实了此次通话，他称，双方同意未来举行"个人"会晤，讨论"采取哪些措施可以让和平变得公平和真正持久。"

据报道，特朗普此前多次称，如果他再次当选美国总统，打算在"一天内结束乌克兰危机"，但目前尚不清楚他将如何解决。

编译案例

◎ 新闻稿 1

Thousands march from Tel Aviv to Jerusalem to protest Israeli government's judicial overhaul plan[1]

Published 4:34 PM　July 21, 2023, AP

JERUSALEM (AP)—Thousands of Israelis joined a march from Tel Aviv to Jerusalem on Friday in the latest protest against Prime Minister Benjamin Netanyahu's vow to push through a controversial overhaul of the judiciary system.

Hundreds of protesters became thousands as Israelis joined the 70-kilometer (roughly 45-mile) march throughout the day in a demonstration against one of Israel's most far-right governments in history.

The demonstrators planned to camp overnight at Shoresh, about 18 kilometers (11 miles) from Jerusalem, before making their way to Israel's parliament on Saturday, the Jewish day of rest.

The march comes a day after Netanyahu vowed to press ahead with the plan, defying demonstrators, growing defections by military reservists and appeals from U.S. President Joe Biden to put the plan on hold.

Ronen Rosenblatt, 58, a high-tech worker who'd joined the march following months of frustration with Netanyahu's government, described the event as jovial, with people united behind a common objective of "stopping this stupidity, this dictatorship."

Protesters carried Israelis flags and political signs in a line four kilometers (2.5 miles) long that wound through olive orchards and farmland. They'd left seaside Tel Aviv on Thursday, camping overnight roughly halfway to Jerusalem near the Latrun Monastery.

Rising on Friday to shared meals and coffee, the protesters dismantled their tents as others prayed with their arms wrapped in tefillin before they all began marching again towards Jerusalem and the Knesset, Israel's parliament.

Lawmakers are expected to vote Monday on a bill that would curtail the Supreme Court's oversight powers by limiting its ability to strike down decisions it deems "unreasonable." The standard is meant as a safeguard to protect against corruption and improper appointments of unqualified people.

1　新闻稿来源：https://apnews.com。

The bill is one of several keystone pieces of the Netanyahu government's judicial overhaul plan. Netanyahu and his allies — a collection of ultranationalist and ultra-Orthodox parties — say the plan is needed to curb what they consider excessive powers of unelected judges.

Critics say the legislation will concentrate power in the hands of Netanyahu and his far-right allies and undermine the country's system of checks and balance. They also say Netanyahu, who is on trial for corruption, has a conflict of interest.

The proposal has bitterly divided the Israeli public and drawn appeals from Biden for Netanyahu to forge a broad national consensus before passing any legislation.

The judicial overhaul plan was announced shortly after Netanyahu took office as prime minister following November's parliamentary elections. It was Israel's fifth election in under four years, with all of the votes serving as a referendum on his leadership.

Presidents of major Israeli universities said they would hold a strike Sunday to protest the bill, local media reported. Doctors held a two-hour "warning strike" Wednesday to protest the overhaul, which they said would wreak havoc on the healthcare system by granting politicians greater control over public health.

They vowed more severe measures if the bill is voted through.

编译稿

以色列数千人游行以表达对政府司法改革计划的不满

美联社7月21日报道，数千名以色列人21日开始大规模游行，以表达对总理内塔尼亚胡拟推动的司法改革计划的不满。

在此之前的一天，内塔尼亚胡无视示威者的要求以及美国总统拜登要求暂停该计划的呼声，誓言将推进司法改革计划。以色列议会24日将对一项相关法案进行投票。该法案旨在削弱以色列最高法院的监督权，限制其撤销不合理决定的权力。

批评人士认为，该法案将导致权力被集中到内塔尼亚胡及其极右翼盟友手中，进而破坏该国的权力制衡体系。

美国总统拜登此前曾呼吁内塔尼亚胡暂停该计划，呼吁其在通过任何立法之前都应首先达成广泛的全国共识。

案例分析

这是一篇针对发生在以色列的一场游行示威的新闻报道，新闻稿采用倒金字塔结构，导语中说明了游行的时间、地点、规模和游行的目的。正文中提供了更多详细的信息，包括游行的路线、背景、游行相关细节、抗议者的心声以及引起的国际社会的反应等。

编译稿同样采用倒金字塔结构，以提供信息为基本原则，重点将游行涉及的基本要素（包括游行的时间、地点、人物、规模、目的、背景、影响等）交代清楚。

◎新闻稿2

Italian PM Meloni, China's Li Qiang discuss closer ties at G20 summit[1]

9:02 PM September 9 2023, Reuters

ROME, Sept 9 (Reuters)—Italian Prime Minister Giorgia Meloni met with China's Premier Li Qiang and discussed deepening ties between the two countries on the sidelines of the G20 summit in New Delhi on Saturday.

During the meeting, the two premiers discussed the common intention to strengthen and deepen the dialogue between Rome and Beijing on key bilateral and international issues, Meloni's office said in a statement.

Italy is seeking ways to resolve a difficult diplomatic call on whether to withdraw from China's Belt and Road Initiative (BRI), a global trade and infrastructure plan modelled on the old Silk Road that linked imperial China and the West.

Beijing is willing to work with Italy to boost mutual trade and investment, but Italian Foreign Minister Antonio Tajani, who visited China earlier this week, reiterated on Thursday that a strategic partnership would be more valuable than the BRI.

"Italy and China share a Global Strategic Partnership whose 20th anniversary will recur next year and which will be the beacon for the advancement of friendship and cooperation ... in every area of common interest", the statement said.

---

1 新闻稿来源：https://www.reuters.com。

编译稿

中国国务院总理李强在二十国集团峰会期间会见意大利总理梅洛尼

英国路透社9月9日报道，中国国务院总理李强9日在二十国集团峰会的间隙会见意大利总理梅洛尼，双方讨论了深化两国关系的问题。

梅洛尼办公室在会谈后发布声明称，两国总理会见期间讨论了双方在重要双边和国际问题上加强和深化对话的共同意愿。明年是中意建立全面战略伙伴关系20周年，这将成为双方在共同关心的各个领域加强友谊与合作的"灯塔"。

目前意大利正试图解决是否要退出"一带一路"倡议这一艰难的外交问题。中国希望促进与意大利的双边贸易和投资，但意大利外长塔尼亚本周访华期间重申，意方认为，建立一种战略伙伴关系将更有价值。

> **案例分析**
>
> 这是一篇有关中意两国总理会晤的政治新闻，此类新闻稿通常包含新闻报道的基本要素，如时间、地点、人物、会谈的内容、良好的合作和未来愿景等。编译此类新闻时通常不需要包含太多细节，只需将新闻中涉及的5W和1H的关键信息编译出来，同时注意选择恰当的措辞。

分析以上政治类新闻稿和编译稿各自的特点，并思考政治类新闻的编译原则。

_____
_____
_____
_____

三、政治类新闻稿的编译原则

在将国际政治新闻编译成中文时，编译者应遵循以下基本原则：

● **符合我国相关政策规定：** 编译时，若原新闻稿涉及我国主权、领土、宗教、民族、意识形态等方面，编译者应仔细核查国家相关政策规定，务必使编译内容准确无误，符合我国的大政方针和原则立场。编译者应保持高度的政治敏锐性，对于某些新闻词语或表达，若无法确定其准确翻译时，应以新华社通稿为准，避免误译或使用任何可能引起歧义或误解的词语。

- **确保新闻事实准确客观**：编译者应准确传达新闻事实，这不仅包括语言的精确表达，还涉及对新闻事件相关背景的正确、深入的理解。这是新闻编译的核心原则之一。
- **高度概括新闻核心信息**：对于国内受众来说，国外的政治新闻似乎离普通读者的生活较远，因此，编译者在编译新闻时可以对新闻事实进行高度概括，省略不必要的细节描述，向读者呈现重要、关键的信息。

总之，在将国外政治新闻编译成中文时，译者必须严格遵循政治类新闻稿编译的基本原则，确保内容符合我国相关政策规定，同时兼顾语言的简洁性和国内读者的文化背景，以实现最佳的传播效果。

四、政治类新闻稿的编译步骤

编译政治类新闻的方法与其他新闻的编译方法相近，不过对于突发性的政治类新闻（如政要遇刺、临时政变等），编译者一般采用与灾难性新闻编译相同的编译手法：

- **梳理新闻要点**：阅读原文并分析新闻事件的核心事实。
- **确定编译结构**：编译稿通常也采用倒金字塔结构，突出最重要的信息。
- **编译导语和正文**：导语应简洁明了，概括最重要的新闻事实；新闻正文需清晰传达政治新闻的关键要素，尤其是事件发生的过程、涉及的相关人物及原因。
- **调整和优化**：编译者完成初稿后要对编译稿进行校对和修改，以确保新闻事实的准确性和表达的流畅性。
- **拟定新闻标题**：标题应凸显最重要的信息，同时要能够吸引读者。

根据上述编译步骤，将以下英语新闻稿编译成汉语新闻稿。

◎ 新闻稿 1

JD Vance slams Kamala Harris during his solo campaign debut as the GOP vice presidential nominee[1]

Updated 10:21 AM GMT+8, July 23, 2024

RADFORD, Va. (AP) — Republican vice presidential nominee JD Vance used his first solo campaign rallies Monday to throw fresh barbs at Vice President Kamala Harris a day after President Joe Biden threw the presidential election into upheaval by dropping out and endorsing his second-in-command to lead Democrats against Donald Trump.

---

1 新闻稿来源：https://apnews.com。

The Ohio senator campaigned at his former high school in Middletown before an evening stop in Radford, Virginia, two venues intended to play up his conservative populist appeal across the Rust Belt and small-town America that he said the Biden-Harris administration has forgotten.

"History will remember Joe Biden as not just a quitter, which he is, but as one of the worst presidents in the history of the United States of America," Vance said in Virginia. "But my friends, Kamala Harris is a million times worse and everybody knows it. She signed up for every single one of Joe Biden's failures, and she lied about his mental capacity to serve as president."

Vance sought to saddle Harris with the administration's record on inflation and immigration, clarifying the lines of attack that the Trump campaign will use even with the change at the top of the Democratic ticket. Harris still must be formally nominated but has quickly consolidated commitments from top party leaders and is now backed by more than half of the delegates needed to win her party's nomination vote, according to an Associated Press survey.

"The border crisis is a Kamala Harris crisis," Vance said, accusing Biden and Harris together of rolling back immigration policies that Trump enacted in his White House term. He added Harris is "even more extreme than Biden" because, Vance alleged, she has designs on abolishing federal immigration enforcement and domestic police forces.

Vance, 39, drew biographical contrasts with Harris, as well, comparing his service in the Marine Corps and small business ownership to Harris "collecting a government paycheck for the last 20 years."

Harris, 59, was a local prosecutor, then California attorney general and a U.S. senator before she ran for president unsuccessfully in 2020 and became Biden's running mate. Vance was elected to the Senate two years ago.

Vance also fulfilled his role as Trump's biggest cheerleader, promising the former president would lead an era of peace and prosperity in a White House encore, while helping Republicans dominate House, Senate and state contests.

"We've got an opportunity to win races up and down the ballot," he said.

He promised: "You're going to see more and more products stamped with that beautiful logo: 'Made in the USA.'" He also asked the crowd: "Who is sick of sending

America's sons and daughters into foreign lands they have no business in?"

The senator carefully stopped short of outright isolationism, however, pledging the U.S. would "punch back hard" when necessary. Vance did not detail any policy approach to the wars that have most vexed the Biden administration: Vladimir Putin's Russian invasion of Ukraine and the Israel-Hamas war in Gaza.

Those arguments are at the core of Trump's "America First" brand and highlight Vance's electoral strengths as the son of Appalachia who first came to national prominence with his memoir, "Hillbilly Elegy." Trump's campaign intends to use him heavily across the Rust Belt and swaths of small town America where voters have moved to the right and remain especially frustrated over decades of what Vance called "bad trade deals."

Earlier Monday in Ohio, Vance tried to deflect the criticism that Trump, who has refused to accept his 2020 loss to Biden and tried to overturn the results, is a threat to democracy. The senator claimed that the real threat came from the push by "elite Democrats" who "decided to throw Joe Biden overboard" and then have the party line up behind a replacement without primary contests.

Democrats, he said in Virginia, lied "for three-and-a-half years" only to "pull a switcheroo."

While Republicans promoted a unifying message at the Republican National Convention where Vance was nominated last week and decried inflammatory language in the wake of the assassination attempt against Trump, one of the first speakers to introduce Vance in Ohio suggested the country may need to come to civil war if Trump loses in November.

"I believe wholeheartedly, Donald Trump and Butler County's JD Vance are the last chance to save our country," said George Lang, a Republican state senator. "Politically, I'm afraid if we lose this one, it's going to take a civil war to save the country and it will be saved. It's the greatest experiment in the history of mankind."

Lang later apologized after Harris' team highlighted his remarks on a post on X.

"I regret the divisive remarks in the excitement of the moment on stage," he said on the same social network. "Especially in light of the assassination attempt on President Trump last week, we should all be mindful of what is said at political events, myself included."

Vance still has work to do raising his profile. A CNN poll conducted in late June found the majority of registered voters had never heard of Vance or had no opinion of him. Just 13% of registered voters said they had a favorable opinion of Vance and 20% had an unfavorable one, according to the poll.

During brief political career, he has morphed from being a harsh Trump critic, at one point likening him to Adolf Hitler, to becoming a staunch defender of the former president.

After Vance was named as Trump's running mate, a startling number of Republican delegates, who are typically party insiders and activists, said they did not know much about the senator.

In his hometown in Ohio, though, he was welcomed as a local star.

Darlene Gooding, 77, of Hamilton, said Vance will provide a welcome contrast to Trump.

"Trump doesn't always come off the best. It's all about him," she said. "JD is wonderful. He gives you the idea he really cares about people."

In Virginia, Trump backers were warming quickly to his new running mate.

Pamela Holloway, who came to see Vance in Radford, described herself as a former Democrat who has gravitated to Republicans. She said she recently bought Vance's book to learn more about how his experiences have shaped his political outlook.

"He's truthful," she said of his writing. "He talks about his mother being an addict. He talks about the hardships with his grandmother" who raised him. "He talks about things that aren't fake."

◎新闻稿2

Shanghai Cooperation Organization Summit Begins in Kazakhstan[1]

04 July 2024, QNA

Astana, July 04 (QNA) — The 24th Meeting of the Council of Heads of State of the Shanghai Cooperation Organization (SCO) began in the Kazakh capital Astana, where a wide range of current issues related to political, trade, economic, cultural, and humanitarian relations will be discussed.

---

1 新闻稿来源：https://www.qna.org.qa。

During the opening speech, President of Kazakhstan Kassym-Jomart Tokayev said, "our countries provide the vector for the development of the entire Eurasian continent. We have turned the SCO into one of the most authoritative and influential structures," noting that the interest in the SCO is growing.

He added that for nearly a quarter century, the Organization has become a significant mechanism in the international relations system, greatly contributing to sustainable growth and comprehensive progress, pointing out that fruitful interaction in politics, security, economy, and culture among member states shapes the development path of the entire Eurasian continent.

During the summit, leaders of member states signed a decision by the Council of Heads of State granting the Republic of Belarus full membership of the SCO.

President of Kazakhstan welcomed Belarus's accession before the signing ceremony.

The Summit brought together leaders of member and observer states, as well as dialogue partners.

New agreements are expected on cooperation in areas such as counter-terrorism, drug control activities, combating organized crime across borders, and ensuring information security.

第三节　经济类新闻的编译

一、经济类新闻的概念

经济类新闻是社会经济生活中新近发生或正在发生的事实的报道。广义的经济类新闻涵盖整个社会经济生活或与经济相关的方方面面，包括经济形势、产业政策、金融市场动态、资本投资、经济决策、企业经营以及与之相关的各种信息。经济活动是人类社会一切活动的基础，不仅决定了个体的生活水平，还深刻影响着政治、文化等许多方面，大到国与国之间的关系和变化，小到公司经营策略的选择、普通个体的衣食住行等，都与经济密切相关。经济类新闻报道涉及的内容非常广泛，主要包括以下方面：

● 经济与国际关系；
● 经济与政治（外交）；

- 经济与产业；
- 经济与人口；
- 经济与科技创新；
- 经济与消费。

总之，与经济相关的各个领域相互交织，共同构成一个复杂而相互依存的经济生态系统。及时、准确、全面地报道经济新闻，可满足公众对经济领域信息的需求，同时还能够有效引导舆论、促进经济发展、提升公众的经济素养，并在政策制定过程中发挥积极的作用。

相较于其他领域的新闻报道，经济类新闻具有以下特征：

- **报道专业性**：经济类新闻具有很强的专业性，包含经济专业术语、专业知识和理论。
- **报道前瞻性**：前瞻性不仅体现在对未来经济趋势的预测上，还包括对政策变化的解读和对这些变化可能带来的影响的评估，对受众有一定的指导意义。
- **报道精准性**：精准性指新闻事实、数据、名称、表述的精确无误。
- **报道多元性**：报道形式多样，包括文字、图表、数据、音视频等。
- **报道通俗性**：通俗性是指采用通俗易懂的话语表达专业概念，或以讲故事的方式讲述新闻事件，以帮助广大受众更好地理解复杂的经济问题。

从内容要素来看，经济类新闻主要分为政经新闻、财经新闻、产经新闻和社经新闻四大类。

- **政经新闻**主要涉及国家经济政策的分析和解读。此类新闻报道的内容包括政策发布的主体（如国家央行、财政部等）、政策的主要内容及变化、政策调整的原因及影响等。
- **财经新闻**涵盖了经济领域的各类消息，包括国际贸易（国贸动态、汇率变动、跨国公司）、金融市场动态与金融监管（利率调整、外汇储备、股票债券）、财政与税收、资本市场（股票、基金、期货）等。此类新闻报道，无论是经济调查报告还是经济时事评论，通常都包括新闻事件主体、核心新闻事实、市场动态变化趋势及相关因素分析和影响。
- **产经新闻**专注于产业经济的发展动态，报道各行业的经济运行情况、最新发展趋势、产业链上下游的发展情况、企业活动（重点企业的经营状况、上市公司并购重组）和市场变化。此类新闻报道通常包括新闻事件主体、核心新闻事实、行业发展趋势及相关因素分析及影响。
- **社经新闻**主要涉及社会经济活动或与经济民生相关的报道，包括就业、消费、教育、医疗、投资理财、社会保障（住房、失业保险）等。此类新闻报道一般包括新闻事件主体、核心新闻事实、对受众产生的影响及相关因素分析。

总之，经济类新闻包罗万象，为受众提供了全面理解经济运行的视角，随着媒介融合和数据驱动的新闻生产时代的发展，经济类新闻的报道形式和内容也在不断创新和丰富。媒体在报道新闻事实的过程中，应努力兼顾新闻的专业性和报道的趣味性，在理性评述的基础上提高报道的可读性，以吸引更多受众的关注。有时，编译者也可将硬性政策信息转化为与百姓生活紧密相关的软性新闻，以取得良好的阅读效果。

二、经济类新闻稿的结构

经济类新闻稿，无论是哪种类型，大多先报道核心新闻事实，再讲述相关的背景、原因及影响，这是由此类新闻的专业性和严谨性所决定的。不过，有时候经济类新闻也采用金字塔结构，从描述人物或从叙述故事开始，以吸引受众关注此类信息，同时突出新闻事件中的人物和故事，使新闻报道更加具有通俗性、趣味性和可接受性。当然，对于具体的新闻事件，有时连续性的新闻报道也采用沙漏式结构。

阅读以下两篇新闻稿，对比分析两篇新闻稿在结构和写作手法上的不同。

◎新闻稿 1

AI Company Pika Raises $55M to Redesign Video Making and Editing[1]

November 28, 2023 07:17 AM Eastern Standard Time

PALO ALTO, Calif.—(BUSINESS WIRE)—Pika, an AI video platform that is redesigning the video-making and editing experience, announced its Series A funding round of $35 million, led by Lightspeed Venture Partners. With this latest round, Pika has raised a total of $55 million in the company's first six months with Pre-Seed and Seed rounds led by Nat Friedman and Daniel Gross. Additional investors include other prominent angel investors in AI, including Elad Gil, Adam D'Angelo (Founder and CEO of Quora), Andrej Karpathy, Clem Delangue (Co-Founder and CEO of Hugging Face and Partner at Factorial Capital), Craig Kallman (Chairman and CEO of Atlantic Records) and Alex Chung (Co-Founder of Giphy), as well as venture firms such as Homebrew, Conviction Capital, SV Angel and Ben's Bites.

Pika also unveiled Pika 1.0, a major product upgrade that includes a new AI model that can generate and edit videos in diverse styles such as 3D animation, anime

---

1 新闻稿来源：https://www.businesswire.com。

or cinematic, and a new web experience that made it easier to use. A video highlighting some of the new features of Pika 1.0 can be found here. You can join the waitlist for Pika 1.0 at https://pika.art.

The first version of Pika launched in beta on Discord in late April of 2023 and today has more than 500,000 users generating millions of videos each week. Top Pika users on Discord spend up to 10 hours a day creating videos with Pika. Pika-generated videos have gone viral on social media: on TikTok alone, the **#pikalabs** hashtag has nearly 30M views.

Video is one of the most widely used creative mediums, dominating social media, entertainment and educational platforms, but it remains complicated and resource-intensive to create. While other AI video tools are primarily focused on professionals and commercial use, Pika has designed a video-making and editing experience that is effortless and accessible to the everyday consumer and creator. Anyone can be a creative director with Pika.

"My Co-Founder and I are creatives at heart. We know firsthand that making high-quality content is difficult and expensive, and we built Pika to give everyone, from home users to film professionals, the tools to bring high-quality video to life," said Demi Guo, Pika co-founder and CEO. "Our vision is to enable anyone to be the director of their stories and to bring out the creator in all of us."

The new Pika 1.0 includes the following:

● A new generative AI model that creates even higher quality video.

● New features that allow you to edit videos with AI, in addition to generating videos in many new styles:

 • Text-to-Video and Image-to-Video: Type a few lines of text or upload an image on Pika, and the platform creates short, high-quality video using AI.

 • Video-to-Video: Transform your existing videos into different styles, including different characters and objects, while maintaining the structure of the video. For example, change a video from live action to an animated video.

 • Expand: Expand the canvas or aspect ratio of a video. For example, change a video from a TikTok 9:16 format to a wide screen 16:9 format, and the AI model will predict the content beyond the border of the original video.

• Change: Edit video content with AI, such as changing someone's clothing, adding in another character, changing the environment or adding in props.

• Extend: Extend the length of an existing video clip using AI.

• New web interface: Now, Pika will be available on both Discord and web (mobile and desktop) at https://pika.art.

"Just as other new AI products have done for text and images, professional-quality video creation will also become democratized by generative AI. We believe Pika will lead that transformation," said Michael Mignano, partner at Lightspeed Venture Partners. "Given such an impressive technical foundation, rooted in an early passion for creativity, the Pika team seems destined to change how we all share our stories visually. At Lightspeed, we couldn't be more excited to support their mission to allow anyone to bring their creative vision to life through video, and we're thrilled to be investing alongside other amazing investors at the forefront of AI."

Pika was founded by two experts in AI: Demi Guo, co-founder and CEO, and Chenlin Meng, co-founder and CTO, both former PhD students hailing from Stanford University's prominent AI Labs. Prior to her time at Stanford, Demi worked as the youngest full-time employee at Meta AI Research as a college sophomore, and won numerous international awards in software development. Chenlin has published more than 28 research papers in the last three years, including Denoising Diffusion Implicit Models (DDIM), which is now a default approach for content generation and has been widely used in OpenAI's DALLE-2, Google's Imagen and Stability AI's Stable Diffusion.

About Pika

Pika is an AI video platform that allows anyone to bring their creative vision to life. The company is redesigning the video-making and editing experience with AI, providing a tool that is effortless and accessible to everyone.

◎新闻稿2

Pika Launches AI Video Editing App And Announces $55 Million In Funding[1]

By Kenrick Cai　Dec 02, 2023, 14:00 PM　Forbes

Last winter, Demi Guo and several Stanford computer science Ph.D. classmates spent their winter break trying to make a movie using generative AI. Buzzy AI video editor startup Runway, which had just hit a $500 million valuation, was offering a $10,000 grand prize for the best submission to its inaugural "AI Film Festival" and they were confident they had a shot.

But Guo's team didn't even place. "We were the most technical team, but we really struggled to make the film," she told *Forbes*. While recent AI breakthroughs had been promising, bringing them to bear on the video-making process itself proved exceedingly cumbersome for Guo, who poured hours into tools like Runway and Adobe's Photoshop with middling success and great frustration. In the end, the awards went to professional creatives. "It just didn't look that good," she says of the film. "I was so frustrated."

So in April, Guo and Chenlin Meng, a fellow Ph.D. student, dropped out of Stanford to launch Pika to build an easier-to-use AI video generator. Since then, some 500,000 people have tried the software and it's now being used to create millions of new videos each week. That explosion in interest has sent Silicon Valley investors into a frenzy and the four-person startup has raised $55 million across three funding rounds in quick succession. The first two were led by former GitHub CEO Nat Friedman, and the latest—a $35 million Series A from Lightspeed Venture Partners—values Pika Labs at between $200 million and $300 million, according to a source with direct knowledge of the matter.

"We're trying to redesign the interface of video-making," said Guo, who serves as the company's CEO. "It's still very hard to make good videos."

Pika's video generation tool has so far only been available through the social messaging app Discord. Users type text into a chat box—for example, "a robot walking on the beach at sunset"—and receive an AI-generated video as a chat reply.

1　新闻稿来源：https://www.forbesmiddleeast.com。

On Tuesday, Pika brought that experience to the Web, and a massive new mainstream audience, with a new app and features to allow for the editing and customizing of objects within a video—adding sunglasses to the aforementioned robot, for example.

> *A startup's biggest weapon and biggest advantage is speed, and this is honestly the fastest moving team I've ever seen.*
>
> Lightspeed partner Michael Mignano

Nat Friedman, who has emerged as one of the leading solo investors in the AI space since he departed GitHub in 2021, first invested in Pika back in April. He told *Forbes* he was impressed by an early demo version that Guo and Meng had cobbled together using a single graphics processing unit (GPU), the hardware chips which power most AI computing tasks. Friedman and frequent coinvestor Daniel Gross have amassed a 2,500-plus GPU cluster they call Andromeda which they make available to startups in which they invest. That helped supercharge Pika's efforts to build a proprietary AI model for video, similar to OpenAI's text-based GPT-4 or Midjourney's image-based models.

In its early days, Pika focused only on generating anime. The founders told Friedman that taking on AI generation of realistic videos would be too difficult, given that larger well-funded companies like Runway and Stability AI already had significant headstarts. Then, there was Adobe, a $280 billion public market behemoth that was moving quickly to add AI functionality to Creative Suite. But Guo and Meng's rapid pace of development surprised investors—and themselves.

One summer afternoon, Friedman suggested they add a way to embed text into videos. He received a text message back at 3 a.m. saying the feature was ready. Friedman recalls being shocked initially, but he soon realized this "very intense" pace was typical of the team. "It was part of what persuaded me to do the next investment," he says. Lightspeed partner Michael Mignano, who invested in September, sees this as a crucial edge for Pika: "A startup's biggest weapon and biggest advantage is speed, and this is honestly the fastest moving team I've ever seen," he told *Forbes*.

The Information was first to report that Lightspeed was in talks to invest.

Indeed, within weeks of Pika's founders telling Friedman realistic video was far too difficult a task for them to pull off, they did just that. And when Mignano brought up the idea of a web app earlier in November, Guo took it as a directive to deliver the product that same month.

We're not trying to build a product for film production. What we're trying to do is something more for everyday consumers.

Pika CEO Demi Guo

Pika is now leasing a few hundred GPUs—some from Friedman's Andromeda cluster, some from other cloud providers—which it used to build a new version of the AI model it debuted today. It's meant to perform better and allow for more refined editing. Founded in April, the four-person startup is already valued by venture capitalists at more than $200 million, using the aspect ratio of a video, for example. Meanwhile, the company is hard at work tinkering with algorithms to further improve the model, and also developing ones for filtering copyrighted materials that have tripped up rivals and dragged them into costly IP litigation. "Right now that's still very exploratory," Guo said.

With new funding in hand, Guo says she plans to expand Pika's team to about 20 people next year, most of them engineers and researchers. Monetizing the product, which is currently free, isn't a key priority yet, though she says the company may eventually introduce a tiered subscription model (pay more for access to more features) for consumers.

That's also how Guo plans to differentiate Pika from its bigger rivals. "We're not trying to build a product for film production," she told *Forbes*. "What we're trying to do is something more for everyday consumers—people like me and [Meng] who are creators at heart, but not that professional." If there had been a tool like Pika a year ago, Guo says her Stanford team might have had a fighting chance in the AI Film Festival. "I think it definitely would've helped a lot," she said.

_____

_____

_____

_____

编译案例

◎ 新闻稿 1

Russia's ruble hits a 17-month low to the dollar as the Ukraine war bites[1]

By Hanna Ziady, CNN Updated 8:16 AM EDT, Mon August 14, 2023

London (CNN)—The ruble hit a 17-month low against the dollar Monday, highlighting the growing squeeze on Russia's economy from Western sanctions and a slump in export revenues.

The Russian currency has lost nearly 40% of its value this year, weakening past 100 rubles to the dollar, as Moscow's war in Ukraine takes a heavy toll.

The fall in the ruble's value is one of several negative indicators for the Russian economy, even as President Vladimir Putin insists that Western sanctions are having a limited effect.

The currency collapsed in the immediate aftermath of Russia's full-scale invasion of Ukraine in February 2022, dropping as low as 136 to the dollar in March 2022. It then soared to around 50 rubles to the dollar in June last year, as oil and natural gas prices surged.

But European economies have since weaned themselves off Russian oil and gas, importing more from the United States, Canada and Norway instead.

That has strained the Russian government's finances, which are also under pressure from a surge in spending to pay for the ongoing war.

The Kremlin has doubled its 2023 defense spending target to more than $100 billion—a third of all public expenditure—a government document reviewed by Reuters showed.

Western sanctions have also depressed foreign investment in the country and knocked exports.

The drop in exports, combined with a jump in imports driven by strong domestic demand, has cheapened the ruble further, according to Russia's central bank governor Elvira Nabiullina.

The central bank said Monday that elevated government "demand" and high rates of lending by Russian banks had boosted overall activity in the economy, placing upward

---

1 新闻稿来源：https://edition.cnn.com。

pressure on inflation and contributing to the ruble's weakness.

It also said it could raise interest rates soon to bring price rises under control. "The Bank of Russia admits the possibility of raising the key interest rate in coming meetings," it said in a statement shared with CNN.

b

Russia rouble: No panic but currency fall will hurt[1]

14 August　BBC

If you switch on Russian state TV today, you'd be forgiven for thinking that the Russian economy is booming.

A presenter on the Rossiya-24 channel did admit that the dollar exchange rate had reached an eye-watering 101 roubles—but, he went on to insist, the Russian economy was still doing marvellously well. Russian GDP—up! Oil and gas revenues—growing!

And in today's copy of *Komsomolskaya Pravda*, the biggest-selling daily newspaper in Russia, an article on page 3 declared: "The Russian economy takes a sharp upward turn."

But the plummeting rouble will still hurt.

It is now at its lowest for 16 months. Pressure is growing on the Russian economy, as imports increase faster than exports and military spending grows.

Economists say it will likely lead to inflation. Foreign travel will become more expensive to ordinary Russians. One travel agency owner in Moscow told me he expected many clients would now opt for taking a holiday inside Russia, instead of travelling abroad.

But going overseas was already very problematic for people here—Western sanctions against Russia's aviation industry make foreign travel very difficult. Many countries have stopped issuing visas for Russians, and financial restrictions mean their bank cards don't work in the vast majority of foreign countries.

Admittedly, Russia has been here before—the rouble fell steeply after the full-scale invasion of Ukraine. But then it recovered, prompting President Putin to declare at a meeting just over a year ago: "The dollar is clearly faltering, and the rouble is strengthening."

1　新闻稿来源：https://www.bbc.com。

But some economists here say that rouble exchange rates are now entirely managed by the Central Bank—and that recovery was artificially engineered.

Chris Weafer, founding partner of Eurasian consultancy firm Macro-Advisory, says last year's economic priority was keeping the rouble's value as high as possible but officials have now chosen to devalue the currency as a means of balancing government spending.

The exchange rate slide therefore reflects these decisions made by officials rather than a specific sign of an "imminent crisis" or a broader collapse of Russia's economy, he adds.

编译稿

俄罗斯卢布大跌 汇率创 17 个月新低

美国有线电视新闻网消息，8 月 14 日，俄罗斯卢布兑美元触及 17 个月低点。分析认为，卢布下跌凸显出西方制裁对于俄罗斯经济造成的压力，以及该国出口收入的下滑。

报道称，俄罗斯卢布汇率 14 日贬破 101 卢布兑 1 美元。这一下跌突显了西方制裁和出口收入下滑对俄罗斯经济的日益挤压。尽管俄总统普京坚称西方制裁效果有限，但卢布贬值是俄罗斯经济的几项负面指标之一。俄罗斯央行行长纳比乌林娜表示，出口下降加上强劲内需推动的进口激增，导致卢布进一步贬值。

另据英国广播公司（BBC）报道，进口增长快于出口加上军费增长令俄罗斯经济面临的压力愈来愈大。经济学家分析，这些情况可能导致通货膨胀，对于一般俄罗斯人来说，出国旅行会变得更贵。莫斯科的旅行业者认为，预计许多人将选择留在俄罗斯度假，而不是出国。

事实上，出国对于俄罗斯人来说已经是一个大问题，西方对俄罗斯航空业的制裁，使得出国旅行变得非常困难，许多国家已经停止向俄罗斯人发放签证，金融限制也意味着他们的银行卡在绝大多数国家都无法使用。

案例分析

这里的两篇新闻稿都是关于俄罗斯卢布大跌的报道，两篇从不同的角度分析了卢布大跌的原因及影响，写作结构大致相同。第一篇采用了典型的倒金字塔结构；第二篇采用了叙述式开头，从一个电视台节目主持人的角度道出了核心新闻事实。编译稿在综合了两篇新闻稿核心内容的基础上，合并了相同的信息，保留各自不同的内容，组合成了一篇新的完整的新闻报道。

◎新闻稿2

Britain to follow U.S. move to halve stock settlement time[1]

By Huw Jones March 29, 2024 4:50 AM GMT

LONDON, March 28 (Reuters)—Britain's stock markets should halve the time it takes to settle a share trade to stay competitive and complete this shift by the end of 2027, a report recommended on Thursday, a step the UK government has backed to play catch up with Wall Street.

Exchanges in the United States, Canada and Mexico move to settlement within one business day—dubbed T+1—at the end of May to cut risk, catching up with India and China, meaning 55% of global equity markets will operate on T+1 or less by the end of this year.

This is piling pressure on Britain and continental Europe to follow suit. The European Union has already said it would do so, though with no date set. Switzerland will have little choice but to switch as well.

Britain's finance ministry commissioned the report into cutting settlement times for trades on the London Stock Exchange and other platforms. This would reduce the time it takes to settle trades for cash to one business day from two currently.

The Accelerated Settlement Taskforce, which produced the report, found there was industry consensus to move to T+1 given that increasing efficiency is essential to maintain international competitiveness.

Taskforce Chair Charlie Geffen said government and regulators needed to push for a coordinated move to T+1 given that it will mean "significant investment", but also bring cost savings and reduce risk.

"It just makes sense to have a timetable and a deadline. If you don't have timelines, stuff doesn't get done," Geffen told Reuters.

"Learning the lessons from the United States is going to be important. I suspect there will be some teething issues to resolve."

European asset managers have already complained about not having enough time to find dollars to pay for U.S. stocks under the new settlement regime which comes into effect in the United States at the end of May.

Switching is costly. In the report, consultants Accenture estimated that in relation to

---

1 新闻稿来源：https://www.reuters.com。

the T+1 switch in the U.S., total investment of $30–50 million a year for three years would be needed by each large financial firm to make the switch.

Geffen recommended setting up a technical group to report by year-end on operational changes that will cost millions of pounds, such as back office automation at banks and asset managers. The industry should complete this by the end of 2025 to get systems ready.

The technical group would decide on a deadline for a mandated switch to T+1 which would be the end of 2027 at the latest.

"I am delighted to confirm that we are accepting all of the recommendations that the report makes to the government," Britain's financial services minister Bim Afolami said in a joint statement with the Taskforce.

Stocks make up 42% the 8.8 trillion pounds ($11.10 trillion) of assets managed out of London, with 32% of this in North American stocks and 19% in European stocks.

ALIGNMENT OR GO IT ALONE?

The stock settlement switch adds to a whole string of regulatory changes the UK finance industry has faced post-Brexit.

Geffen said it had been difficult to achieve consensus on the pace at which Britain should move to T+1, with some wanting EU alignment, while others want the mismatch with Wall Street to be as short as possible.

Britain, the EU and other European jurisdictions should try to work together to try to align the shifts to T+1, the report said.

EU regulators have noted that the bloc has multiple stock exchanges, and clearing and settlement houses, making a switch to T+1 more complicated than for a single jurisdiction.

"If the EU or other European jurisdictions commit to a transition date to T+1 the UK should consider whether it wishes to align with that timeline," the report said.

"However if that cannot be achieved within a suitable timescale the UK should proceed in any event."

Jos Dijsselhof, CEO of SIX Group, which operates the Zurich stock exchange and the Madrid bourse in the EU, said he would like to see Britain, the EU and Switzerland adopt T+1 at the same time. "We don't see much benefits from everybody going individually," he told Reuters.

Whether firms that want to move early to T+1 would be allowed to do so after 2025 is an issue the technical group would work through, Geffen said.

The report also said the technical group should consider a move at a later date to instant settlement or T+0, which was "technically possible today". ($1 = 0.7925 pounds)

编译稿

继美国之后，英国将把股票结算时间减半

路透社 3 月 28 日报道，周四的一份报告建议，为保持竞争力，英国股市应减半股票交易结算时间，并在 2027 年底前完成这一转变。英国政府支持此举，以追赶美国。

放眼全球，美国、加拿大和墨西哥计划 5 月底前将结算周期缩短至一个工作日——即 T+1。同时也这意味着全球将有 55% 的股市采取同一行动。

这给英国和欧洲大陆带来巨大压力。因此英国财政部委托加快交易结算任务组（Accelerated Settlement Taskforce，简称 AST）撰写了这份报告，以缩短伦敦证券交易所和其他平台的交易结算时间，将目前的两个工作日缩短到一个工作日。

报告指出，业界就这一决策达成共识。AST 主席查理·格芬（Charlie Geffen）表示，向 T+1 过渡有利有弊，政府和监管机构需要推动相关进展，并设定最后期限。他还指出，针对相关机构的不满与困难，技术部门要作出相应的调整。

对于是否和欧洲其他国家采取相同的时间规划尚未有定论。

案例分析

这篇新闻稿是有关英国计划缩减股票结算时间的报道，采用倒金字塔结构，导语概括新闻主题，正文说明该计划产生的原因、背景、影响及其他细节。该新闻稿专业性比较强。编译稿在内容选取和表述上特别注意到这一点，仅呈现新闻的核心事实，以传递信息为主，不过多涉及专业性知识，个别地方通过解释更好地帮助读者理解信息。

三、经济类新闻稿的编译原则

根据经济类新闻的性质和特点，编译者在编译此类新闻时应注意以下几点：

- **术语准确性**：编译时应确保信息的准确性，注意专业术语的表达。
- **数据典型性**：编译时应挑选典型的、有全局性的数据进行报道。
- **表述简洁性**：对于政策解读及市场预测与分析的报道，编译时语言表达应力求简洁清晰、有逻辑性。

● **叙事趣味性**：经济类新闻稿大多比较专业，难以被大众读者理解，编译时要考虑受众群体，注意报道的角度和叙事方式，可根据情况使用浅显易懂的语言，以增加报道的趣味性、通俗性、可接受性和吸引力。

● **要素统一性**：编译者有时需要在复杂的信息中突出人物和故事，应注意人（事件主体）、事（新闻事件）、物（事件客体）的统一。

四、经济类新闻稿的编译步骤

编译经济类新闻的方法与编译其他新闻的方法基本相同：

● **梳理新闻要点**：阅读原文并分析新闻事件的核心事实。

● **确定编译结构**：编译政经、财经、产经新闻时多根据原新闻稿采用倒金字塔结构，突出核心信息；编译社经新闻时，有时也可采用金字塔结构，突出人物和故事，增加趣味性。

● **编译导语和正文**：导语应简洁明了，概括最重要的新闻事实；正文可根据不同新闻类型进行结构调整，重点突出新闻的关键要素，或分析、或预测、或评述。

● **调整和优化**：完成初稿后要对编译稿进行校对、修改和润色，确保译文的准确性和流畅性。

● **拟定新闻标题**：新闻标题应凸显最重要的信息，同时要能够吸引读者。

将以下英语新闻稿编译成汉语新闻稿。

◎ 新闻稿 1

India's gold demand to rise in 2024 despite subdued March quarter: World Gold Council[1]

Reuters Updated: Jan 31, 2024, 12:02:00 PM IST

India's gold demand is expected to be subdued in the first quarter of 2024 due to lower jewelry sales. However, annual demand is anticipated to rise as consumers adjust to higher prices. The World Gold Council (WGC) projects that India's gold demand, which has been stuck between 700 and 800 metric tons in the past five years, will break out of this range and rise to between 800 and 900 tons in 2024.

MUMBAI, Jan 31 (Reuters)—India's gold demand is expected to be subdued in the first quarter of 2024 due to lower jewellery sales, but annual demand is anticipated to rise as consumers adjust to higher prices, the World Gold Council (WGC) said on

---

[1] 新闻稿来源：https://economictimes.indiatimes.com。

Wednesday.

Higher purchases in the world's second-biggest gold consumer could support prices which are trading near record highs.

Rising demand for imports could also widen India's trade deficit and put pressure on the rupee.

India's gold demand has been stuck between 700 and 800 metric tons in the past five years, but it is expected to break out of this range and rise to between 800 and 900 tons in 2024, Somasundaram P.R., CEO of WGC's Indian operations told Reuters.

"Given the fact that high prices have now been absorbed and economic growth is robust, demand is resetting its base to 800 to 900 tons," he said.

Indian gold demand fell 3% in 2023 from the prior year to 747.5 tons, the lowest since 2020, as prices rallying to a record high curtailed jewellery demand, the WGC said in a report published on Wednesday.

Switzerland, the United Arab Emirates, Peru, and Ghana are leading gold suppliers to India.

In the March quarter, demand is expected to stay low due to fewer auspicious wedding days, the WGC said.

Weddings are a major driver of gold purchases in India, with bullion in the form of jewellery being a crucial part of a bride's attire and a popular gift from family and guests.

Indian gold consumption in the Oct-Dec quarter fell 4% to 266.2 tons, as a drop in jewellery demand overshadowed higher sales of coins and bars for investment purposes, the WGC said.

Meanwhile, gold smuggling into India gained momentum to approximately around 130 tons from around 110 tons a year ago, Somasundaram said, due to prices reaching record highs.

India's commerce ministry has backed a long-standing demand from the jewellery industry to reduce import tariffs on gold bars, government and industry officials said, amid concern the duties were further harming the country's faltering jewellery exports.

◎新闻稿2

Japan launches ride-hailing services in Tokyo, other areas to follow[1]

KYODO NEWS 2024-04-28

TOKYO—Japan on Monday launched ride-hailing services in Tokyo, with other areas across the country to follow suit in a bid to address a nationwide shortage of taxi drivers.

The country partially lifted a ban on the services earlier this month, allowing drivers with a standard license to offer taxi services on specified days and hours using their own private vehicle, provided they are under the management of a local tax company.

The Tokyo Hire-Taxi Association, one of the operators involved in the project, held a ceremony to commemorate the launch, demonstrating how drivers use a dedicated smartphone app to receive dispatch requests and to input health-related data concerning their fitness to drive.

"We will greatly expand the ride-hailing business and establish it throughout Japan to resolve a shortage of transport providers," transport minister Tetsuo Saito said at the ceremony. He went for a test ride using the service.

About 80 drivers were available as of Monday morning, with the services used around 50 times before 9 a.m., according to the association.

Registered vehicles are dispatched with destinations and fares calculated in advance. Only cashless payments can be accepted in principle.

The services are now available in Tokyo's 23 wards and the suburban areas of Musashino and Mitaka from Monday to Friday from 7 a.m. to before 11 a.m. and from 12 a.m. to before 4 a.m. on Saturday mornings.

The services will later be expanded, with the transport ministry having also allowed their introduction in other large cities such as Kyoto, Osaka, Nagoya and Fukuoka.

The government is aiming to start the services later this month in Kyoto, Nagoya and Yokohama.

---

1 新闻稿来源：https://english.kyodonews.net。

第四节 科技类新闻的编译

一、科技类新闻的概念

科技类新闻，顾名思义，就是报道科学技术领域里新动态、新发明、新发现、新成果、新产品、新趋势、新政策的新闻。这类新闻涉及诸多领域，例如能源、材料、航空航天、网络通信、人工智能、生物医药、信息安全等。科技类新闻向公众迅速及时地报道和传播最新、最前沿的科技信息，这些信息不仅反映了科技的最新发展，还体现了人类对自然界和未知领域的探索与认知。

编译科技类新闻既能够帮助国内专业科技人员了解更多国外科技领域动态和相关技术突破，又能够向广大读者普及科技知识，扩大普通受众的视野，促进我国科技事业的发展进步。

科技类新闻涉及不同的专业和领域，作为新闻报道来说，呈现新闻事实是核心，因此，科技类新闻以写实见长，讲究内容真实、话语朴实，旨在将深奥的科技专业术语大众化，使科学内容通俗化，便于广大读者更好理解和接受。

二、科技类新闻稿的特点

科技类新闻是对科技领域新出现的现象、趋势，或新近发生的科技事件进行科学性、知识性的报道，往往具有以下特点：

● **准确性 (accuracy)**：科技类新闻必须确保文内信息和数据真实可信，即新闻来源要权威、可靠，内容翔实，避免误导读者或传播错误信息。

● **新颖性 (originality)**：科技类新闻关注最新的科技进展、发展趋势和行业的重大变化等，具有新颖性和时效性。

● **通俗性 (popularity)**：科技类新闻报道通常使用通俗易懂的语言，避免过于专业的术语，以提高新闻的可读性和吸引力，便于将科技发展成果更广泛地传播给普通读者。

● **精练性 (conciseness)**：科技类新闻通常使用精练简洁的语言和结构，使读者能够快速获取所需的知识或信息。

● **生动性 (vividness)**：科技类新闻的生动性主要表现为生动形象的报道语言、多元的报道方式、具有感染力的故事，这些都能提高新闻的趣味性，激发读者的好奇心和阅读兴趣，引导或促使读者作出进一步思考。

三、科技类新闻稿的编译原则

科技类新闻通常报道的是各个领域的最新科技成果，其报道内容的专业性和前沿性对编译者提出了较高的要求。要做好科技类新闻编译，编译者必须在"行家"和"读者"之间不断进行身份转换。编译科技类新闻时，编译者应遵循以下原则：

● **信息准确**：准确性是编译科技类新闻的首要原则。编译者应首选来自权威、可靠消息源的新闻，如科技媒体、行业会议等，对于科学研究、技术发展等信息，编译者应确保理解准确、表达精准。

● **重点突出**：科技类新闻往往涉及科技前沿和创新理念，编译者应对新闻内容进行筛选，突出科技的前沿性和创新性，帮助读者了解科技创新对社会和生活带来的影响。

● **语言通俗**：编译科技类新闻时应尽量采用简明的语言风格，使用通俗易懂的语言，必要时可使用恰当的修辞手法来提高新闻的趣味性和可读性，便于读者轻松理解和消化复杂的科技信息，增强科普效果，实现传播目的。

● **形式多元**：科技类新闻多包含事实和数据，有时为了取得更好的传播效果，编译者可采用图表、图片等更为直观、形象的方式，还可以通过比较或对照等方法凸显科技新闻中的亮点。但无论用何种信息呈现形式，编译者都应保持中立，要客观地传递科技信息，避免个人观点和情感色彩的介入。

阅读并对比以下新闻稿及其编译稿，观察并总结各自的特点。

新闻稿	编译稿
Smart Glass Knows When It Needs Another Beer[1] 2002 / 04 / 09 New Scientist Drink up that beer—another will soon be whisked to the table thanks to a hi-tech pint glass that tells bar staff when it needs refilling. Developed by a Japanese electronics company, the intelligent glass is fitted with a radio-frequency coil in its base and emits a signal to a receiver set in the table when it's empty, *New Scientist* magazine reported Thursday. The Glassware system works by coating each glass with a clear, conducting material, enabling it to measure exactly how much liquid has been sipped or guzzled. When empty, the glass sends an electronic cry for more beer from the table to waiters equipped with hand-	樽中酒少杯先知——聪明的智能酒杯 据周四《新科学家》杂志报道，一家日本电子公司研制出了一款智能啤酒杯，有了这种高科技的啤酒杯，无论你坐在酒吧的什么位置，当你的酒杯快要见底的时候，不用你招呼，酒吧的服务生就会马上过来为你斟酒。 据报道，这种智能啤酒杯是将一枚可以发射无线电频率的线圈置于杯子底部，这样当酒杯空了的时候线圈就会向吧台的接收仪器发出信号。 这种智能酒杯的工作原理是给

---

[1] 新闻稿来源：https://www.vbforums.com。

新闻稿	编译稿
held computers on frequencies similar to those used by mobile phones. 　　A team from the Mitsubishi Electric Research Laboratories working in Cambridge, Massachusetts has made the first prototypes, but may find it hard to sell the idea to Britons. 　　"It sounds like a fun idea, but I don't think it would work in our pubs," said a spokesman for J.D. Wetherspoon, which runs over 500 pubs in Britain. 　　"The tradition in Britain is to get up and go to the bar for a round of drinks, not to have a waiter bring beers to the table, no matter how quickly," he said.	酒杯涂上一层光洁的传导材料，这样无论顾客是小啜还是狂饮，这套系统都可以测量出酒杯中还剩下多少酒。 　　当酒杯空了的时候，它就会从顾客坐的桌子发出电子提示声提醒服务生需要添酒了，而服务生手中则拿着可以接收频率的掌中电脑，就和手机发出频率的道理差不多。 　　一个在美国麻省剑桥工作的日本三菱电子实验室研究小组已经成功制造出了第一个这样的智能酒杯。

(1) 新闻稿特点：_____

_____

(2) 编译稿特点：_____

_____

四、科技类新闻稿的编译要点

在编译科技类新闻时，编译者应注意以下几点：

● **突出科技特色**：编译科技类新闻应重点呈现科技信息，对于不同类型的科技新闻，编译的重点略有不同。科技成果类报道涉及科技成果、原理和特点以及科技的创新性、领先性、意义和价值；政策类报道应包括具体措施、实施细节、目标对象、可能产生的影响等；科学研究类报道通常包括研究背景、方法、结果和意义；科技动态类报道应包括现状、进展和发展趋势等；人物类报道应突出动人的故事、学术思想、影响力、对社会的贡献等。

● **满足受众需求**：科技类新闻的编译必须要考虑受众的阅读习惯和对信息的需求，编译时可根据需要对原新闻稿结构进行适当调整，对与受众关系不大的内容可适当删减或省略。

● **增加报道趣味**：编译科技类新闻需充分利用背景材料，提高报道的可读性和趣味性，便于广大读者接受和理解。

编译案例

◎ 新闻稿 1

Meta to start labeling AI-generated content in May[1]

by Alex PIGMAN 2024-04-05 AFP

Facebook and Instagram giant Meta on Friday said it will begin labeling AI-generated media beginning in May, as it tries to reassure users and governments over the risks of deepfakes.

The social media juggernaut added that it will no longer remove manipulated images and audio that don't otherwise break its rules, relying instead on labeling and contextualization, so as to not infringe on freedom of speech.

The changes come as a response to criticism from the tech giant's oversight board, which independently reviews Meta's content moderation decisions.

The board in February requested that Meta urgently overhaul its approach to manipulated media given the huge advances in AI and the ease of manipulating media into highly convincing deepfakes.

The board's warning came amid fears of rampant misuse of artificial intelligence-powered applications for disinformation on platforms in a pivotal election year not only in the United States but worldwide.

Meta's new "Made with AI" labels will identify content created or altered with AI, including video, audio, and images. Additionally, a more prominent label will be used for content deemed at high risk of misleading the public.

"We agree that providing transparency and additional context is now the better way to address this content," Monika Bickert, Meta's Vice President of Content Policy, said in a blog post.

"The labels will cover a broader range of content in addition to the manipulated content that the Oversight Board recommended labeling," she added.

These new labeling techniques are linked to an agreement made in February among major tech giants and AI players to cooperate on ways to crack down on manipulated content intended to deceive voters.

Meta, Google and OpenAI had already agreed to use a common watermarking standard that would invisibly tag images generated by their AI applications. Identifying

---

1 新闻稿来源：https://techxplore.com。

AI content "is better than nothing, but there are bound to be holes," Nicolas Gaudemet, AI Director at Onepoint, told AFP.

He took the example of some open source software, which doesn't always use this type of watermarking adopted by AI's big players.

Biden deepfakes

Meta said its rollout will occur in two phases with AI-generated content labeling beginning in May 2024, while the removal of manipulated media solely based on the old policy will cease in July.

According to the new standard, content, even if manipulated with AI, will remain on the platform unless it violates other rules, such as those prohibiting hate speech or voter interference.

Recent examples of convincing AI deepfakes have only heightened worries about the easily accessible technology.

The board's list of requests was part of its review of Meta's decision to leave a manipulated video of US President Joe Biden online last year.

The video showed Biden voting with his adult granddaughter, but was manipulated to falsely appear that he inappropriately touched her chest.

In a separate incident not linked to Meta, a robocall impersonation of Biden pushed out to tens of thousands of voters urged people to not cast ballots in the New Hampshire primary.

In Pakistan, the party of former prime minister Imran Khan has used AI to generate speeches from their jailed leader.

编译稿

Meta 将用水印标记 AI 生成内容

据法新社 4 月 5 日报道，拥有脸书和照片墙等社交媒体平台的科技巨头元宇宙平台公司 (Meta)5 日表示，将从 5 月开始为人工智能 (AI) 生成的内容贴上标签。该公司正努力打消用户和政府对"深度伪造"技术相关风险的疑虑。

报道称，这家社交媒体巨头还说，将不再删除在其他方面未违反该公司规则的伪造图像和音频，而是通过贴标签和添加背景的方式提醒用户注意。

报道指出，这些变化是这家科技巨头针对其监督委员会所提批评的回应。该委员会独立审查 Meta 的内容审核决定。

今年 2 月，该委员会要求 Meta 紧急调整其应对伪造内容的方式，因为人工智能技术取得巨大进步，可以轻易伪造令人高度信服的内容。

该委员会发出警告的背景是，人们担心，在美国乃至世界多国举行选举的关键一年，人工智能驱动的应用程序被广泛滥用，用于生成在各大平台传播的虚假信息。

Meta 的"Made with AI"（用 AI 制作）新标签将指明由人工智能生成或修改的内容，包括视频、音频和图像。此外，被认为具有高度误导公众风险的内容将被贴上更醒目的标签。

案例分析

新闻稿的主题是 Meta 公司计划于今年 5 月用水印标记 AI 生成内容，报道采用倒金字塔结构，导语说明主题内容，正文介绍此项决定的背景、将标记的内容、计划的具体实施、AI 伪造内容案例等。编译稿也采用了相同的写作结构，先导语后正文，并将原文的信息进行了合并和删减，概述了有关此项计划的几个主要方面，信息呈现更为凝练。

◎新闻稿 2

Tsung-Dao Lee Obituary: boundary breaking physicist who won Nobel prize at just 30[1]

By Robert P. Crease

Outside the Institute of High Energy Physics in Beijing stands a 5-metre-high metal sculpture. The round, swirling shape of 'The Tao of All Matter' invokes the yin and yang of ancient Chinese philosophy—a representation of the inseparable opposites said to form the basis of all things—as well as the ring of the modern particle accelerator a few dozen metres away. The designer was physicist Tsung-Dao (T. D.) Lee. An artistic, inventive and boundary-breaking physicist, in 1957 Lee became one of the youngest winners of a Nobel prize at 30 years old. He shared the award with his compatriot Chen Ning Yang for their work on broken symmetry in particle physics.

Chinese-born but based in the United States for most of his career, Lee, who has died aged 98, promoted engagement between US and Chinese physicists. Lee set up the

---

1 新闻稿来源：https://www.nature.com。

China-US Physics Examination and Application system, through which US physicists set exams for Chinese universities to administer, and then went to China to mark them. On the basis of the results, US universities awarded scholarships to nearly 1,000 Chinese students between 1979 and 1989.

Lee's own education in Shanghai had been interrupted by the 1937 Japanese invasion of China, and by 1945 he was studying physics at the National Southwestern Associated University in Kunming, China. There, at 19 years old, he received a fellowship from the Chinese government to study in the United States, where he completed a PhD at the University of Chicago, Illinois, with the Italian American nuclear physicist and Nobel prizewinner Enrico Fermi as his adviser. He spent the rest of his career at Columbia University in New York City.

Lee earned his own Nobel in one of the most remarkable episodes of twentieth-century science. Physicists were baffled by two particles, known as τ and θ, that were identical except that they decayed in different ways. Treating them as distinct particles created insoluble theoretical problems, whereas treating them as identical defied the fundamental structure of physics known as parity—the idea that objects always behave in the same way as their mirror images.

In 1956, Lee worked on the problem with Yang while the two were spending the summer at Brookhaven National Laboratory in Upton, New York. Colleagues remember hearing them shouting at each other in their offices in Chinese and English, and drawing equations in the sand on visits to the beach. Did physicists, the two asked, really know that parity structured the 'weak interaction' that governed decays of τ and θ? After wading through a 1,000-page book detailing 40 years of work on the subject, they realized that that aspect of parity had not been tested. On 22 June 1956, Lee and Yang sent an article to *Physical Review* with the title 'Is parity conserved in weak interactions?'. The journal's editor insisted that question marks in paper titles were unscientific and changed it to 'Question of parity conservation in weak interactions' (T.D.Lee and C.N.Yang *Phys.Rev.* 104, 254;1956).

Lee and Yang struggled to interest experimenters in testing a hypothesis widely regarded as preposterous. Only Chien-Shiung Wu at Columbia agreed. She set up an experiment to detect β-decay—the emission of β-particles from nuclei—in ultracold radioactive cobalt. At the tail end of 1956, her team announced that parity was indeed violated in the weak interaction. As another Columbia colleague, Nobel-prize winning physicist Isidor Rabi, said at a press conference: "A rather complete theoretical structure has been shattered at the base and we are not sure how the pieces will be put together." By the end of the year, Lee and Yang had been jointly awarded the Nobel Prize in Physics for their discovery. Lee and others felt that Wu deserved a share of the prize, but she never received it.

Lee and Yang's personal relationship did not survive the success of their professional one. To their colleagues' distress and incomprehension, their clashes became so fierce that universities and laboratories took care to invite only one at a time for visits.

Lee was influential in the evolution of the Brookhaven lab when it faced an uncertain future after a huge high-energy accelerator project was cancelled in 1983. He helped the lab to transform that project into another, the Relativistic Heavy Ion Collider (RHIC), which would study the nature of nuclear matter. Lee then established and was first director of the RIKEN BNL Research Center, a pioneering collaboration between Japanese and US scientists at the RHIC.

As an assistant professor at Columbia University in the early 1950s, Lee initiated 'Chinese lunch', a tradition in which, at noon on Mondays, physicists would take a visiting seminar speaker to a local Chinese restaurant. Lee insisted on ordering for everyone, and the conversation was usually so lively that participants would have to race back to campus in time for the seminar to begin at 14:10. His research contributed to an astounding variety of fields, including astrophysics, hydrodynamics, particle physics, condensed-matter physics, relativistic physics and statistical mechanics.

Halfway around the world from Beijing, at the Santa Maria degli Angeli basilica in Rome, is another of Lee's sculptures: 'Galileo Galilei Divine Man'. In it, the revolutionary seventeenth-century astronomer, philosopher, physicist and artist holds a telescope and robes adorned with heavenly bodies. Both sculpted and sculptor were scientists whose work ventured across boundaries: between scientific fields and between the sciences and the arts.

编译稿

打破边界的物理学家李政道，三十岁获诺贝尔奖

著名物理学家李政道于8月4日在美国旧金山去世，享年98岁。他以突破性的研究闻名，并在30岁时成为诺贝尔奖最年轻的获得者之一。

1957年，李政道与杨振宁因在粒子物理学中发现"宇称不守恒"现象而获得诺贝尔物理学奖，此发现挑战了当时物理学中认为粒子行为与其镜像相同的传统观念。

李政道出生于中国，职业生涯大多在美国度过。他不仅在科学领域取得了卓越成就，还致力于推动中美物理学界的交流。他在1979年创立了中美物理考试与申请系统（即中美联合培养物理类研究生计划），帮助成千上万的中国学生获得了前往美国大学深造的机会。

在职业生涯中，李政道的研究领域涵盖了天体物理学、粒子物理学、统计力学等多个领域。他曾担任布鲁克海文国家实验室的顾问，帮助转型并推动重离子对撞机的建设。

此外，李政道还热衷于艺术创作，他设计的两件雕塑作品，北京中科院高能物理研究所前的"物之道"和罗马圣玛丽亚教堂中的"伽利略-神圣之人"展现了科学与艺术的跨界融合。

案例分析

这是一篇科学人物报道，不同于一般性的新闻，这篇报道更像是人物传记。报道的开头和结尾也很特别，从雕塑开始，以雕塑结束，向读者娓娓讲述这位科学家鲜为人知的故事。报道开头简单介绍了李政道的生平、所取得的伟大成就、对中美科技领域交流所作的贡献。之后用倒叙法叙述了李政道的求学和职业生涯，以及他获得诺贝尔物理学奖的故事，语言生动，文字优美。编译稿采用了倒金字塔结构，导语简洁明了地说明了核心新闻事实，突出了李政道的卓越成就。正文概述了他在物理学领域的成就、对推动中美科技与文化交流作出的突出贡献，以及作为科学家所具有的艺术特质。

◎新闻稿3

New funding for development of world's first lung cancer vaccine[1]

2024-03-22

Researchers at the University of Oxford, the Francis Crick Institute and University College London have been granted £1.7 million of funding from Cancer Research UK and the CRIS Cancer Foundation to develop a lung cancer vaccine.

Developed by scientists from the University of Oxford, the Francis Crick Institute

---

1 新闻稿来源：https://www.ox.ac.uk。

and University College London, the 'LungVax' vaccine uses technology similar to the highly successful Oxford/AstraZeneca COVID-19 vaccine.

The team will receive funding for the study over the next 2 years to support lab research and initial manufacturing of 3,000 doses of the vaccine at the Oxford Clinical BioManufacturing Facility.

Lung cancer cells look different from normal cells due to having "red flag" proteins called neoantigens. Neoantigens appear on the surface of the cell because of cancer-causing mutations within the cell's DNA.

The LungVax vaccine will carry a strand of DNA which trains the immune system to recognise these neoantigens on abnormal lung cells. The LungVax vaccine will then activate the immune system to kill these cells and stop lung cancer.

In this study, the scientists are developing this vaccine in the lab to show that it successfully triggers an immune response. If this work is successful, the vaccine will move straight into a clinical trial. If the subsequent early trial delivers promising results, the vaccine could then be scaled up to bigger trials for people at high risk of lung cancer. This could include people aged 55–74 who are current smokers, or have previously smoked, and currently qualify for targeted lung health checks in some parts of the UK.

There are around 48,500 cases of lung cancer every year in the UK. 72% of lung cancers are caused by smoking, which is the biggest preventable cause of cancer worldwide.

Kidani Professor of Immuno-oncology at the University of Oxford and research lead for the LungVax project, Professor Tim Elliott, said: 'Cancer is a disease of our own bodies and it's hard for the immune system to distinguish between what's normal and what's cancer. Getting the immune system to recognise and attack cancer is one of the biggest challenges in cancer research today.

'This research could deliver an off-the-shelf vaccine based on Oxford's vaccine technology, which proved itself in the COVID-19 pandemic. If we can replicate the kind of success seen in trials during the pandemic, we could save the lives of tens of thousands of people every year in the UK alone.'

Professor of Experimental Oncology at the University of Oxford and founder of the LungVax project, Professor Sarah Blagden, said: 'When given to people with cancer at its earliest stages, anti-cancer treatments are more likely to be successful.

'We are developing a vaccine to stop the formation of lung cancer in people at high risk. This is an important step forward in preventing this devastating disease.'

Professor Mariam Jamal-Hanjani of University College London and the Francis Crick Institute, who will be leading the LungVax clinical trial, said: 'Fewer than 10% of people with lung cancer survive their disease for 10 years or more. That must change. This research complements existing efforts through lung health checks to detect lung cancer earlier in people who are at greatest risk.

'We think the vaccine could cover around 90% of all lung cancers, based on our computer models and previous research, and this funding will allow us to take the vital first steps towards trials in patients.

'LungVax will not replace stopping smoking as the best way to reduce your risk of lung cancer. But it could offer a viable route to preventing some of the earliest stage cancers from emerging in the first place.'

Chief Executive of Cancer Research UK, Michelle Mitchell, said: 'The science that successfully steered the world out of the pandemic could soon be guiding us toward a future where people can live longer, better lives free from the fear of cancer.

'Projects like LungVax are a really important step forward into an exciting future, where cancer is much more preventable. We're in a golden age of research and this is one of many projects which we hope will transform lung cancer survival.'

President of CRIS Cancer Foundation, Lola Manterola, said: 'We are at a crucial moment in the history of cancer research and treatment. For the first time, technology and knowledge of the immune system are allowing us to take the first steps towards preventing cancer.

'This groundbreaking study represents a firm step in that direction, and we at CRIS consider it essential to support it.'

编译稿

英科学家研制世界首款肺癌疫苗

据英国牛津大学网站 3 月 22 日消息，英国科学家正在研制世界上首款肺癌疫苗"LungVax"。它发挥作用的机理是训练免疫系统，识别肺癌细胞表面的新抗原并摧毁异常的肺癌细胞，这与牛津大学和阿斯利康制药公司联合研发的新冠疫苗的技术类似。

来自牛津大学、弗朗西斯·克里克研究所和伦敦大学学院的专家，获得了来自英国癌症研究中心和 CRIS 癌症基金会的 170 万英镑的研究资金。研究团队将在未来两年进行实验室研究并初步生产 3000 剂疫苗。如果实验室测试成功，该疫苗将进入临床试验，并可能扩大至高危人群的大规模试验。这些高危人群包括 55-74 岁的当前吸烟者或既往吸烟者。

肺癌是英国最致命的常见癌症，每年约有 5 万例肺癌病例，其中 72% 与吸烟有关。研究负责人、牛津大学免疫肿瘤学教授蒂姆·埃利奥特（Tim Elliott）表示，癌症是一种很难被免疫系统识别的疾病，让免疫系统识别并攻击癌症，是当今癌症研究中面临的最大挑战之一。LungVax 疫苗有望帮助免疫系统更有效地识别和对抗癌症。如果成功，疫苗每年仅在英国就可能挽救数以万计的生命。

项目创始人萨拉·布拉格登（Sarah Blagden）教授指出，早期的抗癌治疗更可能取得成功，而 LungVax 则是防止高危人群肺癌形成的重要一步。该疫苗不会取代戒烟成为降低患肺癌风险的最佳方式，但有望在肺癌早期预防方面发挥重要作用。

案例分析

这篇新闻稿的主题是英国科学家获得资助用以研制世界首款肺癌疫苗，报道采用倒金字塔结构，导语仅透露这项研究所使用的技术与研制新冠疫苗类似，但并未具体说明，而留下的这个悬念在正文中才揭开。正文主要包括该项研究获得资助的事实、研究所采用的技术和作用机理、研究的意义和应用前景、科研团队对研究结果的信心和乐观情绪以及英国肺癌患者的现状等。编译稿虽然同样采用了倒金字塔结构，但导语把正文中的一些内容提到前面，明确了该项研究的主要内容、研究所使用的技术和作用机理以及所获得的研究资助。正文部分也包含了原稿中主要涉及的研究项目内容，不同的是编译稿调整了内容的顺序，这样处理更符合受众的阅读和思维习惯。

将以下英语新闻稿编译成汉语新闻稿。

◎ 新闻稿

Robot disguised as a coyote or fox will scare wildlife away from runways at Alaska airport[1]

Updated 5:11 AM GMT+8, March 30, 2024

ANCHORAGE, Alaska (AP)—A headless robot about the size of a labrador

---

1 新闻稿来源：https://apnews.com。

retriever will be camouflaged as a coyote or fox to ward off migratory birds and other wildlife at Alaska's second largest airport, a state agency said.

The Alaska Department of Transportation and Public Facilities has named the new robot Aurora and said it will be based at the Fairbanks airport to "enhance and augment safety and operations," the *Anchorage Daily News* reported.

The transportation department released a video of the robot climbing rocks, going up stairs and doing something akin to dancing while flashing green lights.

Those dancing skills will be put to use this fall during the migratory bird season when Aurora imitates predator-like movements to keep birds and other wildlife from settling near plane infields.

The plan is to have Aurora patrol an outdoor area near the runway every hour in an attempt to prevent harmful encounters between planes and wildlife, said Ryan Marlow, a program manager with the transportation department.

The robot can be disguised as a coyote or a fox by changing out replaceable panels, he said.

"The sole purpose of this is to act as a predator and allow for us to invoke that response in wildlife without having to use other means," Marlow told legislators last week.

The panels would not be hyper-realistic, and Marlow said the agency decided against using animal fur to make sure Aurora remained waterproof.

The idea of using a robot came after officials rejected a plan to use flying drones spraying a repellent including grape juice.

Previous other deterrent efforts have included officials releasing pigs at a lake near the Anchorage airport in the 1990s, with the hope they would eat waterfowl eggs near plane landing areas.

The test period in Fairbanks will also see how effective of a deterrent Aurora would be with larger animals and to see how moose and bears would respond to the robot, Marlow told the Anchorage newspaper.

Fairbanks "is leading the country with wildlife mitigation through the use of Aurora. Several airports across the country have implemented robots for various tasks such as cleaning, security patrols, and customer service," agency spokesperson Danielle Tessen said in an email to The Associated Press.

> In Alaska, wildlife service teams currently are used to scare birds and other wildlife away from runways with loud sounds, sometimes made with paintball guns.
>
> Last year, there were 92 animal strikes near airports across Alaska, including 10 in Fairbanks, according to an Federal Aviation Administration database.
>
> Most strikes resulted in no damage to the aircraft, but Marlow said the encounters can be expensive and dangerous in the rare instance when a bird is sucked into an engine, potentially causing a crash.
>
> An AWACS jet crashed in 1995 when it hit a flock of geese, killing 24 people at Elmendorf Air Force Base in Anchorage.
>
> If the test proves successful, Marlow said the agency could send similar robots to smaller airports in Alaska, which could be more cost effective than hiring human deterrent teams.
>
> Aurora, which can be controlled from a table, computer or on an automated schedule, will always have a human handler with it, he said. It can navigate through rain or snow.
>
> The robot from Boston Dynamics cost about $70,000 and was paid for with a federal grant.

第五节　教育类新闻的编译

一、教育类新闻的概念

教育类新闻是教育领域发生的各类新闻事件的报道，涉及教育机构、教学活动、人才培养等多方面，涵盖教育政策和实践、教育改革和创新、教育技术发展和应用、教育交流与合作、最新教育动态以及教育问题与社会关注（如教育资源分配、教育公平、学生心理健康）等主题。编译具有社会影响力和重要意义的教育类新闻，有助于国内受众了解和关注国际教育领域的重大事件、热点问题、教育发展趋势等。

二、教育类新闻稿的写作特点

由于各国的文化背景与教育体制差异较大，教育类新闻在写作上呈现多样性和复杂性。教育类新闻常使用多种叙事策略，包括多角度报道、叙事个体化（突出新闻人物）等。有时新闻通过改变叙事焦点使读者成为故事中的一部分，以增强读者的参与感，提高读者兴趣。

根据内容的需要，教育类新闻稿可采用不同的结构：

● **紧急性教育事件**：对于一些需要突出重要性或紧急性的教育新闻事件，英语新闻稿多采用倒金字塔结构，内容上通常是"先果后因"或"先概述后细节"，采用"闪回"或"插叙"等叙事手法。

● **非紧急教育事件**：非紧急教育事件多采用金字塔结构进行报道，按照时间顺序和事件进展逐渐展开。

● **人物类教育新闻**：需要突出新闻人物的报道常采用故事叙事法，报道往往包含有趣的人物故事和引人入胜的细节描写，有时还通过引用对话或场景描述以增强新闻的故事性和吸引力。

● **暴露问题类教育新闻**：此类报道倾向于以批判性的视角关注教育领域中存在的问题，多采用调查性报道的方式，通过大量的采访和数据搜集深入挖掘问题并提供详尽的分析，对于一些长期关注的教育问题或事件，新闻会采用跟踪报道的方式，定期更新事件的最新进展和变化。

此外，教育类新闻报道也很注重新闻的可读性和生动性，会通过细节描写增加现场感、突出人情味、增加趣味性、提高吸引力，此外，报道也重视使用背景材料以增加新闻内容的深度和广度，帮助读者更好地理解新闻事件。

编译案例

◎ 新闻稿

Fontbonne University in Missouri to close due to budget problems and declining enrollment[1]

BY JIM SALTER Updated 5:08 AM GMT+8, March 14, 2024 (AP news)

A sign for Fontbonne University is displayed Thursday, Nov. 30, 2023, at its campus in Clayton, a suburb of St. Louis. The 100-year-old university in Missouri will shut down next year, its president said Monday, March 11, 2024, citing declining enrollment and ongoing budget problems that made it impossible to keep going.

A century-old university in suburban St. Louis will shut down next year, its president said Monday, citing declining enrollment and ongoing budget problems.

Fontbonne University, in Clayton, was founded by the Sisters of St. Joseph of Carondelet in 1923, first as a place to educate young Catholic women. Enrollment for the fall semester was 874 students, including 650 undergraduates. A decade ago, Fontbonne's

---

1 新闻稿来源：https://apnews.com。

enrollment was about 2,000 students, the St. Louis Post-Dispatch reported.

University President Nancy Blattner said in a statement that Fontbonne will not accept freshmen for the fall 2024 semester, but will continue with classes through summer 2025. University leaders will work with faculty and staff to help them find new positions elsewhere, she said.

"After many years of declining enrollments and a shrinking endowment, the financial position of the university is no longer able to be sustained for the long term," Blattner said.

Many universities are facing similar struggles. Public and private colleges and universities across the country have announced mass layoffs in recent months, as well as program eliminations and campus closures. Budget shortfalls are blamed on declining enrollment, the end of federal pandemic funding and other factors.

In December, the University of Arizona unveiled a financial recovery plan to address a shortfall that now stands at $177 million in the current operating budget. Earlier last year, four of the 14 universities in the Big Ten Conference—Penn State, Nebraska, Minnesota and Rutgers—announced significant budget shortfalls. Bradley University, a private school in Illinois, faced a $13 million budget shortfall representing 10% of its total operating budget.

Blattner said Fontbonne leaders have worked for years to try and turn things around.

"Despite our best efforts to cut costs, create new academic programs and launch athletic teams, the university is unable to recover from years of declining enrollments and budget deficits," she said.

The university's 16-acre campus sits next to Washington University in St. Louis. Washington University announced Monday that it agreed to purchase the Fontbonne campus but doesn't have definitive plans for the property.

编译稿

创校 101 年 圣路易芳邦大学走入历史

据美联社 3 月 14 日消息，位于密苏里州圣路易斯郊区的芳邦大学 3 月 11 日宣布该校将于 2025 年夏季学期关闭。芳邦大学校长南希·布拉特纳表示，因多年招生人数下降和财务困难，学校董事会决定关闭这所具有百年历史的天主教大学，占地 16 英亩的校园将出售于邻近的华盛顿大学，出售价格没有披露。

布拉特纳校长说，芳邦大学将在 2024 年秋季停止招收新生，但会继续教学上课，尽可能让现有的学生毕业。对于无法完成学业毕业的学生，学校也将尽可能安排学生在其他学校继续就读完成学位。

芳邦大学始建于1923年，开办初期是一所女子学院，校名来自圣约翰·芳邦修女（St. John Fontbonne），2002年芳邦学院正式改制成为芳邦大学。芳邦大学一直以来与当地华人社区关系良好，招收的学生中有许多来自中国。据了解，过去15年里，芳邦大学的学生入学人数下降了70%以上，从全盛时期的3000余人到现在不到800名学生。大学关闭对社区和学生都是一个极大的损失。

报道称，芳邦大学并非唯一面临困境的高校，许多公立和私立大学近期都宣布了大规模裁员和关闭校园的消息，美国大学正面临前所未有的压力。

案例分析

本新闻稿采用倒金字塔结构，即按照"呈现结果 – 分析原因 – 提供背景"的顺序安排内容，详细分析了芳邦大学将作出关闭决定的过程，以及后续的一些安排。编译稿也采用了与原文一样的倒金字塔结构，还特别提到芳邦大学与中国的渊源，考虑到了受众的需求。

三、教育类新闻稿的编译要点

在编译教育类新闻稿时，编译者应注意以下几点：

- **信息准确**：无论原新闻稿是涉及教育政策还是教育技术、学术动态，编译者都必须确保理解并准确传递原文信息。在理解方面，编译者应主动了解原新闻稿涉及的国家和地区的文化和政策背景，避免偏见和刻板印象；编译时要注意表达的准确性。
- **语言简练**：教育类新闻通常涉及广泛的普通读者群体，因此编译者应注意在编译时做到语言简洁明了、逻辑清晰、重点突出，尽量避免使用过多的专业术语。
- **读者导向**：在编译此类新闻的时候，编译者应有读者意识，清楚了解读者的阅读习惯，以及读者对此类新闻的关注点和需求，以便对原文信息进行恰当的筛选和组织。

新闻编译入门　Approach to News Transediting

编译案例

◎新闻稿 1

TOEFL iBT Approved for Canada's Student Direct Stream[1]

30 May, 2023, 10:00 BST

PRINCETON, N.J. (PRNewswire) —ETS announced today that the TOEFL iBT test has been approved by Immigration, Refugees and Citizenship Canada (IRCC) for use in Canada's Student Direct Stream (SDS), an expedited study permit processing program for international students from 14 countries who plan to enroll in one of Canada's postsecondary designated learning institutions.

Previously, only one English-language testing option was authorized for the SDS route. The expansion to include TOEFL iBT is a welcome change for test takers who now have the option to select which test works best for them.

"We are thrilled to be unlocking more opportunities for students to access one of the world's most desirable study abroad destinations," said Rohit Sharma, Senior Vice President of Global Higher Education and Workskills at ETS. "Not only will the addition of TOEFL benefit the hundreds of thousands of students who take advantage of the SDS route each year, but institutions can feel confident knowing that they can access a wider pool of applicants who can demonstrate their skills with the premier test of English-language proficiency."

Students can begin sending TOEFL iBT scores as part of their SDS application beginning August 10, 2023. This is available to legal residents in Antigua and Barbuda; Brazil; China; Colombia; Costa Rica; India; Morocco; Pakistan; Peru; Philippines; Senegal; Saint Vincent and the Grenadines; Trinidad and Tobago; and Vietnam.

The TOEFL iBT test is already accepted by 100% of Canadian universities and is also the world's most widely accepted English-language test, used by more than 12,000 institutions in more than 160 countries worldwide.

Today's announcement follows a recent announcement from ETS that it is enhancing the TOEFL iBT test beginning July 2023, in which test takers will experience a shortened test, a simplified registration process and increased score transparency.

To learn more about applying for SDS, including eligibility criteria, please visit the Government of Canada website. For more information on TOEFL iBT, including how to

---

1　新闻稿来源：https://www.prnewswire.com。

register, access to practice materials and more, visit www.ets.org/toefl.

编译稿

托福成绩可申请加拿大学生直入计划

美通社 5 月 30 日消息，美国考试服务中心（ETS）日前宣布托福 iBT 考试已被加拿大官方批准用于申请加拿大学生直入计划（Student Direct Stream，简称 SDS）。该计划为国际学生申请进入加拿大指定院校就读提供快速学习签证申请，适用于包括中国在内的 14 个国家的国际学生。

据悉，此前仅有一种英语测试被批准用于申请 SDS。现在，托福 iBT 考试也可用于申请，考生因此拥有更多的自主选择权，选择最适合自己的英语考试。从 2023 年 8 月 10 日起，中国考生可通过提交托福 iBT 成绩递交 SDS 申请，达到 83 分即可用于申请 SDS。

ETS 相关负责人表示，托福考试被纳入加拿大学生直入计划（SDS），不仅能有效证明申请人的英语语言水平，使每年通过 SDS 通道递交申请的学生受益，还能帮助当地院校接触到更多申请者。

案例分析

本新闻稿是有关托福考试政策变化的报道，采用倒金字塔结构，导语明确了计划的出台、好处和影响。正文内容涉及该变化的背景、受益学生群体、涉及的国家和其他相关信息。编译稿采用了相同的写作结构，内容涵盖了原文中的主要信息，此外，编译稿中还增加了一些与中国考生相关的内容，可满足受众的需求。

◎**新闻稿 2**

Nightly sleep is key to student success: A new study finds[1]

By Stacy Kish February 13, 2023

College is a time of transition for young adults. It may be the first time students have the freedom to determine how to spend their time, but this freedom comes with competing interests from academics, social events and even sleep.

---

[1] 新闻稿来源：https://www.sciencedaily.com。

A multi-institutional team of researchers conducted the first study to evaluate how the duration of nightly sleep early in the semester affects first year college students end-of-semester grade point average (GPA). Using Fitbit sleep trackers, they found that students on average sleep 6.5 hours a night, but negative outcomes accumulate when students received less than six hours of sleep a night. The results are available in the Feb. 13 issue of the *Proceedings of the National Academy of Sciences*.

Previous studies have shown that total sleep is an important predictor for a broad range of health and performance outcomes. Sleep guidelines recommend teenagers get 8 to 10 hours of sleep every night. Many college students experience irregular and insufficient sleep.

David Creswell, the William S. Dietrich II Professor in Psychology and Neuroscience at the Dietrich College of Humanities and Social Sciences, led a team of researchers to evaluate the relationship between sleep and GPA. College students often push themselves to achieve, and GPA is the important marker of academic success.

"Animal studies have shown how critical sleep is for learning and memory," said Creswell. "Here we show how this work translates to humans. The less nightly sleep a first year college student gets at the beginning of the school term predicts lower GPA at the end of the term, some five to nine weeks later. Lack of sleep may be hurting students' ability to learn in their college classrooms."

Past work with animals has shown that memories that form during the day are consolidated during sleep. When normal sleep patterns are interrupted, the content learned during the day is lost. Extending this logic to students, the researchers were curious if interrupted or inadequate sleep could impair their academic learning and if this would be apparent by academic achievement.

The study evaluated more than 600 first-year students across five studies at three universities. The students wore wrist Fitbit devices to monitor and record their sleep patterns. The researchers found that students in the study sleep on average 6.5 hours a night.

More surprising, the researchers found that students who receive less than six hours of sleep experienced a pronounced decline in academic performance. In addition, each hour of sleep lost corresponded to a 0.07 decrease in end-of-term GPA.

"Once you start dipping below six hours, you are starting to accumulate massive sleep debt that can impair a student's health and study habits, compromising the whole system," said Creswell. "Most surprising to me was that no matter what we did to make the effect go away, it persisted."

The study controlled for past academic performance, daytime napping, race, gender and first-generation status. Several of the studies also controlled for total academic course load. None of these factors affected the overall impact of nightly sleep on GPA.

"A popular belief among college students is value studying more or partying more over nightly sleep," said Creswell. "Our work here suggests that there are potentially real costs to reducing your nightly sleep on your ability to learn and achieve in college. There's real value in budgeting for the importance of nightly sleep."

This works suggests the importance of building structured programs and interventions at institutions of learning that encourage undergraduate students to focus on their sleep.

Creswell was joined by Stephen Price, Sheldon Cohen, Janine M. Dutcher, Daniella Villalba, Kasey Creswell and Marsha Lovett at CMU; Michael J. Tumminia at the University of Pittsburgh; Yasaman Sefidgar, Jennifer Brown Jennifer Mankoff, Yiyi Ren, Anind K. Dey and Xuhai Xu at the University of Washington; Afsaneh Doryab at the University of Virginia and Stephen Mattingly, Aaron Striegel, Gonzalo Martinez and David Hachen at the University of Notre Dame on the project titled, "Nightly sleep duration predicts grade point average in the first year of college." The project received funding from the National Science Foundation and the National Institute on Disability, Independent Living and Rehabilitation Research.

编译稿

研究发现充足的夜间睡眠是学生学业成功的关键

大学是年轻人的一个过渡时期。这可能是学生第一次有自由决定如何度过他们的时间，但这种自由伴随着来自学术、社会活动甚至睡眠的竞争利益。据美国每日科学网站报道，一个由多个机构组成的研究小组进行了一项研究，评估学期初的夜间睡眠时间如何影响大学新生的期末平均成绩（GPA）。

迪特里希人文和社会科学学院的大卫·克雷斯韦尔教授带领该研究小组对三所大学600多名新生的睡眠和GPA之间的关系进行了评估。通过使用Fitbit睡眠追踪器，科研人员发现学生平均每晚仅睡 6.5 个小时，当学生每晚的睡眠时间少于 6 小时的时候，负面结果就会累积，学习成绩明显下降，每损失 1 个小时的睡眠，期末的 GPA 就会下降 0.07。该研究结果发表在 2 月 13 日出版的《美国国家科学院院刊》上。

克雷斯韦尔教授指出，动物研究表明睡眠对学习和记忆十分关键，对于人类也一样。睡眠不足可能会损害学生的健康、学习习惯甚至整个系统，最终伤害到学生在大学课堂上的学习能力，无论做什么消除这种影响都无济于事。减少夜间睡眠对大学生的学习和学业成就存在潜在的实际成本。这项研究提示我们，在学习机构建立结构化的方案和干预措施、鼓励本科生关注他们的睡眠质量非常重要。

> **案例分析**
>
> 这篇新闻稿报道了国外科研人员关于睡眠对大学生学业影响的研究成果，报道采用倒金字塔结构，先呈现研究结果，然后再陈述研究的过程，包括研究对象、研究方法、研究结论，最后根据研究结论提出相关的建议并补充背景信息。编译稿采用了相同的报道结构，将原文中所涉及的与该项研究相关的主要内容概括性地呈现给读者。

将以下英语新闻稿编译成汉语新闻稿。

University of Bristol collaboration secures nearly £2 million for technical experts[1]

By Angela Chau 26/03/2024

A pioneering new project that will develop the abilities of Research Technical Professionals (RTPs) and support them to build the skills to work with industrial partners to address real-world challenges and opportunities has been awarded £1.97 million.

The funding from UK Research and Innovation (UKRI) and the Engineering and Physical Sciences Research Council (EPSRC) has been secured by the GW4 Alliance universities of Bath, Bristol, Cardiff and Exeter.

RTPs are highly knowledgeable technical experts, with a unique set of skills and specialisms, but often lack both the time and opportunities to pursue tailored

---

1 新闻稿来源：https://www.sciencedaily.com。

professional development. Simultaneously, industry research and development can often be significantly accelerated through access to capabilities and technical expertise in universities, however these links are often missing or hidden within academic research programmes, meaning that many RTPs miss out on the chance to engage with industry directly to showcase and share their expertise.

Greg Kemble, X-CITED Co-Lead and Technical Services Manager at the University of Bristol said: "I look forward to working on the X-CITED programme to develop new and effective approaches to Research Technical Professional training, and continuous professional development. Achieving this, through solving current and pressing challenges, will directly benefit individuals, the project teams they are deployed too and those they originate from."

Delivered over three years, it is hoped that the X-CITED programme will become a regional demonstrator for new approaches to professional skills development for the sector. The scheme will focus on several core activities, including harnessing talent from across the GW4 universities to create peer networks and Communities of Practice, building a rich research ecosystem and generating a regional knowledge exchange based around key technology specialisms. The innovative programme will also build a mechanism for industrial partners to work with RTPs and progress industry challenges through a series of discussion forums and Industry Challenge Projects, bridging the gap between academia and industry, and delivering real-world impact.

Alongside this, X-CITED will establish a Talent Bank of trainee RTPs, training them in a range of techniques, maximising their engagement in collaborative projects with industry partners, and fostering more diverse pathways into technical careers. The Talent Bank approach will also support existing RTPs to release time for their own professional development, bolstering the resilience and sustainability of university research facilities.

The X-CITED programme is being delivered as part of GW4WARD, an initiative designed to drive forward the professional development of technical staff across GW4. The programme is closely aligned to the GW4 universities' pledge to the Technician Commitment, which aims to support all Research Technical Professionals across GW4 to gain recognition, visibility, and career development opportunities, and responds to many of the recommendations in the TALENT Commission Report.

> GW4 Alliance Director, Dr Joanna Jenkinson MBE, said: "Research Technical Professionals play a critical role in helping to drive forward our research and innovation programmes. We have around 1300 technical staff across our four institutions, often acting as the linchpin in any University department, operating and maintaining facilities and providing valuable expertise and intellectual input to enable high quality teaching and research. The X-CITED programme will allow us to further support the GW4 RTP communities, offering skills development, building links with industry, and demonstrating that the technical competencies present in higher education institutions are both applicable and valuable to the industrial sector."
>
> X-CITED will form part of a network of 11 Strategic Technical Platforms, funded by EPSRC and UKRI Digital Research Infrastructure (DRI) investment, as part of a £16 million initiative to support strategic investments for systematic support, training and development to promote, enable and empower the RTP community in UK universities.
>
> All 11 projects will benefit from the EPSRC's extensive experience in supporting research software engineers, data wrangling, facility managers, and equipment specialists, as well as community development.
>
> Jane Nicholson, Research Base Director at EPSRC, said: "Through these 11 new projects, the Strategic Technical Platform funding will help cultivate a thriving, dynamic, and vibrant community of research technicians. This community will not only support and elevate cutting-edge research in the UK, but also foster a sizeable, highly skilled and esteemed research technician network. The UK is a world leader in high-tech research and development and it's essential that we fully support the full breadth of skills needed for the workforce that deliver this innovation."

第六节　社会类新闻的编译

一、社会类新闻的概念

社会类新闻报道主要涉及社会事件、社会现象、社会问题等，比如社会福利、老龄化、网络安全、环境问题。不同于时政新闻等硬新闻，社会类新闻属于软新闻，对时效性的要求不是太高。但社会类新闻关联到日常生活的方方面面，涉及范围广，内容丰富，可有趣，也可严肃。因此，在选取社会类新闻编译素材时，应着重考虑新闻事件是否具有显著性、普遍性、趣味性、新奇性、接近性等特点。社会类新闻报道写作方式灵活，需要根据报道的内容组织安排结构，通常都会包含新闻的六大基本要素。

二、社会类新闻稿的结构

社会类新闻报道写作方式灵活，有些会采用倒金字塔结构，有些则会采用延缓性导语，或以故事开头，突出人物和事件。

编译案例

◎新闻稿1

Greece is moving some workers toward a 6-day workweek[1]

June 25, 2024 at 12:01 AM GMT+8

The workweek is about to get a lot longer for some employees in Greece.

Starting July 1, workers in the private sector could be going into the office six days a week—as the 48-hour workweek goes into effect.

Select industrial and manufacturing facilities, along with businesses that provide 24/7 services, are eligible to extend the workweek beyond five days under new labor laws. Food service and tourism workers are not included in the longer workweeks.

The change to the labor laws was approved last September following productivity issues in the country, which have led many workers to put in extra hours and often not be compensated for the time. Officials also note there has been a shortage of skilled workers due to a shrinking population.

Workers who do put in the extra time will receive 40% extra during the additional eight hours—and 115% of their normal salary if they work on a holiday.

Employers who decide to embrace the 48-hour workweek will be required to notify employees at least 24 hours before the shift begins. No additional overtime beyond the eight hours is allowed.

The new rules were not met with widespread acceptance ahead of their approval. The day before the bill was passed, public sector workers, such as teachers, doctors, and transportation workers, walked off the job in protest, calling the overhaul an affront to workers' rights that could create "barbaric" conditions.

---

1 新闻稿来源：https://www.fortune.com。

Workers in Greece already work more than those in the U.S. and most of Europe. The Organisation for Economic Co-operation and Development (OECD) notes Greeks worked an average of 1,886 hours in 2022, compared to 1,811 in the U.S. and the European Union average of 1,571.

Greece's unorthodox approach to labor comes as many other regions are experimenting with a four-day workweek. Last year, the results of the world's largest trial of the shorter schedule showed workers who put in four days were just as productive as they were during a five-day week. The nonprofit that ran the pilot program called it a "resounding success on virtually every dimension."

Last March, one member of California's legislature floated legislation for a 32-hour workweek to become national law, with the backing of the AFL-CIO and the Economic Policy Institute. The bill failed to find traction.

编译稿

7月1日起希腊新劳动法将允许部分企业要求员工一周工作6天 遭反对

一些希腊人下个月开始要每周上6天班了。

据美国《财富》杂志6月25日报道，希腊将从7月1日起对部分私营企业以及公共部门实行每周6天工作制，工时延长至每周48小时。希腊新劳动法规定，特定的工业、制造业企业以及提供24小时全天候服务企业将延长工作周至6天，但餐饮服务和旅游业不包括在其中。

据报道，为了应对该国因人口减少、技术工人短缺出现的劳动力问题，以及很多员工不得不在没有加班费的情况下加班的现状，希腊政府于去年9月修改了劳动法，引入新工作制。

新规在批准前引发了教师、医生和运输工人的广泛抗议，认为此举会损害工人权益，是对工人权利的侮辱，可能会导致"野蛮"的工作条件产生。

希腊工人的年均工作时长已超过美国和大多数欧洲国家，正当希腊尝试延长工作时间的时候，另一些国家正在试行每周四天工作制。

> **案例分析**
>
> 原新闻稿采用倒金字塔结构，开门见山点出最核心的新闻事实，然后具体说明该新规的细节及社会反应，最后补充了一些相关的背景信息。从内容上看，虽然这个新闻事件发生在希腊，但是工作时长一直是"上班族"热议的话题，选择该新闻稿作为编译素材同样会引起目标读者的兴趣。编译稿也采用相同的结构，涵盖原文的主要内容，并按照新闻要素的重要性排列信息。

◎新闻稿2

Fukushima Nuclear Plant's Diluted Treated Water Release Begins from 1 P.M. for 17-Day Discharge[1]

August 24, 2023　17:12 JST

For the first time since the 2011 meltdowns at the Fukushima No. 1 nuclear power plant, diluted treated water from the facility is being discharged into the ocean, Tokyo Electric Power Company Holdings, Inc. announced Thursday.

Ahead of the release, TEPCO determined that there were no problems regarding matters such as the dilution of the treated water as well as the weather and sea conditions.

The operation to release the water started at 1:03 p.m. Thursday with the activation of pumps. This first discharge will run for 17 days, with about 7,800 tons of treated water, or about 460 tons per day, being released.

Treated water is contaminated water that has been purified to remove most radioactive materials other than tritium. This contaminated water is being generated because water is used to cool the nuclear fuel that melted and solidified in the reactor cores that melted down following the 2011 Great East Japan Earthquake and tsunami.

According to TEPCO's overall plan, the treated water will be diluted with seawater to a concentration of 1,500 becquerels of tritium per liter before discharge, whereas the national standard allows up to 60,000 becquerels. Using extreme caution, TEPCO is diluting the treated water for this first discharge so that the tritium concentration will be about 190 becquerels per liter.

The diluted water is being discharged through an undersea tunnel that leads to an

---

1　新闻稿来源：https://japannews.yomiuri.co.jp。

opening about 1 kilometer offshore from the plant.

TEPCO said that through the fiscal year ending March 2024, it plans to release about 31,200 tons of treated water, or about 2% of total amount of such water stored at the facility. The current discharge is the first of four such operations this fiscal year.

The treated water discharge will continue over a period of about 30 years, an important step toward the decommissioning of the crippled power plant, which the government and TEPCO aim to complete in 2041–51.

Since Tuesday, TEPCO has checked the dilution process, diluting about 1 ton of treated water with about 1,200 tons of seawater. According to TEPCO, the tritium concentration had dropped, with a maximum of 63 becquerels per liter measured.

The Japan Atomic Energy Agency also conducted its own third-party test and found the tritium concentration was in line with the results of TEPCO's test.

"We are handling matters with a heightened sense of urgency," said Junichi Matsumoto, a TEPCO corporate officer in charge of treated water discharge operations, during a press conference held at the Fukushima No.1 nuclear power plant on Thursday.

From Friday, government and TEPCO websites will announce the results from the radiation monitoring of the sea around the plant.

编译稿

日本福岛核电站开始核污水排放

日本读卖新闻8月24日报道，日本福岛第一核电站运营商东京电力公司24日宣布，已于当天下午1时开始向海洋排放核污染水。这将是自2011年福岛第一核电站核反应堆核心熔毁以来，该电站首次向海洋排放核污染水。

根据计划，首次排放将持续17天，共排放约7800吨的核污染水，每日排放量约460吨。经处理的核污染水是指经过净化的、去除氚以外的大多数放射性物质的水。2011年东日本大地震发生后，福岛第一核电站反应堆堆芯中的核燃料熔毁。东京电力公司利用水冷却这些核燃料，核污染水由此产生。

东京电力公司表示，到2024年3月底，将分4个阶段排放总量约3.12万吨的核污染水，这将占福岛第一核电站核污染水存放总量的2%。根据东京电力公司的计划，最终被排入大海的水中氚浓度将被稀释到每升1,500贝克勒尔以下，排放标准约为日本安全限制（每升不高于60,000贝克勒尔）的1/40。核污染水排放将持续约30年。

> **案例分析**
>
> 新闻稿是关于日本核污水排海事件的报道，该事件不仅涉及日本一个国家，还将波及邻国乃至世界各个国家，其影响也不仅仅是海洋环境，还可能涉及生态平衡、渔业发展、食品安全等许多方面，属于热点新闻。新闻稿采用倒金字塔结构进行报道，先说核心，再说细节和背景。编译稿也采用相同的结构，对原稿中的报道内容进行了提炼，只呈现最核心的新闻信息，考虑到了受众对新闻信息的心理需求。

三、社会类新闻稿的编译步骤

在编译社会类新闻稿时，编译者往往应遵循以下步骤：

- **梳理新闻要点**：阅读原文，提炼核心新闻事实，理清新闻稿的文体结构。
- **确定编译结构**：社会类新闻稿有时采用延缓性导语，编译时可根据内容需要用故事或人物描述进入主题，也可采用倒金字塔结构。
- **编译导语和正文**：编译导语时应注意用简洁明了的语言呈现最核心的信息；正文应根据受众需求呈现相关信息。有时，导语可不交代具体事实，旨在引导读者阅读完全文。
- **调整和优化**：初稿完成后，编译者还需要进行调整和优化，以确保信息准确、表达流畅。
- **拟定新闻标题**：新闻标题应醒目，并能激发读者的阅读兴趣。

将以下英语新闻稿分别编译成汉语新闻稿。

◎新闻稿1

Why fewer people are choosing to have kids[1]

Updated 9:03 AM EDT, Fri July 26, 2024

(CNN)—Becky Hayden and her husband, Seth, have spent 21 years of marriage being fully active members of their community in California.

The Haydens have run a local scholarship program, they have kept a closetful of prom dresses to loan out to students in need, they are mentors in their community—and they have never had kids of their own.

---

[1] 新闻稿来源：https://edition.cnn.com。

"A lot of people make the assumption because we don't have kids, we're not fulfilled," Becky Hayden said. "And it's not right."

The proportion of adults in the United States younger than 50 years old who do not have children is growing—leaping from 37% in 2018 to 47% in 2023, according to a new Pew Research Center survey published Thursday.

The new Pew study comes as comments resurfaced from Ohio Sen. JD Vance, the Republican candidate for vice president, who told former Fox News host Tucker Carlson in 2021 that the country was being run by "a bunch of childless cat ladies who are miserable at their own lives and the choices that they've made and so they want to make the rest of the country miserable, too."

But with more people not having children, Pew researchers wanted to investigate whether the unhappy childless adult characterization is actually true.

"We wanted to learn more about the reasons adults don't have children, their experiences, how it impacts their relationships," said Rachel Minkin, a report coauthor and Pew research associate.

The latest poll surveyed more than 3,300 adults who do not have children and say they are not likely to have them. While researchers did find that those surveyed reported some difficulties and pressure, they also found that people without children also reported ways in which their experiences were full and connected.

"We see majorities … saying having a fulfilling life doesn't have much to do with whether someone does or doesn't have children," Minkin said.

The reasons people aren't having kids

There were many reasons why people said they didn't have kids, including financial concerns, infertility, or that it just didn't happen, according to the research. For people younger than 50, the top reason reported for not having children was that they don't want to.

"It is completely normal and valid to not want to have children," said licensed psychologist Dr. Linda Baggett, owner of Well Woman Psychology in Manhattan Beach, California, in an email. "I think current generations are feeling more empowered to be open about and act on this preference, whereas in past generations people may have been more likely to have children anyway due to societal expectations, economic/labor factors, and religious beliefs.

"It is a myth that everyone, especially women, want to have children," said Baggett, who was not involved in the research.

In her practice, psychotherapist Carissa Strohecker Hannum sees a lot of people saying that they feel hesitant to bring children into the world when they are so concerned about the state of it. Other clients have had such bad experiences with their relationships with their own parents that they are worried about repeating the pattern. Hannum, clinical director at Monarch Wellness in the Washington, DC, area, was not involved in the research.

People tell her, "Before I consider raising a child in this world, I really want to work on my mental health. And I really want to make sure that I'd be bringing a child into a different sort of emotional environment."

Societal pressure to have kids

When Hayden meets someone new or runs into someone she hasn't seen since high school, the question often comes up: How old are your kids?

And when she answers that she doesn't have any, Hayden said she often sees an expression flash across their face that communicates that she is less than or incomplete.

Many of the cons people reported in the Pew survey related to not having children come from the outside.

For those older than 50 who responded and are employed, 33% said they are expected to take on extra work because they don't have children and 32% say they are left out of conversation of coworkers who have kids, the data showed.

Women were especially likely to say that they felt pressure from society to have children, Minkin said.

"I hear this a lot, and it is unfortunate," Baggett said.

She recommends setting a kind but firm boundary with loved ones about how they talk about the decision not to have kids and remind them that it isn't up for discussion.

"It's OK to validate that the other person may be disappointed, but that doesn't mean your feelings and decisions are up for debate," she added.

Living a full life

For people who choose not to have children, there is a lot of potential for happiness and fulfillment.

"Embrace and own this decision," Baggett said. "You have to do what's best for you and honestly, it serves no one, especially the child, to bring an unwanted child into the world."

People who responded to the Pew survey said that not having children gave them more resources to advance in their career and pursue their hobbies and passions.

Hayden said she has found her passion using the resources she and her husband have built to support their community members who might not have the things they need—whether that be educational support, properly fitting shoes or a present to bring to a friends' birthday party.

"I'm just so lucky that I have found a passion," she said. "At the end of the day, I don't feel like your life has to be your children."

◎新闻稿2

PUNCHING AND PUMPING IRON, CHINESE WOMEN GO 'YOLO'[1]

March 8, 2024 Reuters

Without a job, friends or direction in life, a 30-something woman decides to take up boxing, triggering a physical transformation that is the narrative of the biggest box office for any movie in China this year.

"YOLO," starring and directed by Jia Ling, has made the equivalent of US$475 million since last month in theaters. Critics say this remake of a 2014 Japanese movie hit a nerve with Chinese audiences with its spin on the intense training sequence which echoes Sylvester Stallone's "Rocky" film series and is usually reserved for male action stars.

The film has also tapped into a growing trend. From throwing punches to pumping iron, Chinese women with time and money are taking up sports that had once been considered fringe in a challenge to the commercialised ideal that women should aspire to be fair, slim and youthful.

1　新闻稿来源：https://www.success-street.com。

A 35-year-old boxing trainer and owner of a gym in central Beijing who goes by the professional nickname A-Nan says some clients who were inspired by the movie have dropped out quickly when they realized the difficulty of training.

Even so, her gym has been enrolling more women than men to train over the past several years and the proportion of female memberships at her gym is higher. Many of the women looking to train have jobs in finance, law and accounting.

"They have a stronger sense of determination," she said. "Another crucial factor is competitiveness: to excel in a high efficiency job, you need not only a good education and intelligence but also a healthy body."

Body building only opened to female professional competition in China in 1996. Even now, female competitors are often widely referred to as "King Kong Barbies".

"There are indeed cultural changes happening," said Wu Xiaoying, a China-based sociologist and specialist in gender studies. "I believe the aesthetic preferences of women today are becoming more diverse."

Xie Tong, a 29-year-old who balances a career in finance with her passion for bodybuilding, says lifting has liberated her. "If I look back, exercise used to be about conforming to others' aesthetics, about becoming thin, about punishing myself, about doing things I didn't want to do," she told Reuters.

第三部分

汉英新闻编译

第六章
汉英新闻编译概述

第一节 汉英新闻编译和对外新闻报道

一、汉英新闻编译的界定

汉英新闻编译是把用汉语写成的新闻（或汉语新闻信息）通过翻译和编辑的方法处理成英语新闻进行对外传播的新闻报道形式。汉英新闻编译是对外新闻报道的主要形式，集英语新闻写作、翻译、编辑于一体，也是一种特殊的新闻写作。汉英新闻编译在我国对外新闻报道机构（如新华社对外部、《中国日报》等英文报纸、外文出版局有关下属单位、中央广播电视总台英语频道、英语广播及各网络媒体的英语新闻网站等）被广泛采用。对外新闻和对外传播是汉英新闻编译中的两个重要概念。

对外新闻是中国新闻机构发布的以国外读者为对象的有关中国的新闻。对外新闻报道的根本任务是全面完整地反映中国共产党和中国政府的对内对外政策，正确反映中国在国际社会中的形象，为中国的现代化建设创造一个良好的国际环境。

对外传播是通过中国人自主创办或与外国人合作的报纸、刊物、广播、电视、通讯社和网站等传播媒体，以境外人士为主要传播对象，以让世界了解中国为最终目的而进行的新闻传播活动。

二、对外传播过程的基本要素

1948年，美国传播学家哈罗德·拉斯韦尔(Harold Lasswell)发表了一篇传播学研究论文《社会传播的结构与功能》。在这篇文章中，他全面论述了社会传播的过程、结构及其功能，并清晰地阐释了传播过程的五个基本构成要素，这些要素也被称为"5W传播模式"，具体包括以下内容：

- 谁说 (who)；
- 说什么 (what)；
- 通过什么渠道 (in which channel)；
- 对谁说 (to whom)；

- 取得什么效果 (with what effect)。

简单地说，这五个要素分别对应的是传播者、传播内容、媒介、受众和传播效果。这个模式简明而清晰，奠定了传播学研究的基本内容：控制分析、内容分析、媒介分析、受众分析和效果分析。

汉英新闻编译是一种重要的对外传播方式，因此编译人员在编译过程中要始终保持对外传播意识，思考编译的角度，选择编译的内容，充分考虑受众的需求和编译的效果。

三、我国对外新闻报道的发展

从中华人民共和国成立至今，我国的对外宣传主要经历了四个发展阶段：

- **初步建设阶段（1949—1978）**。在这一阶段，我国开始逐步建立起全国性的对外宣传体系，如创办《人民中国》《人民画报》等对外宣传刊物，成立了新闻总署国际新闻局。这一时期的对外宣传工作注重配合新中国外交方面的活动，大力宣传我国的和平外交政策。
- **初步发展阶段（1978—1999）**。在这一阶段，我国对外传播事业开始发展，以对外宣传小组成立为起点，对外宣职能部门进行体制改革与业务重组，确定了以经济建设为中心、服务国家发展与现代化建设的外宣思想路线。在这一时期，对外传播呈现出从"宣传"向"传播"理念转型的特点。
- **高速发展阶段（2000—2017）**。这一阶段以我国政府实施文化"走出去"战略为起点，对外传播主体呈现多元化发展，媒体产业格局再升级。在中央国际传播规划的指引下，"央媒"纵向深入海外市场，逐渐向建成具有一定国际影响力的现代传播体系发展。在新兴信息传播技术的影响下，对外传播话语逻辑与形态呈现出向"跨文化传播""精准传播"理念过渡的趋势。
- **全媒体发展阶段（2018年至今）**。2018年中央电视台（中国国际电视台）、中央人民广播电台、中国国际广播电台实行"三台合一"，以此为起点，媒体融合步入新阶段，全媒体格局加速发展，在国际传播舞台发挥着越来越大的作用。

目前，我国的主要新闻机构及相关网络媒体包括：

- 新华通讯社（简称新华社）；
- 《中国日报》；
- 《环球时报》（人民日报社主办）；
- 《今日中国》《中国画报》（中国外文局下属的英语传媒）；
- 中央电视台新闻频道；
- 中国国际广播电台；

- 新华网 (www.xinhuanet.com)；
- 人民网 (www.peopledaily.com.cn)；
- 中国日报网 (www.chinadaily.com.cn)；
- 中国国际广播电台网站 (www.cri.com.cn)；
- 央视网 (www.cctv.com)；
- 中国网 (www.china.com.cn，国务院新闻办公室主管，外文局主办)；
- 中国新闻网 (www.ecns.cn)；
- 环球网 (www.globaltimes.cn)。

阅读以下新闻稿，思考将其编译成英语新闻稿时应着重考虑哪些因素、传播什么信息。

2025QS世界大学排名发布，北大、清华跻身全球前20[1]

新京报　2024-06-05　17:54

新京报讯 6 月 5 日，国际高等教育研究机构 QS Quacquarelli Symonds 正式发布了 2025QS 世界大学排名。麻省理工学院连续 13 年蝉联榜首，帝国理工学院自 2014 年后再次回到综合排名全球第二的位置。牛津大学排名第三，哈佛大学排名第四，剑桥大学位列第五。北京大学和清华大学跻身全球前 20，北京大学排名由去年的全球第 17 上升至全球第 14 名，清华大学位列全球第 20。

中国内地高校排名表现方面，总计有 71 所中国内地高校进入本次 QS 世界大学排名。其中 48 所（68%）高校的排名较去年有所提升，只有 16% 的大学排名有所下降。近一半（46%）上榜的中国内地大学位列全球前 500。值得注意的是，中国内地高等教育强调增强研究能力的战略持续取得成功，在 QS 研究影响力衡量标准的"师均论文引用"指标中，全球前 100 的大学中有 24 所来自中国内地，其中 6 所更是进入全球前 20。

其中，上海交通大学重返全球前 50，从第 51 位上升到第 45 位。浙江大学排名全球第 47 名。中国内地前 10 中有 7 所学校的排名较去年有所上升，提升最大的是同济大学，排名从全球第 216 位跃升至 192 位，这也是同济大学首次跻身全球前 200 名。本次排名中，近 7 成中国内地大学排名上升，清华大学重返全球前 20，北京大学排名进一步攀升。五所中国内地高校跻身全球前 50，其中 4 所排名有所上升。中国内地高校在研究影响力方面表现出色，彰显雄厚研究实力。

1　新闻稿来源：https://baijiahao.baidu.com。

> 从世界范围来看，英国拥有最多数量排名靠前的大学，在全球 Top5 中占据 3 个席位，并且在国际学生比例方面表现出色。美国成功保持了其在雇主和学术界的良好声誉。加拿大的高等教育在可持续发展方面表现出色。澳大利亚在亚太地区的国际研究网络指标中处于领先地位。新加坡拥有亚洲地区唯一一所跻身全球前 10 的高校——新加坡国立大学，排名全球第八。日本是所有主要亚洲高等教育体系中下降最明显的国家，63% 的上榜大学排名下降，延续了长达十年的下滑趋势。
>
> 据了解，本次排名覆盖来自 106 个高等教育体系的 1500 所大学，排名基于 1700 万篇研究论文、1.76 亿次引用（不包括自引）、190 万份学术回应、66 万份雇主回应、来自全球 5600 所院校的数据、23 万个单独的数据点、175798 名学者和 105476 名雇主的深度洞察。
>
> _____
>
> _____
>
> _____

第二节　汉英新闻编译的选题和选材

汉英新闻编译就是把汉语新闻稿编译成英语新闻稿供国外读者阅读，因而就需要考虑国外受众的需求，同时新闻编译的选题与新闻的价值要素密切相关。新闻编译的选题和选材指的是选取什么题材进行编译、选取什么新闻事实（新闻材料）支持主题。一般来说，在选取汉英新闻编译的题材时，应遵循以下原则。

一、遵循新闻报道的规律

当今世界瞬息万变，新闻事件层出不穷。编译者首先应遵循新闻报道的规律，即按照新闻事件的价值选择适合编译的题材；对于重大新闻事件或具有对外报道价值的新闻事件，都应及时编译，进行客观报道。

国外学者曾把判断新闻价值的标准浓缩为三个词，即 relevance、usefulness、interest（有关、有用、有趣），并具体把它们演化成六条标准：Impact（冲击力）、Prominence（显要度）、Conflict（冲突性）、Proximity（接近性）、Novelty（新颖性）、Timeliness（时效性）。

中国新闻学院前常务副院长周立方教授则将新闻价值的判断标准总结为新闻性、特殊性、政策性、知识性、重要性、关联性、监督性和趣味性等。中外学者对新闻价值的界定略有不同，但重要性（冲击力）、冲突性、显要度和时效性等都是选题中需要重点考虑的方面。

二、遵循国家的外宣方针

汉英新闻编译就是把大量有关中国的各种新闻信息从汉语编译成英语进行二次传播，这是外宣工作的一个重要组成部分，因而要符合国家的外宣方针，贴近中国发展的实际，帮助世界更好地读懂中国。一般来说，能体现中国立场、中国的对外政策、中国文化、中国的科技发展、中国的大国担当、中国的热会热点等选题都可以作为汉英新闻编译的选题。

三、考虑外国读者的阅读需求

汉英新闻编译除了要遵循翻译工作都需要遵循的"信、达、雅"原则之外，还需"贴近国外受众对中国信息的需求、贴近国外受众的思维习惯"。从事外宣工作的新闻编译者应善于发现和分析中外文化的差异和特点，充分考虑外国读者的阅读需求，对汉语新闻原文进行适当的加工，使编译稿能够发挥传播和交际的功能。

确定编译选题后就要对这些新闻事实进行编译和加工，编译者可根据主题需要和受众需求对新闻材料进行选择和适当的增删。选材的原则主要包括以下几点：

- 选材应服务于选定的主题；
- 选材应符合编译的方针；
- 选材应考虑国际传播的效果。

对照以下新闻报道及其英语编译稿，说明此篇新闻稿在编译过程中如何体现选题和选材原则。

◎ 新闻稿

朱鹮保护创造拯救濒危物种成功范例[1]

本报记者 张蕾 张哲浩 **通讯员** 赵侠 《光明日报》（2023年02月10日01版）

本报西安2月9日电 一个世上仅存7个成员的物种，竟然能"起死回生"！记者从陕西省林业局了解到，最新数字显示，历经40年精心保护，曾极度濒危的朱鹮，数量已经从1981年的7只增至9000余只，栖息地面积由不足5平方

---

1 新闻稿来源：https://epaper.gmw.cn。

公里扩展到 1.6 万平方公里。中国的朱鹮保护,成为世界拯救濒危物种的成功范例。

朱鹮,古称朱鹭,在地球上已经生存超过 6000 万年。它姿态优雅,体形端庄,翩然若仙,自古以来被视为幸福吉祥之鸟。有学者认为,先秦典籍《鹖冠子·度万》"凤凰者,鹑火之禽,阳之精也"中"火凤凰"的形象,就来自面颊双腿朱红、翅带粉红的朱鹮。

朱鹮曾广泛生存于东亚地区,但由于人类过度使用农药,加之滥捕滥杀,多个国家和地区相继宣布灭种。从 1978 年起,我国在全国范围内展开野生朱鹮调查,历时近 3 年、行程 5 万多公里,足迹遍布 14 个省份,才在秦岭深处的陕西洋县姚家沟发现了当时世界上仅存的 7 只野生朱鹮。随即,对洋县朱鹮出没地区实施封山育林,开启对朱鹮的全方位保护。

"朱鹮种群恢复经历了非常艰难的过程。"陕西师范大学生命科学学院教授于晓平介绍,1981 年至 1990 年,由于种群基数小,加之缺乏科学手段,朱鹮种群恢复极为缓慢,始终未能突破 20 只;1991 年至 2000 年,随着保护体系不断完善,人工饲养繁殖和疾病防治技术日趋成熟,朱鹮数量突破 100 只。"进入 21 世纪,特别是最近 10 年来,随着一系列生态工程实施,秦岭生态系统多样性、稳定性和持续性显著增强,朱鹮栖息地状况得到极大改善,而朱鹮保护、繁育和野化放归技术又接连取得重大突破,朱鹮营巢地逐渐超过 700 处,数量接近万只关口。"

随着朱鹮数量增长,为了缓解洋县承载压力、解决近亲繁殖等问题,朱鹮"易地保护""野化放归"相继启动。朱鹮栖息地由大山深处向丘陵平川扩展,由洋县一隅向秦巴全域扩展,由长江流域向黄河流域扩展,由陕西向全国扩展,并通过捐赠等方式向东亚国家扩展……

"目前,陕西已成功繁育朱鹮 10 余代,建立人工繁育种群 5 个、野化种群 6 个。在陕西之外的 9 个人工繁育基地也相继建成,通过野化放归,将朱鹮重新引入历史分布区,建立可自我维持的野生种群。目前,已形成以在陕野生种群为'源种群'、各地放飞种群为'卫星群'的中国朱鹮种群新样态。"陕西省林业局局长党双忍说。

编译稿

China's protection of crested ibises serves as global model for saving endangered species

(People's Daily Online) 13:36, February 16, 2023

China has increased the number of crested ibis. The animal was once a critically endangered bird species. It has been brought back to a stable number after falling to an all-time low population of seven in 1981 to more than 9,000 today.

Moreover, the birds' habitat area has been successfully expanded from less than 5 square kilometers to 16,000 square kilometers, according to the forestry authority of northwest China's Shaanxi Province.

Crested ibises have lived on earth for more than 60 million years. They are graceful as well as demure and have been regarded as a symbol of happiness and auspiciousness in China since ancient times.

Crested ibises have been widely distributed in East Asia but were declared extinct in many countries and regions due to the overuse of pesticides and excessive and indiscriminate hunting by human beings.

Since 1978, China has conducted nationwide investigations into wild crested ibises. After nearly three years of efforts, researchers finally found seven wild crested ibises in Yaojiagou village, Yangxian county, Shaanxi Province. The seven wild birds that nested deep in the Qinling Mountains in Shaanxi were the only living crested ibises in the world at that time.

Since these birds were discovered, immediate efforts were made to protect them in an all-round way, including closing mountains for forest restoration.

During the first decade since China started the comprehensive protection of crested ibises, the population of the bird species recovered slowly, owing to the small base population and a lack of scientific measures, according to Yu Xiaoping, a professor at the College of Life Science, Shaanxi Normal University.

As China's system for crested ibises protection and technologies for artificial rearing and breeding of crested ibises as well as disease prevention and treatment improved continuously between 1991 and 2000, the number of crested ibises in the country exceeded 100 in the period, Yu said.

"Since the beginning of the 21st century, especially during the recent 10 years as a series of projects have been implemented for ecological conservation, there has been significant improvement in the biodiversity, stability, and sustainability of the ecosystems of the Qinling Mountains, and the environment of the habitats of crested ibises has been improved greatly," Yu noted.

In addition, major breakthroughs in the technologies concerning the protection, breeding, and rewilding of crested ibises have been achieved over the recent decade, which have helped increase the population of the birds to nearly 10,000, Yu added.

To relieve the pressure on Yangxian county and address problems hindering the expansion of the birds' population, including inbreeding, China has kicked off projects for the ex-situ conservation and rewilding of the birds.

Thanks to these projects, the habitats of crested ibises have extended from deep mountains to hills and plains and from Yangxian county to the whole country. Moreover, the country has also donated crested ibises to other countries in East Asia to extend the habitats of the birds further.

"So far, Shaanxi has successfully bred more than 10 generations of crested ibises, developed five populations of artificially-bred crested ibises and six populations of rewilded crested ibises. We have also built nine bases for artificial breeding of the birds outside Shaanxi," said Dang Shuangren, head of the Shaanxi provincial forestry bureau.

"By releasing crested ibises into the wild after rewilding training, we reintroduce the bird species to its old distribution areas for the establishment of self-sustaining wild populations," Dang noted.

第三节　汉英新闻编译的原则

在编译汉语新闻稿编译成英文时，编译者通常应遵循以下原则：
- 应准确传递原新闻稿件的内容；
- 应采用英语新闻媒体常用的行文体例；
- 应注重语言表达的准确和地道；
- 应符合目标读者的思维和阅读习惯；
- 应体现新闻传播的意图和效果；
- 应保持原新闻稿的文体风格。

就新闻稿各个部分来说，编译者在进行汉英新闻编译时还应注意：
- 编译标题要尽量与原文一样简短传神；
- 编译导语应概括原新闻稿主旨，说明最核心的新闻事实；
- 编译正文要力求语言平实、行文简明。

对比以下新闻稿及其编译稿，思考新闻稿是否体现了汉英新闻编译的原则，并在符合编译原则的项目后打√。

◎新闻稿

仅乒乓球大的"心脏"上岗开工！[1]

人民资讯　2022-03-17　05:56　本文转自：中国新闻网

3月14日，南京市第一医院副院长、心胸血管外科主任陈鑫带领团队为一名患者成功实施超小型磁悬浮离心式心室辅助装置植入术。这是我国自主研发，世界上体积最小、质量最轻的磁悬浮离心式"人工心脏"，它直径仅34毫米、重90克，如一颗乒乓球般大小。这是江苏省首次进行此款"人工心脏"植入手术。

为什么要植入"人工心脏"？药物难控制，心脏移植供体受限

患者肖先生今年56岁，最近三个月胸口憋闷，感觉喘不过气来，辗转江苏多家医院治疗，被诊断为扩张性心肌病，心功能Ⅳ级，病情危重。

南京市第一医院心胸血管外科专家细致检查和分析，认为肖先生患"终末期心脏病"，药物治疗的作用已不大。频发的心衰使得肖先生的病情已不容等

---

[1] 新闻稿来源：https://baijiahao.baidu.com。

待，经医院专家会诊后，决定为他植入最新型Corheart 6植入式左心室辅助装置。

据南京市第一医院陈鑫教授介绍，对于重症心衰患者而言，心脏移植是最有力的治疗手段。目前我国心衰患者约1000万人，但供体数量有限，我国每年心脏移植手术量约为500至600台，很多患者等不到可以救自己的那颗心。

而"人工心脏"有其独特优势：它可以作为等待心脏移植的过渡；也可以为急性心衰患者提供短期替代治疗。终末期心衰患者可携带"人工心脏"长期生存。

超小型"人工心脏"有多小？仅乒乓球大小，重量减少60%

本次手术所用的超小型磁悬浮离心式人工心脏名叫"Corheart 6"。这是江苏省首次进行此款"人工心脏"的手术。经过术前精心准备，3月14日，陈鑫主任、邱志兵副主任带领其手术团队，经过两个小时的努力，将磁悬浮人工心脏植入患者体内。机械心帮心脏把血泵出来，重新建立一个循环系统。患者顺利脱离体外循环辅助，生命体征趋于平稳，手术圆满成功。术后第三天，肖先生就可以在床旁进行康复锻炼，活动耐量良好。这颗机械心现在正有条不紊地在肖先生身体里工作着。

"人工心脏"被誉为"医疗器械皇冠上的宝石"，全球"人工心脏"植入量已经超过14000例，用人造器官代替自然器官的临床技术也逐渐成熟。

相关数据显示，本次手术所用的超小型磁悬浮离心式人工心脏（Corheart 6）只有乒乓球大小，它的直径34毫米，厚度26毫米，仅有90克重。比现有的磁悬浮"人工心脏"直径缩小40%，重量减少60%。在感染风险防控、装置可靠性、血液相容性等性能上，这块超小型"人工心脏"都表现出色。

超小型磁悬浮离心式人工心脏植入术的成功实施，标志着我国在应用"人工心脏"救治心力衰竭的领域迈入世界领先行列。

编译稿

Artificial heart about size of a ping pong ball gives hope to patient

On March 14, a medical team from Nanjing First Hospital in Nanjing, east China's Jiangsu Province successfully implanted an artificial heart into a patient. The artificial heart, having a diameter of only 34 millimeters and weighing 90 grams, is about the size of a ping pong ball.

It is the first time that an artificial heart transplant of this type has ever been performed in Jiangsu Province. Called Corheart 6, the medical device functions as a pump to circulate blood throughout the patient's whole body, thus significantly alleviating the symptoms of heart failure. The device is powered by magnetic and fluid levitation technologies.

Xiao, 56, had been suffering from chest tightness and shortness of breath in the past three months. He was diagnosed with end-stage heart disease after doctors from the cardiothoracic surgery department of Nanjing First Hospital performed a thorough physical examination. The doctors thought that drugs would not be able to alleviate Xiao's symptoms since he was in a critical condition. After a specialist consultation, the doctors decided to implant a device into the patient to replace his failed organ.

The operation was a success, and three days after the operation, Xiao could stand up and perform rehabilitation exercises around his hospital bed. Now, the device is functioning normally in Xiao's body.

For patients with severe heart failure, heart implantation is the most effective means of treatment, according to Chen Xin, a professor with Nanjing First Hospital.

China has about 10 million heart failure patients, but due to a lack of donors, only between 500 and 600 heart transplants are able to be performed each year. An artificial heart can help prolong the life of a patient until he or she receives a healthy donor heart, while for patients diagnosed with end-stage heart failure, an artificial heart can replace the failed organ of the patient and enable the patient to live normally.

Corheart 6, with a diameter 40 percent shorter and weighing 60 percent less than a regular artificial heart has demonstrated its capabilities in preventing and controlling risks of infection, is more reliable and causes less damage to the patient's blood than other types of artificial hearts.

序号	编译原则	是否体现编译原则
1	应准确传递原新闻稿件的内容	
2	应采用英语新闻媒体常用的行文体例	
3	应注重语言表达的准确和地道	
4	应符合目标读者阅读习惯	
5	应体现新闻传播的意图和效果	

第四节　英语新闻稿的行文体例

新闻稿的行文体例指新闻稿的写作或编译格式。英语新闻媒体一般都有自己的行文体例。一般来说，新闻机构制定统一的新闻写作体例至少有三个方面的作用：1）方便记者写作或编译；2）方便编辑编改；3）方便读者阅读。目前，世界多数英文媒体都接受或采用美联社的新闻写作体例。美联社写作体例的规定全部汇集在不断更新的《美联社新闻写作体例手册》(AP Style book) 里面。

汉英新闻编译与英语新闻写作一样，应有统一的行文体例。在将汉语新闻稿编译成英语新闻稿时，编译者也应考虑主流英文媒体的常用写作体例。

阅读以下新闻稿及其编译稿，分析新闻稿和编译稿在行文体例上有何不同。

◎新闻稿

恭喜，他们结婚了！这种形式引网友热议[1]

光明网 2024-04-16 11:21

近期，浙江嘉兴平湖一对新人举办了一场只花了 5000 元钱的"极简婚礼"，不仅得到在场亲友的点赞，也引起网友集体热议。

没有豪华车队、没有伴郎伴娘、没有司仪跟妆，也没有花哨的灯光音响……这场"极简婚礼"由新郎黄涛和新娘卫雅侨亲自主持，他们在婚礼上讲述了相知相爱的故事和对婚姻的理解。

新娘卫雅侨表示，二人在生活中也是比较喜欢简单、简约、关注自身感受的生活方式，所以他们选择举办一个简约的婚礼。

卫雅侨介绍，当他们把办"极简婚礼"的想法告诉双方父母时，一开始家长不太认可，认为婚礼是两个新人乃至两个家庭的组合，要隆重一点，但是二人的坚持最终让双方父母放下了成见。到场的所有亲朋好友也点赞这种做法，朋友们都觉得他们很有勇气并且非常幸福。

卫雅侨和黄涛之所以选择"极简婚礼"，也与当地婚俗改革密不可分。一个偶然的机会，他们看到当地政府发布的一篇题为《婚俗改革让婚礼习俗更纯粹更美好》的微信推文，从而受到启发。他们决定不要接亲环节，不邀伴郎伴娘，放弃高档酒店，把婚宴放在镇上的友邻中心。

之所以能被热议，卫雅侨觉得，一方面是因为年轻人有自己的想法并坚持执行感染了大家。另一方面，长辈们能改变传统观念，支持年轻人移风易俗，

---

[1] 新闻稿来源：https://baijiahao.baidu.com。

用新方式拥抱新生活的态度得到了大家的认可。

花费5000元的"极简婚礼"话题火热之后，很多网友表示赞同。大家认为这样的婚礼极大降低了经济负担，也减轻了年轻人面对烦琐复杂婚礼流程的心理压力，是追求个性化、自由化以及简约舒适生活方式的体现。

类似的案例也出现在安徽宿州市萧县。

31岁的新郎陈伟健和28岁的新娘黄多艺最近也选择了"三无婚礼"。没彩礼、没礼炮，婚车是装饰了喜庆拉花和多彩气球的共享电动车。

新娘黄多艺表示，每辆共享单车都是朋友提前准备精心装饰的，并且两人选择了"零彩礼"为爱减负，为爱情增添甜蜜，他们要通过自己的努力，创造更加美好的未来。

同样不办婚宴的还有出生于1998年的冯宁宁和男友。

两人都是吉林人，由于工作原因两人定居在四川。冯宁宁表示，两人计划不办婚宴，将费用节省下来去旅行，既浪漫，又更具性价比。

冯宁宁发现，身边的一些朋友同学在筹备婚礼时，需要起个大早准备化妆、接亲等步骤，从早上忙到晚上，感觉办一个婚礼又费时间又费钱。于是她设想，自己的婚礼不办婚宴，把费用省下来，夫妻二人去旅行，通过旅拍去记录这一路的所见所闻。

"极简婚礼"受青睐凸显年轻人婚姻观的转变。随着时代的变迁，婚礼形式也在不断推陈出新，比如80年代的"三转一响"，90年代讲究星级酒店、豪华婚车的排场。如今，鲜明的风格和个性更受推崇。

中山大学社会学与社会工作系副教授裴谕新分析，"极简婚礼"实际上是去掉传统婚礼中的繁文缛节，加上年轻人的创意，让婚礼变得更适合自己，并且可以减少时间和金钱的投入，同时又能获得一种情感上的体验。

裴谕新教授认为，年轻人虽然把婚礼中不必要的社会应酬，以及家庭之间社会资本的交换这部分省略掉了，但对于张扬自己的个性，以及展现双方情感链接的不可替代性还是非常关注的。

对此，不少网友表示这样的方式很好，是做了自己当时想做却没有做的事。但也有网友表示，什么形式结婚全靠自愿，不能要求每个人如此。

编译稿

Simple weddings reflect youth authenticity

By Bi Mengying Published: Apr 09, 2024 09:35 PM

For generations, weddings in China, as in many cultures around the world, have been lavish affairs. They served not only as a celebration of union but also as a display of family status and prosperity.

The typical Chinese wedding, with its elaborate rituals, extensive guest lists, and opulent banquets, symbolizes not just the merging of two hearts but of two families, their social standing, and their wealth. However, young Chinese couples are redefining what it means to celebrate their union.

They focus on the core essence of the celebration: the love between the couple, shared with close family and friends in a more intimate, meaningful and even eco-friendly setting.

Recently, a couple in Pinghu, East China's Zhejiang Province, held a "minimalist wedding" that cost only 5,000 yuan ($691). According to the couple, this type of wedding saved them no less than 100,000 yuan. There was no luxury motorcade, no groomsmen and bridesmaids.

This "minimalist wedding" was personally hosted by the groom Huang Tao and the bride Wei Yaqiao. They shared the story of getting to know each other and falling in love with each other at the wedding with short-listed guests.

Wei said that the two of them also prefer a simple lifestyle that focuses on their own feelings in life and inner world, so they chose to hold a simple wedding. When they first shared their idea of a simple wedding with their parents, they didn't receive much approval from the older generation.

With the pair's explanation and persistence, both parents eventually let go of their prejudices. The relatives and friends who showed up at the special wedding also praised this practice.

In addition to this praise, the couple also stirred discussions among netizens. The pair is not alone as more and more young Chinese couples are opting for simple weddings.

Yang Yin held her wedding ceremony in Shanghai during the National Day holidays in 2023, a traditional wedding peak in China. The wedding, in her words, "couldn't have been simpler, more environmentally friendly and low-cost."

The party took a bus to the hotel where they dined. The new couple wore ordinary hoodies rather than formal clothing.

Amid the growing popularity of "carbon neutral weddings" among young couples in China, some decorate wedding venues with recyclable materials, some offer the guests vegetarian or vegan dishes, and some purchase offsets for the carbon emissions their weddings produced.

This trend of minimal, simple and eco-friendly weddings, stripping away the extravagance traditionally associated with matrimonial ceremonies, is emblematic of a broader shift in social values and aspirations among young Chinese.

It signals a departure from ostentation and conformity toward authenticity and individuality. This trend is driven by various factors, reflecting broader social changes.

Economically, the exorbitant cost of traditional weddings has become a significant burden for young couples. The minimalist wedding approach offers a financially sensible alternative, allowing couples to prioritize their future lives together over a single day of extravagance.

By embracing simplicity and innovation, these new wedding trends encourage more couples to take the leap into marriage unencumbered by extravagant costs, allowing them to contribute to offsetting the worrying trend of low marriage rates.

Environmentally, the trend aligns with growing awareness and concern over the impact of human activities on our planet. By reducing the scale of celebrations, couples are also lessening their carbon footprint—a small but meaningful contribution to global sustainability efforts.

Culturally, this shift speaks volumes about how values are changing among China's younger generations. There's a growing desire to celebrate one's union in a way that truly reflects personal preferences, rather than adhering strictly to social expectations.

This is a generation that values authenticity over performance, seeking to create wedding experiences that are not only unique but also deeply personal and emotionally resonant. Government and social institutions have not been mere observers in this cultural shift.

In various localities, initiatives aimed at promoting simpler, more economical weddings have been introduced, recognizing the need to alleviate the social and financial pressures associated with traditional weddings.

For instance, Pinghu city was selected into the second batch of wedding custom reform experimental regions in Zhejiang Province in August 2022. Local authorities have launched various measures such as holding special collective weddings. The Pinghu Women's Federation also held lectures to promote simple wedding. These efforts, while rooted in practical concerns, also subtly endorse the evolving perceptions of marriage, love, and celebration among the populace.

The rise of "simple weddings" in China is more than a mere change in wedding fashion. As young couples across the nation choose to celebrate their love in more understated, personal, and meaningful ways, they are crafting a new fashion for marriage—one that prioritizes the essence of the bond over the grand display of the celebration.

第七章
汉英新闻标题和导语的编译

第一节　汉英新闻标题的编译原则

在编译汉语新闻标题时，编译者首先要保证准确传递原文信息，在准确的基础上力求文字简练、地道和精彩，使编译文符合目标读者的表达习惯。从语言表达方面来看，新闻标题的编译相当于新闻标题的写作，因此编译者也应了解和掌握英语新闻标题的特点。编译后的新闻标题同样能够概括新闻内容，能够尽可能多地提供新闻要素。标题都应独立成句，最好采用主谓宾结构。为了节省空间，凡能省略的字词均应省略。编译时，除了参考原标题的结构外，编译者还可参考导语中提供的主要信息和关键字词。事实上，参考导语进行编译的做法非常普遍，因为标题往往就是导语内容的进一步浓缩。下面列举的例子体现了标题和导语之间的紧密联系：

A　China's Pan Zhanle crushes his own world record in 100 freestyle

In a men's 100-meter freestyle final that wasn't particularly close, Pan Zhanle of China prevailed as the Olympic gold medalist, shattering his own world record in 46.40 seconds.

B　New data shows US job growth has been far weaker than initially reported

US job growth during much of the past year was significantly weaker than initially estimated, according to new data released Wednesday.

C　Biden drops out of the 2024 presidential race, endorses Vice President Kamala Harris for nomination

President Biden announced Sunday that he is dropping out of the 2024 presidential race and threw his support behind Vice President Kamala Harris.

熟悉并掌握汉英新闻标题的共同点和差异将有助于汉语新闻标题的编译工作。下文列举的例子展示了新华社等国内主流媒体在国内报道和对外报道中所使用的标题。

A 世行：中国宏观经济前景依然良好（新华社）
   WB sees China's economy grow 10.4% this year (Xinhua)

B 中国外交部强烈抗议日首相岸田文雄参拜靖国神社（新华社）
   China strongly protests against Kishida's visit to Yasukuni Shrine (Xinhua)
   Kishida's provocation condemned (China Daily)

C 中国足球协会原主席陈戌源受贿一审被判无期徒刑（新华社）
   Former head of Chinese Football Association sentenced to life in prison for bribery (Xinhua)
   China's Former Soccer Chief Gets Life in Prison for Bribery (Yicai Global)

D 刷读书类短视频成潮流，全网四千万粉丝的读书博主做对了什么（新浪财经）
   Book-reading bloggers become a trend (China Daily)

E 博鳌报告：亚洲经济增长动能仍然强劲（新华社）
   BFA report: Asia continues to drive the global economic growth (China Daily)
   BFA report: Asia continues to fuel global economy (Global Times)

对照观察以上几组新闻标题，会发现通讯社汉语标题一般信息量较大；英语标题多有省略，结构相对简单，虚词很少，采用主谓宾结构和主动语态。此外，在标点符号使用方面，编译者要特别注意英语新闻标题习惯用单引号代替双引号。

第二节　汉英新闻导语的编译原则

在将汉语新闻导语编译成英语时，编译者应遵循以下原则：

- 确定编译新闻的主题，并筛选出最能说明主题的新闻事实；
- 确定导语的主要新闻要素（包括 who、what、when、where 等），合并原语新闻中与给定主题关系不大的新闻材料；
- 尽量使用 SVO 结构（即主语 – 动词 – 宾语）写作，符合英语新闻导语的表达习惯；
- 关于导语中的"时间"(when) 问题，应尽量使用"今天"或与"今天"相当的时间因素；
- 表达应言简意赅，原则上越短越好；
- 尽量在导语中提供新闻来源（即信源）；
- 编译好之后，务必核实新闻人物、新闻机构的名称及其拼写，确保信息准确。

编译案例

◎ 新闻稿 1

中国灵活就业者已达 2 亿人 线上工作受到年轻人追捧[1]

02/09/2022　07:59　《人民日报》(海外版)

视频制作、网络主播、文案写手……平台经济、共享经济蓬勃发展，孕育出丰富的就业方式，灵活就业也成为当下年轻人的就业新选择。国家统计局相关负责人日前表示，截至 2021 年底，中国灵活就业人员已经达到 2 亿人，其中从事主播及相关从业人员 160 多万人，较 2020 年增加近 3 倍。

求职者选择更丰富

"现在回想起来，我的事业正是从灵活就业开始的。"已经毕业 5 年的柳蓁是一名视频特效制作员，她所在的团队在业界小有名气。毕业之初，柳蓁选择以视频"UP 主"（上传者）的身份进入社会，她制作的各类特效视频深受网友喜爱，播放量节节攀升，最终拿到进入专业团队的"敲门砖"。

中国灵活就业人数明显增加，思维活跃、擅长创新的大学毕业生群体成为灵活就业的主力军。根据全国高等学校学生信息咨询与就业指导中心数据统计，2020 年和 2021 年全国高校毕业生的灵活就业率均超过 16%。

"选择灵活就业不等于找不到工作，也不是随便'打零工'，而是一种全新的就业模式。"柳蓁认为，灵活就业给了求职者选择"单飞"的机会，可以充分发挥个人优势和兴趣，创作出优质的作品和成果，为自己搭建展现能力的舞台，在增长专业技术的同时，摸索职业发展方向。

灵活就业不仅成为毕业生的一个就业途径，也为企业选人用人提供了便利。中国人民大学灵活用工课题组等发布的《中国灵活用工发展报告（2022）》蓝皮书显示，2021 年中国有 61.14% 的企业在使用灵活用工，比 2020 年增加 5.46%，企业倾向于扩大灵活用工规模。

相较于传统的长期就业模式，灵活就业的优势在于相对宽松的准入和退出机制。对求职者而言，灵活就业获取工作机会的门槛更低，不合适也可以随时离职；对企业来说，在选人用人以及如何用、用多久等方面也都比较灵活。因此，无论是求职者还是企业，灵活就业都为其提供了更多的尝试空间和选择机会。

---

[1] 新闻稿来源：http://www.news.cn。

"多面型"人才副业途径多

"人类目前对火山还知之甚少,我们虽然明白火山爆发的原理,但准确预测几乎是不可能的,这也是需要持续推进研究工作的原因。"1月14日,汤加火山爆发的消息在网络上受到广泛关注。在某短视频平台上,主播李东祺制作的一条科普视频回答了网友们关心的问题,播放量突破2万次。

"做短视频只能算是副业,我的本职工作是一名地质研究员。"李东祺告诉记者,搞地质研究需要经常到全国各地进行实地勘测,他便会借机制作视频来展现工作日常,没想到收获了一批忠实粉丝,也获得了可观的额外收入。"后来我就开始做简单的科普视频,同时把相关联的专业性内容以文章形式在知识平台发表,为网友尤其是学生群体了解地质相关知识提供一个窗口,播放量和阅读量都还不错。"

随着智能化时代的到来,灵活就业的方式也为李东祺这样的"多面型"人才提供了副业创新、创造价值的新途径。目前,越来越多的人拥有多方面的知识和能力储备,可以同时满足不同企业的需求。一些人还凭借一技之长在新经济领域进行创新,创造出一系列有价值的作品、产品,为自己带来更广阔的发展空间。国务院近日印发的《"十四五"数字经济发展规划》明确提出,鼓励个人利用社交软件、知识分享、音视频网站等新型平台就业创业,促进灵活就业、副业创新。

"我希望通过做视频、写文章把地质研究的相关知识和心得分享给大家,也希望能够激发在校学生的兴趣,让更多人加入科研队伍,一起来探索未知。"李东祺说。

让灵活就业者更有干劲

国家对于灵活就业人群的保障制度及相关措施近年来逐步完善,2021年7月,人社部等8部门共同印发《关于维护新就业形态劳动者劳动保障权益的指导意见》,对维护好新就业形态劳动者的劳动报酬、合理休息、社会保险、劳动安全等权益作出明确要求。此次发布的《"十四五"数字经济发展规划》也提出,将进一步健全灵活就业人员参加社会保险制度和劳动者权益保障制度,推进灵活就业人员参加住房公积金制度试点。

针对即将面临就业的大学毕业生,人社部就业促进司相关负责人表示,将运用社保补贴政策,支持毕业生多渠道灵活就业、新业态就业。对有意愿、有能力创业的毕业生,人社部将给予倾斜支持,精准开展创业培训、创业服务,提供创业担保贷款、创业补贴、场地支持等政策。

此外,也有高校推出设置创新创业学分、放宽学生修业年限等一系列措施,着力培养学生在创新创业方面的能力和意识,支持学生选择灵活就业。部分高校还设立了"种子基金""学生创业园"等计划和平台,为选择灵活就业、创新创业的学生提供资金、场地及生活保障等方面的支持。

专家表示，在不断完善的政策支持与保障下，各种新型就业模式将吸纳更多劳动力就业，让灵活就业者更有干劲。

编译稿

China records 200 million flexible workers

The diverse new labor forms developed by the booming platform economy and sharing economy are offering new choices for young people in China. According to the National Bureau of Statistics, China had recorded 200 million flexible workers by the end of 2021, nearly three times more than there had been in 2020.

Flexible employment offering more choices for job seekers

University graduates, known for their innovative ways of thinking, make up the majority of China's flexible workers. Over 16 percent of graduating college students in the past two years opted for flexible jobs, said the China Higher Education Student Information and Career Center.

"Doing flexible jobs doesn't necessarily mean that we can't find a job or that we are not being serious about employment," said Liu Zhen, who graduated from university five years ago and now runs a channel about special effects, or SFX, on a video platform.

Liu believes that flexible employment offers job seekers an opportunity to start their own businesses and helps them make a difference with their specialties. It builds a platform for people to showcase their capabilities and helps them pave a road for their future careers, she said.

Flexible employment is not only to the benefit of university graduates, but also facilitates enterprises in terms of recruitment. According to a report issued by the Renmin University of China, flexible employment was adopted by 61.14 percent of enterprises in China last year, up 5.46 percent from a year ago. The report also found that enterprises were planning to expand flexible employment.

Creating abundant opportunities for multifaceted talents

"People still know too little about volcanoes. Though we understand why they erupt, we can barely predict when. This is why we must continue our research," says video blogger Li Dongqi in a clip he uploaded after a series of violent volcanic eruptions broke out in Tonga on Jan. 4. The clip was viewed over 20,000 times.

"Short video blogging is just a side gig, and I'm a geological researcher," Li said. At first, he was just filming to share his frequent field investigations on the Internet, but later he unexpectedly obtained a batch of loyal followers, and considerable extra income, too.

"So I started making science popularization videos, and I also publish relevant articles on knowledge sharing platforms. These contents offer the audience, especially students, a source where they can learn about geology," he told People's Daily Overseas Edition.

In the era of intelligentization, flexible income is building new channels for multifaceted talents like Li to work on side projects and make extra income.

Currently, more and more people are becoming multifaceted and are qualified to work for different types of enterprises. To promote flexible employment on social, knowledge sharing, as well as video and audio platforms is encouraged by a recent development plan on digital economy issued by the State Council.

案例分析

原新闻稿的标题采用前后两段式，既突出了灵活就业者人数多，又说明了灵活就业的趋势。

编译稿中只翻译了原标题的前半部分，重点突出了数量。原新闻稿的导语概括说明了灵活就业的类型、原因和迅猛发展的态势。编译稿的导语基本与新闻稿导语对应，但是并没有明确说明灵活就业有哪些类型，而是突出了灵活就业的迅猛发展之势。

◎新闻稿2

全球首台无人驾驶"空中的士"首次上架售卖[1]

2024年03月18日 16:23 来源：中国新闻网

中新网3月18日 动漫里的无人驾驶飞行器，能在城市低空中穿梭的"飞行的士"离人类社会还有多远？科幻电影里的场景，正成为现实。

记者获悉，3月18日，全球首个获得适航认证的国产自主研发的"空中的士"亿航EH216-S无人驾驶载人航空器在某电商平台上线，标价每一架239万元，已经完成适航取证，并在全球开展商业化试运行。

---

1 新闻稿来源：https://www.chinanews.com.cn。

据介绍，EH216-S 可搭载两人，长 6.05 米，宽 5.73 米，高 1.93 米，由 16 个螺旋桨组成；为全智能无人驾驶航空器，能够垂直起降，完全不需要跑道，主要在低空空域飞行。单次飞行的最长里程为空中直线 30 公里，最大飞行速度可达 130 公里每小时，通过地面指挥调度系统管理，多架航空器可以在空中完成井然有序的无人驾驶飞行。

外形上，亿航 EH216-S 像一架长满螺旋桨的直升机，但和传统直升机单独旋翼相比，亿航 EH216-S 共有 8 个轴多达 16 个旋翼，远看上去像是章鱼博士的触手。这架航空器最大的亮点是每个关键部件都用了多备份的设计理念，充分保障了安全平稳飞行。

"和人们普遍印象中的直升机还是差别很大，"亿航智能副总裁贺天星介绍，"亿航这款 EH216-S 是由多个旋翼提供升力，通过调整各旋翼转速来控制姿态及巡飞。同时，16 个旋翼及飞控等各关键部件都是多备份设计，充分保证了安全性。即使飞行过程中某个部件失灵，其备份也能及时顶替，以充分保证飞行安全性。"

贺天星表示："会针对购买客户的情况进行专业团队服务，为大家在城市空域审批、飞行航线设置、航空器保养、工程师培训等方面做好保障，在符合当下监管要求的城市，可以开展飞行。"

记者还获悉，该电商平台上线的另一型号长航距 VT-30 航空器产品，空中飞行航程达 300 公里，目前已经完成了所有整体构型的验证和试飞，今年内也将进行适航申请。

编译稿

World's first unmanned flying taxi goes on sale

(People's Daily Online) 10:50, March 22, 2024

The EH216-S, the world's first unmanned passenger-carrying flying taxi to obtain a certificate of airworthiness, independently developed by Chinese company EHang, was made available for purchase on an e-commerce platform on March 18.

The aircraft, priced at 2.39 million yuan ($332,000), is now undergoing global commercial trial operations.

The electric vertical takeoff and landing (eVTOL) aircraft doesn't need a runway and can carry two passengers up to 30 kilometers at 130 kilometers per hour. It measures 6.05 meters in length, 5.73 meters in width, and 1.93 meters in height.

Powered by 16 propellers, the EH216-S operates fully autonomously in low-altitude airspace. It is controlled via a ground command and dispatch system, which enables multiple aircraft to operate at the same time.

A key safety feature of the aircraft is that every critical component has multiple backups, fully ensuring stable and safe flight even if certain parts malfunction.

"It's quite different from traditional helicopters," said He Tianxing, vice president of EHang.

"Our professional teams will assist buyers with airspace authorization, flight route planning, maintenance, and engineer training," He said.

Another long-range model, launched by EHang on the same e-commerce platform, the VT-30, featuring a flight range of 300 kilometers, has completed its configuration verification and test flights, according to a credible source. It will apply for airworthiness certification this year.

案例分析

新闻稿和编译稿的标题基本对应，不同的是新闻稿的标题中使用了双引号，编译稿的标题则未作特殊处理。新闻稿的导语包括两个小段，第一段描述了动漫中的"飞的"场景，通过一个问题吸引读者继续阅读；第二段中才真正涉及有关"空中的士"的具体信息，包括型号、价格、目前的商业运行阶段和该产品的意义。编译稿中的导语也包括两个小段，其内容对应的是原文第二段的内容，合并了原文第一段中的引子，这也符合英语新闻导语的写作特点。

◎ 新闻稿 3

山东能源、潍柴动力、山东高速等 6 家鲁企上榜世界 500 强[1]

山东商报·速豹新闻网记者　丁一凡　2022-08-04　12:46　山东

8月3日，2022年《财富》世界500强排行榜正式发布。榜单中，中国大陆（含香港）公司数量相比去年增长了1家，达到136家。加上台湾地区企业，中国共有145家公司上榜，大公司数量继续位居各国之首。

在上榜鲁企方面，今年山东共有6家企业上榜，分别是山东能源集团、山东魏桥创业集团、山东钢铁集团、海尔智家、潍柴动力以及山东高速集团。其中，山东高速集团为今年新上榜的企业。

整体来看，除了新上榜鲁企外，其余5家山东企业在排名方面有升有降。

---
[1] 新闻稿来源：https://baijiahao.baidu.com。

其中，山东能源集团以 1200.12 亿美元的营业收入，位列榜单第 69 位，同比去年上升 1 位。山东魏桥创业集团则以 637.38 亿美元的营业收入，位列榜单第 199 位，同比去年上升 83 位。紧随其后的是山东钢铁集团，以 413.18 亿美元的收入，位列榜单第 332 位，同比去年上升 52 位。

以山东能源集团为例，2021 年，公司营业收入、利润、税金均居山东省属企业首位，是山东省唯一一家资产、营收"双 7500 亿"企业，被国务院国资委评为"国有企业公司治理示范企业"。

此外，海尔智家和潍柴动力，则分别以 352.78 亿美元、315.56 亿美元的营业收入，位列榜单第 405 位、452 位。而值得注意的是，山东高速集团今年成功跻身榜单之中，以 311.35 亿美元的营收位列榜单第 458 位。

山东商报·速豹新闻网记者了解到，山东高速集团是山东省基础设施领域的国有资本投资公司，注册资本 459 亿元，资产总额突破 1 万亿元。集团大力发展基础设施核心业务，致力于打造主业突出、核心竞争力强的基础设施投资建设运营服务商和行业龙头企业，为"交通强省"建设提供有力支撑。

从地域上看，此次上榜企业中，山东能源集团、山东钢铁集团、山东高速集团的总部所在城市为济南，而山东魏桥创业集团、海尔智家、潍柴动力的总部所在城市分别为滨州、青岛、潍坊。

在新上榜企业方面，此次《财富》世界 500 强排行榜一共有 44 家新上榜和重新上榜公司，其中就包括山东高速集团在内的 14 家中国公司。

14 家中国公司分别是：中国中化控股有限责任公司、苏商建设集团有限公司、杭州钢铁集团有限公司、蜀道投资集团有限责任公司、中国航空油料集团有限公司、湖南钢铁集团有限公司、潞安化工集团有限公司、新疆中泰（集团）有限责任公司、比亚迪股份有限公司、顺丰控股股份有限公司、山东高速集团有限公司、成都兴城投资集团有限公司、上海德龙钢铁集团有限公司、台湾中油股份有限公司。

编译稿

Weifang's Weichai Power and Other Five Shandong Companies on Fortune Global 500 list

Six enterprises from east China's Shandong province made it into the 2022 Fortune Global 500 list, including Weichai Power, a combustion engine company headquartered in Weifang.

The rest five are Shandong Energy Group, Weiqiao Pioneering, Shandong Iron and

Steel Group, Haier and Shandong High-Speed Company Limited.

It was the first time for Shandong High-Speed Company Limited to be listed.

Shandong High-Speed Company Limited is a state-owned investment company in infrastructure. Boasting a registered capital of 45.9 billion yuan ($6.77 billion), it has total assets of over a trillion yuan.

It is reported that 44 companies were newly- or re-listed this time.

With revenue of $120 billion, Shandong Energy Group ranked 69th on the list, the highest among all six Shandong enterprises. Last year, the enterprise's income, profit and tax ranked first among all entities registered in Shandong province.

Weichai Power from Weifang ranked 452nd, reporting revenue of nearly $31.6 billion.

The 2022 Fortune Global 500 list was published on Aug. 3. A total of 145 Chinese companies were on the list, the highest among all countries, including nine from China's Taiwan region.

案例分析

新闻稿和编译稿的标题基本对应，区别是新闻稿的标题列举了三个山东企业，而编译稿出于标题长度的考虑仅列举了一个企业。新闻稿的导语包括前三段，第一段概述了世界《财富》500强中国上榜企业总体情况，第二段重点说明山东企业上榜情况，第三段是鲁企排名的名次变化。编译稿的导语也包括三个小段，但是原导语中第一段的内容并未体现，直接从原导语第二段山东上榜企业开始。

这篇新闻稿是山东潍坊宣传部门海外落地稿件，编译时需考虑被传播的对象，对编译内容进行一定的筛选。

将以下汉语新闻报道的标题编译成英语。

(1) 台北101大楼如何抵御花莲强震

_____

(2) 南京大学将开通全国高校首家 AI 课程

_____

(3) 275 天环球邮轮泊天津 近 2000 名各国游客开启京津游

(4) 研究发现充足的夜间睡眠是学生学业成功的关键

(5) 国安部：自媒体运营者绝不能为流量有损国家安全

阅读以下三篇新闻稿，并将标题和导语编译成英语。

◎ 新闻稿 1

各种跨界联名"玩 IP" 谁会成为月饼界的酱香拿铁？[1]

2023 年 09 月 25 日　09:24　来源：重庆晨报

当中秋遇上国庆，月饼市场大年就这么来了。要问当下最热的创意营销方式是什么，那就是 IP 联名。如今，跨界联名产品成为新的"流量密码"，在今年的月饼行业，也不例外。

文博月饼、大白兔月饼……无论是外观设计、食材口味，还是文化创新，推陈出新成为今年月饼市场的主旋律。"酱香拿铁"出圈在前，不知道月饼界能否木棱在后，复制其"酱香拿铁"的火爆。

各大博物馆文创月饼上新

当博物馆遇见中秋节，当国宝碰上月饼，各大博物馆的文创月饼也卷起来了。

故宫博物院旗下的"故宫淘宝"则以馆藏文物乾隆印章"绘月有色水有声"为题，结合中国传统色彩推出了国潮古风文创月饼。

三星堆博物馆今年延续以"体验＋互动＋沉浸"为主题的系列，以馆藏文物青铜神树为灵感，联名成都本土烘焙品牌打造了"神鸟的世界"文创月饼。礼盒外观融入了山海经中的神鸟元素，月饼造型也不落俗，采用了青铜大面具与青铜太阳轮两种图案作为饼面。

苏州博物馆今年以馆藏《月下桂兔图》为灵感，与当地餐饮老字号松鹤楼携手推出了"桂兔望月"中秋礼盒。

1　新闻稿来源：https://www.chinanews.com。

国家博物馆推出"秋月夜"主题月饼。"秋月夜"取材自国博馆藏唐代"月宫铜镜"与清代"剔红山水楼阁人物纹双联提盒",将月色、山水、草木、湖光、玉兔融为一体。

南海博物馆联合海南老字号品牌推出了两款联名款文创月饼,包装源自南海博物馆馆藏文物"明黑漆嵌螺钿四层小撞盒"和"南海鲸灵——馆藏鲸类标本展",顺应了"新国潮"。

南京博物院、洛阳博物馆、北京艺术博物馆等博物馆也推出了自己的文创月饼。文创与月饼的碰撞,不仅满足了消费者的胃,更让文物借由月饼走入公众视野,再次"活"起来。

今年月饼流行跨界组 CP

要问当下最热的创意营销方式是什么,那就是跨界联名。作为烘焙细分领域的月饼行业进入门槛较低,但市场规模呈逐年上升趋势,庞大的月饼市场吸引了众多消费头部公司跨界涉足。

今年中秋节前,大白兔跨界冠生园推出首款月饼礼盒。大白兔月饼礼盒采用经典的大白兔铁皮包装。打开之后,内含 6 颗月饼,分别是大白兔厚乳流心、桂花流心、抹茶流心、巧克力流心、咖啡流心和奶黄流心口味,每颗月饼味道都不相同,但月饼上方都印有一个可爱的兔子图形。其中,大白兔厚乳流心更接近大白兔奶糖的味道,轻轻一口,记忆中的奶糖味便伴随流心月饼在唇齿间融化,回味无穷。

网红雪糕品牌钟薛高与熊猫工厂合作,推出了以熊猫元素为创新概念的中秋礼盒——"花好月圆"月饼冰激淋礼盒;9 月初,生鲜电商叮咚买菜推出新品"微醺冰皮果酒月饼",同时还推出定制原老上海荠菜马蹄鲜肉月饼;近期,乳企光明乳业联合泸州老窖推出酒香巧克力冰激淋月饼中秋礼盒,这也是头部品牌跨界入局月饼市场的又一案例。

星巴克、奈雪的茶、由心咖啡等饮料行业商家也推出了各自的月饼产品。9 月 14 日,新式茶饮品牌奈雪的茶与数字潮玩收藏平台薄盒 App 推出了范特西联名款月饼礼盒,以"黑胶唱片"为款式设计而成。

不少 A 股上市公司也在投资者互动平台透露跨界动作,布局月饼赛道。8 月 18 日,宏辉果蔬在互动平台表示,公司近日推出产品"丰收哥猫山王榴梿冰皮月饼"和"丰收哥猫山王榴梿水晶饼";黑芝麻 9 月 12 日在互动平台直言,公司已研发并小批量生产黑芝麻月饼系列产品,在部分渠道试销。

中国食品产业分析师朱丹蓬表示，当前，许多品牌为了与新生代建立更好的联系和互动，选择跨界合作成为他们的方式之一。此外，月饼市场的利润空间仍然非常可观，这也是许多企业纷纷涉足月饼市场的主要原因。"整体看，今年月饼消费市场，跨界产品中具备高性价比或者网红品牌联名款的产品有望迎来大卖。"

月饼市场竞争愈发加剧

众多行业头部品牌的跨界涌入，也让月饼市场竞争愈发加剧。五芳斋有着A股"粽子第一股"的称号，月饼也是其发展的重点之一。2023年上半年，该公司实现营收18.66亿元，同比增加3.15%；净利润约2.56亿元，同比增加5.78%，其中公司月饼系列收入1.02万元，去年同期为13.49万元，销量下滑明显。

不过，五芳斋在接受机构调研时表示，月饼市场不同于粽子市场，它的发展空间更大，虽然竞争很激烈，但也更欢迎新晋玩家的加入。目前大部分月饼企业仍然局限于区域市场，华东地区真正实现品牌化连锁的本土月饼企业相对较少，这也是公司的机会。

月饼也是老字号餐企广州酒家的主力产品。2022年，广州酒家月饼系列产品实现收入15.19亿元，占营收比重超37%；今年上半年，公司月饼系列产品收入2985万元，同比下降33.8%。在9月初举行的业绩说明会上，广州酒家董事长徐伟兵坦言，"今年虽然是'月饼大年'，但公司对于今年月饼的生产销售持谨慎乐观态度。"

另外，由于月饼消费时令性明显，产品销售旺季一般在三季度，如何安排好今年月饼产品的经营和库存问题，一些月饼企业已经有了经验。业内人士表示，现在一些月饼制作商会早早采取"以销定产"的策略，在月饼开始制作前，公司就会根据接单、排单情况进行今年月饼的产品制作，尽量节前两周内售完，以免产生库存堆积。五芳斋也表示，公司严控库存，根据市场环境制定主流终端政策，聚焦优势渠道，在现有资源和费用投入下产生最大化销售。

在顾客消费习惯的改变等多种因素的影响下，近来元祖股份也进行着线上化渠道转型。另有行业人士指出，元祖股份喊出要"做365天都能卖的产品"，一定程度可以弥补节令品销售的不稳定性。此外，凭借品牌优势、礼品属性以及渠道优势所衍生的各类礼盒券将有助于公司净利率的提升。

数据显示，我国现存月饼相关企业有2.1万余家。在业内看来，超百亿的月饼行业内卷已经十分激烈,新的烘焙品牌不断涌现,越来越多其他行业的品牌参与联名、跨界,在中秋时节短期销售月饼,也来跨界月饼分一杯羹。

◎ 新闻稿2

我国年轻人肥胖相关癌症发病率急剧上升[1]

新浪财经　2024-08-25　16:20

北京首都医科大学内分泌学家杨金奎与合作者研究发现,2007年至2021年间,中国与肥胖相关的癌症发病率以惊人的速度每年增长3.6%,而与肥胖无关的癌症发病率则保持稳定。而且,这一增长在年轻人中尤为明显,这突显了改善公共卫生政策以解决中国日益增长的超重和肥胖率的迫切需要。相关研究8月23日发表于 *Med* 期刊。

"如果我们不彻底改变肥胖的流行趋势,与肥胖相关的癌症发病率将不可避免地继续上升。"论文通讯作者杨金奎说,"这将给中国经济和医疗体系带来巨大负担。"

在中国,癌症仍然是导致死亡的主要原因之一,其中肺癌是最常见的类型。然而,与肥胖有关的癌症,如结直肠癌、乳腺癌、甲状腺癌,正在迅速增加。之前有研究表明,肥胖将很快超过吸烟,成为癌症的主要危险因素。

"尽管公共卫生服务采取诸多措施提高人们的意识,但中国儿童和青少年的超重和肥胖率正在接近美国的儿童和青少年的超重和肥胖率。"杨金奎说,"展望未来,我们迫切需要更有效和积极的方法,可能包括药物和卡路里标签,以减少中国的肥胖问题。"

杨金奎团队分析了2007年至2021年间中国所有新诊断的癌症。结果记录了超过65.1万例癌症病例,其中约48%的病例被确定为世界卫生组织认定的12种与肥胖相关的癌症类型。

值得注意的是,2007年至2021年间,肥胖相关癌症发病率每年增长3.6%,

---

[1] 新闻稿来源:https://baijiahao.baidu.com。

而与肥胖无关的癌症（如肺癌和膀胱癌）的发病率保持稳定。此外，研究人员还发现，随着年龄的增长，肥胖相关癌症发病率上升得更快。对于60岁至65岁的人来说，肥胖相关癌症发病率每年增长不到1.6%。在25岁至29岁的人群中，相关发病率每年增长超过15%。此外，1997年至2001年出生的人被诊断患有与肥胖相关的癌症的可能性是1962年至1966年出生的人的25倍。

结直肠癌、乳腺癌、甲状腺癌、肾癌和子宫癌是年轻人中增长最快的与肥胖相关的癌症类型。杨金奎说："这一趋势与中国年轻人中超重和肥胖率的增长是一致的。"

肉类和酒精消费增加等生活方式导致了中国肥胖患病率的上升。截至2019年，34%的中国成年人超重，16%的被归类为肥胖。这种情况在儿童和青少年中尤其令人担忧，他们超重和肥胖率的增长速度更快。

该团队预测，如果不采取积极的公共卫生措施，中国与肥胖相关的癌症发病率预计将在未来十年翻一番。

◎ 新闻稿3

商务部召开会议听取专家对提高大排量燃油车进口关税意见建议[1]

中国青年网　2024-08-23　12:14

8月23日，商务部财务司负责同志主持召开会议，听取业界和专家学者对提高大排量燃油车进口关税的意见建议。有关行业组织、研究机构和汽车企业代表参会。

---

1 新闻稿来源：https://baijiahao.baidu.com。

第八章
汉语新闻正文的编译

第一节　汉英新闻正文对比

英语新闻稿的主体部分一般由一系列新闻事实组成，这些新闻事实根据其新闻价值由高到低排列。为了使这些新闻事实逻辑严密、浑然一体，使读者读起来感到流畅自然，新闻写作者通常会在导语与新闻主体之间以及各个新闻事实之间使用一些过渡性字词、短语、句子或段落。在编译汉语新闻稿时，编译者也应注意这一点，有时为了帮助读者更好地理解新闻报道的内容，领会其深层含义，还要提供必要的背景信息和解释。

英语和汉语新闻报道在正文的篇幅、段落、句子等方面有所区别（见表8.1），了解这些区别也有助于编译者更好地进行编译。

表 8.1　汉英新闻正文对比

对比范畴	英语新闻稿	汉语新闻稿
篇幅	大	小
段落	短	长
句子	长	短
分句	多	少
信息量	与同篇幅汉语新闻稿大体相当	与同篇幅英语新闻稿大体相当

第二节　汉语新闻正文的编译要点

将汉语新闻报道的正文编译成英语的时候，编译者应特别注意以下几点：

● **筛选材料**：选择与新闻主题关系最为密切的新闻事实，按其重要程度由高到低排列，删除与主题相关性不大的材料。

● **提供背景**：根据需要提供必要的背景或解释。

● **保留引语**：保留重要的直接引语。

● **做好衔接**：做好新闻事实与新闻事实、段与段之间的过渡和衔接。

- **编译结尾**：根据情况编译结尾，一般情况下硬新闻不需要专门的结尾。
- **截短段落**：段落应保持简短，一段一层意思；句子表达应符合英语表达习惯，繁简结合，根据需要可变换句式结构，避免句子形式单一。

编译案例

◎新闻稿 1

泉州世界遗产金银纪念币来了！7 月 25 日发行[1]

人民网　2022-07-18　09:02

人民网北京 7 月 18 日电　人民银行将于 7 月 25 日发行世界遗产（泉州：宋元中国的世界海洋商贸中心）金银纪念币一套。该套金银纪念币共 4 枚，其中金质纪念币 2 枚，银质纪念币 2 枚，均为中华人民共和国法定货币。

据介绍，该套金银纪念币正面图案均为中华人民共和国国徽，并刊国名、年号。

150 克圆形金质纪念币背面图案为泉州天后宫妈祖造像，辅以天后宫正殿造型、水纹、宋元泉州海岸线局部轮廓组合设计，并刊"泉州：宋元中国的世界海洋商贸中心"字样及面额；8 克圆形金质纪念币背面图案为泉州九日山祈风石刻、宋代泉州商船造型，辅以祥云、海浪等组合设计，并刊"泉州：宋元中国的世界海洋商贸中心"字样及面额；500 克圆形银质纪念币背面图案为泉州洛阳桥及开元寺双塔，辅以刺桐花、船等组合设计，并刊"泉州：宋元中国的世界海洋商贸中心"字样及面额；30 克圆形银质纪念币背面图案为泉州老君岩造像，辅以树、山等组合设计，并刊"泉州：宋元中国的世界海洋商贸中心"字样及面额。

纪念币规格和发行量方面，150 克圆形金质纪念币直径 60 毫米，面额 2000 元，最大发行量 1000 枚；8 克圆形金质纪念币直径 22 毫米，面额 100 元，最大发行量 10000 枚；500 克圆形银质纪念币直径 90 毫米，面额 150 元，最大发行量 3000 枚；30 克圆形银质纪念币直径 40 毫米，面额 10 元，最大发行量 20000 枚。

编译稿

China to issue commemorative coins for new world heritage site of Quanzhou

(People's Daily Online) 13:22, July 19, 2022

The People's Bank of China, China's central bank, is going to issue on July 25 a set of commemorative coins featuring "Quanzhou: Emporium of the World in Song-Yuan

---

[1] 新闻稿来源：https://baijiahao.baidu.com。

China," which is a UNESCO World Heritage serial site that illustrates the vibrancy of Quanzhou, in southeast China's Fujian Province, as a maritime emporium during China's Song and Yuan dynasties (10th–14th centuries CE) and its interconnections with the country's hinterland.

The set will include two gold and two silver coins, with all of them being round in shape and legal tender. All the coins will feature the national emblem, the country name and year of issuance on the obverse; and the reverse side will meanwhile be inscribed with the various denominations, Chinese characters reading "Quanzhou: Emporium of the World in Song-Yuan China," and combinations of pictures and elements from some of the 22 sites that together make up the heritage attraction of "Quanzhou: Emporium of the World in Song-Yuan China."

One of the two gold coins will be 60 mm in diameter, contain 150 grams of pure gold and have a face value of 2,000 yuan (about $296.4). The reverse side of this gold coin will feature images of a statue of the Chinese sea goddess Mazu inside the Tianhou Temple in Quanzhou, which was originally built in 1196 CE during the Song Dynasty to worship Mazu, as well as the main hall of Tianhou Temple, water and Quanzhou's coastline during the Song and Yuan dynasties.

The other gold coin, with a diameter of 22 mm and 8 grams of pure gold, will have a denomination of 100 yuan. The reverse side of the gold coin will feature images of the Jiuri Mountain Wind-Praying Inscriptions found in Nan'an county of Quanzhou city, local merchant ships of Quanzhou from the Song Dynasty, auspicious clouds and waves on the high seas.

The maximum issuing numbers of the 150-gram and 8-gram gold coins will be 1,000 and 10,000, respectively.

One of the silver coins will contain 500 grams of pure silver and have a diameter of 90 mm and a denomination of 150 yuan. The reverse of this silver coin will feature images of Quanzhou's Luoyang Bridge and the east and west pagodas of Kaiyuan Temple in Quanzhou, as well as oriental variegated coralbean flowers and ships.

The other silver coin, which will have a face value of 10 yuan, will contain 30 grams of pure silver and will be 40 mm in diameter. Its reverse side will feature images of the Statue of Lao Tze in Fengze district of Quanzhou, trees, and mountains.

The maximum issuing numbers of the 500-gram and 30-gram silver coins will be 3,000 and 20,000, respectively.

> **案例分析**
>
> 新闻稿共有四个小段，前两段是导语部分，说明核心新闻事实，即时间、发行机构、发行的纪念币数量、种类、基本特征等。第三段具体介绍了纪念币的设计、图案，最后一段介绍发行量、面额和规格等信息。编译稿结构和内容安排总体与原稿一致。导语也是两段，正文部分对纪念金币和银币分别进行介绍，因此段落顺序有微调，同时段落数量有所增加，段落长度相应缩短，符合英语新闻稿的写作习惯。另外，编译稿根据受众的情况，适当地补充了一些背景信息，以帮助读者更好地理解报道内容。

◎新闻稿 2

400 公里之上，天宫课堂开讲[1]

本报记者　余建斌　冯华《人民日报》（2021 年 12 月 10 日　第 12 版）

12 月 9 日，离地面 400 公里的中国空间站，"天宫课堂"第一课正式开讲。这是时隔 8 年之后，中国航天员再次进行太空授课，也是中国空间站首次太空授课活动。

在约 60 分钟的授课中，神舟十三号飞行乘组航天员翟志刚、王亚平、叶光富为广大青少年带来了一场精彩的太空科普课。

天地连线
感受航天员的空间站生活
【镜头一】

在中国科技馆地面主课堂的大屏幕上，实时画面从绕着蓝色地球飞行的空间站转换到了宽敞整洁的空间站核心舱中，一个黄色陀螺旋转着出现在镜头中，王亚平的声音响起：

"太空探索永无止境，随着不断旋转的陀螺，我们已经从神舟十号任务，进入了空间站时代。欢迎来到'天宫课堂'！"王亚平和同学们打起招呼，并风趣地介绍身边的"感觉良好乘组"。

"嗨，同学们好，我是指令长翟志刚。""同学们好，我是航天员叶光富。"

明亮的空间站核心舱中，王亚平带着同学们逛起了"太空之家"。核心舱的小柱段有 3 个睡眠区。王亚平的睡眠区里贴着家人的照片，挂着自己喜欢的小物品，十

---
[1] 新闻稿来源：http://paper.people.com.cn。

分温馨。透过舷窗，太空和地球美景尽收眼底。

"失重环境，血液分布和地面不同，下部的血液上涌，所以我们的脸会看起来胖胖的。这会影响健康，所以我们要通过很多种锻炼方法对抗失重生理效应。"王亚平演示了如何使用太空跑步机、太空自行车。

在太空厨房，太空橱柜里有加热装置、饮水分配器、食品冷藏箱。王亚平轻轻拉开食品冷藏箱，掏出一个新鲜的苹果。饮水分配器是取用生活用水的地方。王亚平说，随着技术的进步，空间站舱内的生活用水已经实现了再生，每滴水都会做到物尽其用。

为了展示如何对抗太空失重，叶光富给翟志刚当起了模特。翟志刚介绍，为了防止失重造成的肌肉萎缩，除了锻炼工具，还有个"秘密武器"，就是穿在叶光富身上的"企鹅服"。它有很多拉带让肌肉保持张力，对抗肌肉萎缩。"小小服装背后，浓缩着航天科技专家的巧思妙想。"翟志刚说。

随着王亚平的"导览"，空间站仿佛就在人们眼前，地面课堂不时响起阵阵掌声。

天地实验
乒乓球停留在了太空的水杯中
【镜头二】

"在太空能正常行走吗？"为了回答这个问题，王亚平请叶光富尝试像在地面一样走路。叶光富"踩"了几下，就不由自主地飘了起来，引起大家一阵笑声。"在太空没有重力，无法像在地面一样正常行走。"王亚平揭示了答案。

"不光是走路，太空转身也和地面有很大差别，我们在太空转身很难。"王亚平请叶光富示范太空转身的难度，游泳式、吹气式都不行，最后举起单臂不断转圈，终于转身成功。

天地互动中，还同做了一个小实验。

地面课堂上，同学们把乒乓球放在水杯里，球浮了起来。而空间站里，王亚平把乒乓球放在水杯里，球却停留在了水中。"这是因为失重环境下浮力几乎消失。"

随后，王亚平拿出她和女儿在地球上一起准备的花朵折纸放入厚水膜中，花朵边旋转边"开"了起来，"我们得到了一朵在太空中盛开的花，非常美丽。看到这朵花，我就想到了我的女儿。"王亚平动情地说。

王亚平勉励同学们："你们都是祖国的花朵，含苞待放，未来是你们的，希望你们的梦想都能在这广袤的宇宙中绽放。"

接下来是"太空欢乐球"。王亚平往水膜里不断加水，利用失重环境下水的表面张力，做出一个在地面上无法做出的水球。随后她注入蓝色颜料，放入半片普通的维生素泡腾片。瞬间,水球变成了蓝色。气泡不断产生,但并没有离开水球。

"为什么气泡没有离开水球呢?"王亚平说,这是因为,在失重环境中浮力消失,气泡不再上浮,而是相互挤压。

王亚平说:"这个蓝色的小球像不像我们的地球?地球是人类在宇宙中的摇篮,但人类不可能永远生活在摇篮里。如今我们有了自己的空间站,将来中国人的脚步会踏入月球、火星和更远的深空。"

天地互动
天宫课堂点燃科学梦想
【镜头三】
"我们能发电子邮件给你们吗?"澳门地面分课堂的同学提问。

"我们目前在核心舱可以和地面发邮件,也可以视频。平时我们可以看电影、看小说、听音乐,还可以看电视,频道非常丰富。周末休息的时候,还可以和家人双向通话。不过,目前我们与地面的邮件通信需要特殊处理,还暂时收不到同学们发来的邮件。不过大家有什么想法,都可以在网上给我们留言,也欢迎大家积极评论!"叶光富回答。

太空实验让人意犹未尽,天地之间继续着精彩互动。

"在空间站里,氧气和二氧化碳是怎么循环的呢?"广西地面分课堂的同学问。

叶光富回答,空间站利用电解制氧子系统产生氧气,二氧化碳去除系统去除二氧化碳。后续还会配备二氧化碳还原子系统,它可以将电解制氧产生的氢气和人体产生的二氧化碳反应产生水。"这样就可以大大提高我们空间站的物资循环能力啦。"

不知不觉中,"太空教师"们要和地面课堂的同学们说再见了。每位航天员都为同学们送上一句太空寄语——

"同学们,太空科技,奥秘无穷,未来属于你们!"翟志刚说。

"星空浩瀚无比,探索永无止境,希望同学们张开梦想的风帆,向无尽的宇宙远航。"这是叶光富的祝愿。

"飞天梦永不失重,科学梦张力无限!同学们,期待下次再见。"王亚平说。

神奇的"天宫课堂",点燃了孩子们的科学梦想。

北京市人大附中朝阳分校六年级学生徐楷祺说:"'天宫课堂'让我了解了空间站的结构,还跟着航天员参观了空间站,知道航天员在空间站干什么。原来航天知识如此有趣!"

北京市清华附中科技办公室主任谭洪政老师说:"期待同学们在后续能够提出更有想象力的问题,设计出极具创造力的实验,希望未来我们的实验方案能够进入天宫。"

编译稿

Shenzhou-13 crew gives first science class from China's space station

By Yu Jianbin, Feng Hua (People's Daily) 09:08, December 14, 2021

On Dec. 9, crew members of China's Shenzhou-13 manned spaceflight mission, Chinese astronauts Zhai Zhigang, Wang Yaping, and Ye Guangfu, delivered a wonderful 60-minute science class 400 kilometers above Earth at China's Tiangong space station to elementary and middle school students.

The livestreamed lecture was the first lecture conducted by Chinese astronauts from space in eight years since the last space class was given in 2013, and also the first lecture given from China's space station.

At the main classroom set at the China Science and Technology Museum, students interacted with their "space teachers" in real time via a large screen.

As the live scene on the screen shifted from the space station orbiting the blue Earth to the roomy and uncluttered core module of the space station, a spinning yellow top appeared on the screen, which was followed by an introduction to the lecture made by Wang.

"There is no end for space exploration. As the top spins continuously, we have moved from the Shenzhou-10 mission to the construction of China's space station. Welcome to the 'Tiangong Class'," said Wang, greeting students attending the class in different cities of the country. She then introduced to students her crewmates, Zhai and Ye, who also said hello to the whole class.

Wang gave students a virtual tour of the brightly lit core module of the Tiangong space station. The sleeping zone of the core module is equipped with three bedrooms. With photos of her family and some little ornaments, Wang's bedroom looked warm and sweet. The porthole in the bedroom gave a splendid view of the universe and Earth.

"In zero-gravity environment, our blood distribution is different from that on Earth. Blood in the lower part of our body flows upward, so we look a little chubby and puffy. It can affect our health. Therefore we need to counter the physiological effects of weightlessness through a lot of exercise methods," Wang said. She showed students how to use treadmill and spin bike in space.

In the kitchen of the core module, which is equipped with devices like microwave, water dispenser and refrigerator, Wang took out a fresh apple from the refrigerator.

The water dispenser is used to draw water for drinking and cooking, according to Wang, who said that with technological advances, the space station has realized regeneration of water for drinking and cooking and that every drop of water is made full use of in the space station.

Ye and Zhai demonstrated to students how they resist the physiological effects of weightlessness in space during the class.

Besides exercise equipment, astronauts also have a "secret weapon" that can help prevent muscular atrophy caused by weightlessness, said Zhai, referring to the "penguin jump suit" Ye was wearing during the class.

It has multiple elastic bands inside to help the astronauts maintain their muscle strength, said Zhai, who considers the suit a valuable fruit of the ingenuity of space science and technology experts.

During the class, students in the classrooms on Earth put a ping-pong ball in a glass of water and the ball floated. When Wang did the same thing in the space station, the ball stayed in water. "The reason is that buoyancy almost disappears in zero-gravity environment," Wang explained.

"Can we send an e-mail to you?" a student attending the class from a classroom in China's Macao Special Administrative Region asked.

"We can communicate with the ground control by e-mail and video call from the core module. In our spare time, we are able to watch movies, read novels and listen to music. We also have a lot of TV channels here. We can also have two-way phone calls with our family during the weekend break. Currently, since our e-mail to the ground team requires special handling, we can't receive your e-mail now. But you can leave messages for us online, and we are looking forward to your comments," Ye answered.

案例分析

新闻稿开头两段是导语部分，总体介绍了天宫课堂的情况，包括时间、地点、时长、天宫老师等信息，接下来通过三个小标题（即三个镜头）介绍了课程的内容：空间站的生活、空间站试验、天地互动等。原文包含较多的直接引语，增加了现场感和真实感。编译稿结构和内容顺序安排基本与原稿一致，只是没有使用小标题。前两段为导语，后面按照天宫老师各自负责的授课内容串联起来。编译稿也保留了一些直接引语，以生动形象地展示课堂的热烈气氛。

◎新闻稿 3

我们的照片真是体育老师拍的![1]

中央广电总台中国之声　　2024 年 01 月 16 日　　09:11　　北京

　　张煜，一位变身"摄影师"的体育老师。从 2014 年来到浙江衢州柯城区新华小学下村校区当体育老师以来，近 10 年间他为孩子们拍摄了超过 10 万张照片。

　　张煜回忆，2014 年 10 月份的那天阳光特别好，打在孩子们的脸上，他们天真的笑容和忘我的状态很吸引人，他便非常自然地拍下了 6 个孩子站在墙根前的照片。

　　这张照片获得了无数好评，也让张煜从此开始"兼职"摄影师，随时随地拿起手机记录美好。

　　快门记录下的瞬间，有孩子们欢呼雀跃的兴奋、羞涩扭捏的天真，有奔跑打闹的俏皮、大口扒饭时的憨态可掬，也有被老师批评时的小委屈，还有刻苦学习时的认真。

　　这些照片伴随着孩子们儿时的记忆，有的被写在日记里，有的被用在作文里……学生梅子杰回忆起他最喜欢的一张照片。"大家躺在草地上，阳光刚好穿过桑叶，照在我们脸上。"

　　升上初二的学生郑嘉乐说，"当时我蹲在枫树下面，张煜老师就拍了。照片里光线很亮，（枫叶）黄的，绿的，他拍得很可爱，感觉有人在记录我的童年。"

　　张煜刚参加工作时比较严肃，孩子们都有点怕他。

　　摄影便成了他与孩子们沟通的桥梁。"孩子们看到自己的照片，也会觉得非常可爱有趣，慢慢跟我越来越亲近，对我的教学也有很大帮助。"

　　热身、跑操、丢手绢、萝卜蹲……在张煜的体育课上，"玩"是精髓，孩子们不仅可以在广袤的天空下释放纯真快乐的天性，还有张煜老师摄影镜头的陪伴。

　　如今，每到六一儿童节、校运动会等节日和重要活动，学校其他老师也会情不自禁地拿起手机，记录孩子们展现自我的样子，以此作为礼物送给孩子们。张煜老师也乐于分享自己的摄影经验，传递"快乐教育"的理念。

　　长期拍摄孩子们，让张煜学会以一个温和的观察者姿态出现在孩子的世界，他也在引导孩子们保持专注、乐观。

　　张煜说，他抓拍到的学生常常是污泥沾衣、满头大汗，但他们很真实。童年就是这样有趣、快乐、无邪。"希望能出个小画册或者办个小小的摄影展，让那些毕业的孩子看到这些照片时，回忆起那段快乐的童年时光，也让更多人回想起自己的金色童年。"

---

1 新闻稿来源：https://mp.weixin.qq.com。

编译稿

Chinese PE teacher doubles as photographer, capturing vibrant snapshots of childhood

(People's Daily Online) 14:13, January 18, 2024

Zhang Yu, a physical education (PE) teacher at an elementary school in Kecheng district, Quzhou city, east China's Zhejiang Province, doubles as an unofficial photographer, capturing and preserving his students' childhood memories.

His journey as a photographer began in October 2014, shortly after he started working at the school. He captured a spontaneous moment of six children playing with sycamore leaves in front of a mottled wall on a sunny day. He has been photographing his students for nearly a decade, creating a vast archive.

The first picture of the six children, some using sycamore leaves to shield themselves from the sun while others peer through the leaves at the sky, received widespread praise. This encouraged Zhang to continue capturing everyday moments of his students' school life, using his mobile phone.

So far, Zhang has amassed a collection of over 100,000 photos, documenting the unguarded moments of his students—their joy, messiness during meals, moments of shyness or upset, and concentration on schoolwork.

Zhang's images have become a cherished part of the students' experiences, often referenced in their diaries and writing assignments.

"We were all lying in the grass with dappled sunlight across our faces," recalled Mei Zijie, a student, about his favorite photo.

"I was crouching under a maple tree when my teacher took the picture. The light was bright, and the maple leaves were beautifully yellow and green. The picture is so lovely. It makes me feel like someone was recording my childhood," said Zheng Jiale, now an eighth-grader.

"I hope to publish a photo album someday or hold a photography exhibition. I want the photos to remind students who have graduated from our school of the happy moments from their childhood and to help more people recall their own golden years as children," Zhang said.

案例分析

新闻稿的题目就很吸引人。开头第一段是导语部分，点出新闻核心事实，包括时间、地点、人物、事件等新闻要素。后面通过重点介绍几张照片以及照片中学生的心情，说明这位"摄影师"体育老师对教育、对孩子的爱。原文中包含一些直接引语，增加了新闻的真实感和生动性。编译稿结构和内容安排与原稿一致，第一段是导语，概述新闻事实，呈现新闻基本要素。正文具体讲述了体育老师如何开始拍摄孩子们的日程，记录他们的成长。编译稿也保留了一些直接引语，以增加真实感、提高新闻的可读性。

将以下汉语新闻报道编译成英语，编译时考虑对外传播的五个要素。

◎新闻稿1

2024世界机器人大会开幕 展出600余件创新产品[1]

中国新闻 2024-08-21 13:33

中新网北京8月21日电 2024世界机器人大会今日上午在北京经济技术开发区亦创国际会展中心开幕，将持续至8月25日。

大会以"共育新质生产力 共享智能新未来"为主题，同期举办论坛、博览会、大赛及配套活动。论坛突出尖端引领与融通合作，举办3天主论坛、20余场专题论坛，吸引包括国内外顶尖科学家、国际组织代表、院士和企业家等共计416位演讲和重要活动嘉宾。

博览会突出技术创新与应用成效，169家企业将展出600余件创新产品，其中首发新品60余款。27款人形机器人整机将在博览会亮相，创历届之最。

大赛突出技能提升与人才培养，共举办4大赛事，来自10余个国家的7000余支赛队的13000余名精英赛手现场竞技，将展示"互动性"强的科研类竞赛成果，比拼"观赏性"强的优质竞赛项目，内容涵盖协作机器人、康复机器人、特种机器人、智能人机交互、脑机接口等技术领域。

大会还将围绕政企对接、供需对接、投融资对接、产业链对接、产教对接等举办多场配套活动。

---

[1] 新闻稿来源：https://baijiahao.baidu.com。

◎新闻稿 2

涉及杭州！1 次购买、3 段乘坐、7 天有效！30 天内未乘车可全额退款[1]

杭州综合频道　2024 年 08 月 26 日　15:05　浙江

记者近日从中国铁路上海局集团有限公司（下简称上海局集团公司）获悉，为进一步满足差异化旅游出行需求，促进长三角地区旅游消费，长三角铁路结合管内旅游客流出行特点，创新客票服务举措，加大客运产品供给，于 2024 年 8 月 26 日起推出 3 款高铁旅游计次票产品，为旅客"量身打造"7 日游遍 3 城的乘车新体验。

此次推出的"上海＋东台＋扬州""杭州＋千岛湖＋黄山""南京＋淮安＋盐城"等 3 款高铁旅游计次票产品，以"1 次购买、3 段乘坐、7 天有效"的全新组合售卖模式，为广大旅客提供便利、优惠、自由的乘车新体验。

记者了解到，旅客持高铁旅游计次票不限定具体车次，可选择乘坐任意停靠相应区间的各等级动车组列车二等座。产品票价在综合各区间动车组列车执行票价的基础上执行优惠。旅客购买产品后，30 天内未乘车的，产品自动失效并全额退款。同时，遇有临时调整行程等情况时，持有高铁旅游计次票的旅客可以免收退票费，享受旅游计次票产品诸多惠民功能。

从产品购买方式看，乘车人可使用 12306 网站、"铁路 12306"手机 App 或自助售票机等，提前预约产品所对应发到站及席别的席位。预约席位后，乘车人持购买产品时所使用的有效身份证件原件进站检票乘车。

此外，考虑到广大旅客"快旅慢游"等出行习惯，东台、扬州、千岛湖、黄山、淮安、盐城等地自由行游玩时间一般都在 2 至 3 天左右，为让旅客游玩时间更加从容，上海局集团公司将 3 款旅游计次票产品使用期限设为自首次乘车之日起 7 天（含当日）有效，不仅免去了不少家庭"特种兵式"旅游的匆忙，也可减少沿途购票次数，充分享受高铁出现带来的生活便利。

推出高铁旅游计次票产品，将更好发挥高铁运输时效优势，便利沿线经济交流和人员往来，进一步促进长三角区域经济、县域经济、文旅经济深化发展，助力长三角一体化高质量发展。

1　新闻稿来源：https://mp.weixin.qq.com。

第九章
不同题材的汉语新闻编译

基于前述的理论与方法，本章将对不同主题的汉英新闻编译案例进行分析。鉴于本书第二部分已经对不同题材的新闻报道的概念、分类和特点进行了详细的介绍，本章对此将不再赘述。

需要特别强调的是，在汉英新闻编译实践中一定要保持对外传播意识，始终牢记"5W"传播模式，即谁说、说什么、怎么说、说给谁听、效果如何。下文将分主题对编译案例进行分析。

第一节 灾难类新闻的编译

编译案例

◎新闻稿

辽宁葫芦岛强降雨已造成 10 人遇难 1 人因公牺牲 14 人失联[1]

新京报　2024-08-23　22:25

据央视新闻消息，8 月 23 日晚，辽宁省葫芦岛市召开防汛抗洪救灾新闻发布会。发布会上介绍，此轮强降雨给葫芦岛市，特别是建昌县、绥中县造成极其严重的破坏，道路、电力、通信、房屋、农作物等受灾严重。初步统计，葫芦岛市受灾人口达到 188757 人，因灾损失 103 亿元；8 条国省干线、210 条农村公路不同程度受损中断，桥梁受损 187 座；电力总停线路 40 条、总停台区 3560 个，29 个乡镇 286 个村 128580 户居民用户受到影响；全市 6 条干线通信光缆损毁，县、乡、村 1301 处接入光缆中断。

随着道路、通信基本抢通，经过几轮逐户逐人排查，此次灾情已造成 10 人遇难、14 人失联，此外还有 1 名基层干部因救人牺牲，对于失联人员正在全力搜救。

---

1 新闻稿来源：https://baijiahao.baidu.com。

编译稿

Huludao rainfall causes 10 deaths, 14 missing

By Wu Yong | chinadaily.com.cn | Updated: 2024-08-24 10:56

The recent heavy rainfall in Huludao of Liaoning province has resulted in 10 deaths and 14 people missing as of 10pm on Friday, according to the flood control and disaster relief news conference held by the Huludao municipal government on Friday night.

Additionally, one official died while engaged in rescue operations. Efforts are ongoing to search for the missing individuals.

A total of 934 rescue teams had been deployed across the city, rescuing a total of 769 people so far.

Since Aug 19, Huludao city has experienced continuous heavy rainfall, with both the total precipitation and its intensity breaking historical records since meteorological observations began.

案例分析

这是一篇简短的有关暴雨引发山洪的新闻报道，标题已经道出了新闻的核心信息。报道共有两段，第一段首先发布了洪灾的总体情况，包括影响范围及造成的影响，即受灾人口、设施、道路交通、电力供应和灾害带来的损失。第二段说明遇难和失联人员及救援情况。编译稿的标题直指新闻核心，内容安排与原新闻稿的顺序有所不同，全文共四段，前两段是导语，说明了具体的遇难失踪人数和救援情况。第三段则用数字呈现救援细节，最后一段是有关此次洪灾发生的背景介绍。这样组织内容也符合英语新闻的报道方式。

编译以下汉语新闻稿，编译时考虑对外传播的五个基本要素。

陕西柞水高速公路桥梁垮塌事件：已确认坠河车辆 25 辆、遇难 38 人、失联 24 人[1]

2024-08-02　20:07　来源：上观新闻　作者：新华社

记者从陕西省商洛市获悉，7月19日20时40分许，丹宁高速水阳段公路桥梁因突发山洪发生局部单侧垮塌，陕西省、商洛市立即组织各方力量全力开

---

[1] 新闻稿来源：https://www.jfdaily.com。

展救援处置工作。截至8月2日18时，已确认坠河车辆25辆、遇难38人、失联24人，1人获救。

连日来，有关国家部委、解放军和武警部队、多省消防救援队伍和多支社会救援力量等，调集专业人员3408名和舟艇、无人机、探测仪、水下机器人等专业设备，在当地干部群众支持帮助下，克服河道大部分在高山峡谷之间，河水湍急、改道，库区水面漂浮物淤积、水下情况复杂，不利气象条件、山体垮塌等困难，对下游沿线约100公里的河道、水库进行了多轮次持续搜救。

目前，搜寻和善后等各项工作仍在有序进行中。

第二节　政治类新闻的编译

编译案例

◎ 新闻稿

《北京宣言》，让巴勒斯坦内部团结了起来[1]

发表日期：2024年07月24日　作者：新京报评论

据央视新闻客户端报道，7月21日至23日，巴勒斯坦各派别内部和解对话在北京举行。7月23日上午，巴勒斯坦各派别内部和解对话闭幕式举行。巴勒斯坦各派别代表签署了关于结束分裂、加强巴勒斯坦团结的《北京宣言》。

这是包括长期敌对的法塔赫、哈马斯在内，巴勒斯坦14个派别首次齐聚北京举行和解对话，同时也是自2007年6月反目后，迄今为止巴勒斯坦各派系，尤其是法塔赫与哈马斯间最明显、最重要的和解信号，由此备受各方关注与期待。

在7月23日的中国外交部例行记者会上，发言人毛宁对此表示，《北京宣言》的签署，为饱受苦难的巴勒斯坦人民带来了宝贵希望，中方真诚期待巴勒斯坦各派在内部和解的基础上，早日实现巴勒斯坦民族团结统一和独立建国。

这其实也是长期以来国际社会的共同期待，而此次《北京宣言》无疑就是一个良好的开始。

巴勒斯坦派别冲突由来已久

跟巴以问题一样，巴勒斯坦内部派别问题，也由来已久。

---

1 新闻稿来源：https://www.zgcsswdx.cn。

自1947年11月29日联大通过第181号决议后，巴勒斯坦人就致力于"团结自己"和"对抗以色列"两大使命，并于1964年成立了统一的巴勒斯坦抵抗运动——巴勒斯坦解放组织（简称巴解，PLO）。

1993年8月20日，《奥斯陆协议》达成。1996年1月20日，在巴解框架下，本着"巴以分别建国"和"建立统一的巴勒斯坦国"原则，巴勒斯坦成立了具有政府性质的巴勒斯坦民族权力机构，并首次建立了巴勒斯坦的行政自治实体。

但此时，巴勒斯坦各派别间分歧、矛盾凸显。

成立于1959年的法塔赫，对以色列持相对温和立场，主张走和平、合法斗争道路。该派别历史甚至比巴解组织还长，以"巴解主流派"自居，但其主体为长期流落在外的巴勒斯坦人。

有穆斯林兄弟会血脉的哈马斯，则成立于1987年，成员几乎都是巴勒斯坦本土居民。这一派别则长期坚持不承认以色列，主张强硬立场，坚持暴力手段。

这两个主要派别，分别以约旦河西岸和加沙地带为大本营明争暗斗，法塔赫长期占据主席职位，而哈马斯则在巴勒斯坦立法委员会中影响力与日俱增。

2006年1月25日，巴勒斯坦立法选举，哈马斯以44.45%的选票获得全部132个议席中的74席，力压法塔赫，获得组阁权，并提名哈尼亚为总理。

但此时，两派矛盾进一步激化。同年6月14日，法塔赫的自治权力机构主席阿巴斯宣布解散内阁，解除哈尼亚职务。

同年7月，哈马斯在自己的大本营加沙地带驱逐全部法塔赫人马。自此，法塔赫与哈马斯分别控制约旦河西岸与加沙地带，本就长期难圆独立建国梦想的巴勒斯坦人民，又不得不长期忍受仅有的两块自治领土相互对立之苦。

多国都曾介入斡旋但效果平平

内部的长期分裂，让本就处于对以弱势的巴勒斯坦势力两败俱伤。

法塔赫虽被西方和以色列视为"正式打交道的对手"，却长期被藐视，美以也对"巴勒斯坦建国时间表"和"以色列放弃定居点"等得到国际认可的巴方关键诉求始终回避。

以色列内塔尼亚胡内阁上台后，变本加厉地在西岸扩建定居点，更令法塔赫的主张日益尴尬，其在饱受屈辱的巴勒斯坦人中号召力不断下降。

与此同时，哈马斯的暴力抵抗虽赢得众多被占领土巴勒斯坦人的喝彩，却也因此被一些国家和国际组织视为"恐怖势力"，影响了巴勒斯坦建国事业的国际口碑。

法塔赫和哈马斯的内部对立，更对巴勒斯坦建国事业构成致命影响——得到国际间广泛承认的法塔赫，在巴勒斯坦人中越来越缺乏代表性，而在自治区域和被占领土上有不少拥趸的哈马斯,却难以跻身国际间解决巴勒斯坦问题的各种折冲樽俎场合。

为摆脱这种尴尬、被动的局面,各派和一些国际力量曾多次作出努力:2017年10月12日,法塔赫和哈马斯曾达成"开罗协议",同意进行和解,前者对后者开放议会和内阁,后者则对前者重开加沙地带。但该协议最终变成一纸空文。

而在过去几年间,土耳其、阿尔及利亚、埃及等国,也都曾介入斡旋,并牵头召开了多次各派系和解会议,但均效果平平。

2023年10月7日,哈马斯对以色列发动大规模袭击后,以色列大举进攻加沙地带。以色列的强硬报复行动,令被占领土和自治区域中巴勒斯坦人共同感受到"大敌当前"的压力,法塔赫、哈马斯等各巴勒斯坦派别都面临着生存危机。

这一共同危机,也促使巴勒斯坦各派别不得不以前所未有的积极态度谋求和解与团结,以共御其侮。这也是中国等区域外有国际影响力的国家再次积极介入斡旋的契机。

《北京宣言》是一个良好开始

事实上,此次哈以冲突爆发后,中国等国就介入了相关斡旋,积极寻求和平之路。

2024年4月,中国公开承认法塔赫与哈马斯代表在北京举行了"关于推进巴勒斯坦内部和解并进行深入、坦诚对话的磋商"。

这是继今年2月莫斯科磋商后,巴勒斯坦两大派系在中东之外密集举行的又一次和解磋商。

7月中旬,多家国际媒体披露,中国"正在斡旋哈马斯和法塔赫在北京举行和谈",但一些欧美观察家认为,"两派分歧尖锐,不能抱太大希望"。

然而,继2017年10月开罗会议后,多达14个巴勒斯坦主要派别再次齐聚一堂,尤其《北京宣言》的最终达成,显示巴勒斯坦自2006年分裂后近20年来首次显示出如此广泛、如此重要的共识,已远远超过各方预期。

据中国外交部王毅部长在此次和解对话闭幕式上的致辞,针对当前加沙冲突困境,中方提出了三步走的倡议。

第一步是推动加沙地带尽快实现全面持久、可持续停火,确保人道援助和救援顺畅准入;第二步是秉持巴人治巴原则,携手推进加沙战后治理;第三步是推动巴勒斯坦成为联合国正式会员国,并着手落实两国方案。

这三步,可谓是巴勒斯坦各派争取内部和解,并早日实现巴勒斯坦民族团结统一和独立建国的务实路径,同时也如王毅外长所说,这三步走环环相扣、缺一不可。

这无疑需要法塔赫、哈马斯和所有巴勒斯坦派别、民众在共同的危机和压力下,拿出更多妥协的艺术和团结的勇气。

此外还需注意的是，巴以问题绕不开美国。而目前美国总统选情不断出现戏剧性场面，其中的变数对巴以、中东和平影响几何尚待观察，其对巴勒斯坦内部的"分"与"合"影响，也不容忽视。

这也意味着，作为中东和平的重要组成部分，巴勒斯坦的内部和解，仍需国际社会有关各方的不懈努力和更多耐心。但无论如何，此次《北京宣言》都是一个良好的开始，值得期待。

编译稿

Beijing Declaration turns a new page for Palestine

By Ke Rongyi | chinadaily.com.cn | Updated: 2024-07-26 21:50

The Beijing Declaration on Ending Division and Strengthening Palestinian National Unity, signed by representatives from 14 Palestinian factions after reconciliation talks in Beijing on July 23, marks the first time these groups, including long-standing adversaries Fatah and Hamas, joined together for reconciliation since their falling apart in 2007.

On the very day of the signing of the Beijing Declaration, spokesperson for the Chinese Ministry of Foreign Affairs, Mao Ning, said that the signing of the declaration brings precious hope to the suffering Palestinian people and China sincerely hopes that, based on internal reconciliation, the Palestinian factions will soon achieve national unity and independence for the nation.

Palestine was near national unity in January 1996, when the Palestinian National Authority was established. However, differences and contradictions among the various factions became prominent. Fatah adopted a relatively moderate stance towards Israel, advocating for a peaceful path, while Hamas had long maintained a refusal to recognize Israel, holding a hardline position that includes the use of violence. The two main factions have been competing openly and covertly, with Fatah long occupying the presidency and Hamas increasingly gaining influence in the Palestinian Legislative Council.

In the January 2006 Palestinian legislative elections, Hamas won 74 of the 132 seats, outperforming Fatah, which further escalated the conflict between the two factions. In June of the same year, Fatah's chairperson announced the dissolution of the government, and then in July, Hamas expelled all Fatah personnel from their stronghold in Gaza. Since then, Fatah and Hamas have controlled the West Bank and Gaza respectively, leaving the

Palestinian people, who have long struggled for independence, to endure the hardship of living with two autonomous territories at odds with each other.

The prolonged internal division has left the Palestinian forces, which were already disadvantaged against Israel, even weaker. Although Fatah is considered a formal adversary by Israel and Western countries, it has been marginalized due to weak internal support. Particularly, the Netanyahu administration's intensified settlement expansion in the West Bank embarrassed Fatah's peaceful stance, diminishing its appeal among Palestinians. Conversely, Hamas's violent resistance, which earned applause from Palestinians on occupied territories, drew opposition from some countries and international organizations.

To break free from this deadlock, Fatah and Hamas reached an agreement in Cairo in October 2017, but the agreement ultimately proved to be ineffective. In the latest round of the Israeli-Palestinian conflict, harsh Israeli retaliatory actions threatened the survival of all Palestinian factions, including Fatah and Hamas, prompting the two to seek reconciliation and unity. This was also an opportunity for China, among other influential regional countries with international clout, to actively mediate again.

In April 2024, China publicly acknowledged that representatives from Fatah and Hamas had held consultations in Beijing on promoting intra-Palestine reconciliation and engaging in deep and honest dialogue. The finalization of the Beijing Declaration signifies that after nearly 20 years since the split in 2006, Palestine has demonstrated broad and significant consensus for the first time, surpassing the expectations of all parties involved.

Addressing the current conflict in Gaza, China proposed a three-step initiative. The first step is to encourage a comprehensive, lasting, and sustainable ceasefire in Gaza to ensure unimpeded humanitarian aid and relief. The second step is to adhere to the principle of self-rule by the Palestinians while working together on post-Gaza governance. The third step is to promote Palestine's accession as a full member of the United Nations and to begin implementing the two-state solution.

These steps represent a realistic path forward for Palestinian factions to strive for internal reconciliation and to realize national unity and independence as soon as possible. Achieving this, however, undoubtedly requires more compromise and courage for solidarity from Fatah, Hamas, and all Palestinian factions amid common crises and pressures.

At the same time, as an important part of achieving peace in the Middle East, continuous efforts and patience from relevant parties around the world are still needed for Palestine's internal reconciliation. Nevertheless, regardless of this, the Beijing Declaration marks a positive beginning that deserves anticipation.

> **案例分析**
>
> 　　原新闻稿是一篇典型的政治新闻报道，标题非常醒目地点出了核心新闻信息。前四段可以看作是导语，包含了所有的新闻要素。正文通过三个小标题讲明了巴勒斯坦内部分裂及政治派别形成的前因后果，也说明了《北京宣言》所带来的和平希望。编译稿比较简洁，标题同样点明主题，前两段是导语，概括了新闻核心事件，包含了所有的新闻要素，正文按照时间顺序简要地回顾了巴勒斯坦分裂局面的形成，指出中国为巴勒斯坦各派别达成和解、实现中东和平所付出的努力。编译稿的结构与原新闻稿基本一致。

编译以下汉语新闻稿，编译时考虑对外传播的五个基本要素。

第六届中非媒体合作论坛暨中非智库高端对话在京举行[1]

2024-08-22　来源：北京日报、新闻联播

　　8月21日，第六届中非媒体合作论坛暨中非智库高端对话在北京举行。中共中央政治局委员、中宣部部长李书磊出席开幕式并致辞。

　　与会嘉宾表示，在习近平主席和非方领导人的战略引领下，中非关系进入共筑高水平中非命运共同体新阶段。中非合作论坛峰会即将隆重举行，这将是加强中非友好团结的又一次盛会。媒体智库人士要弘扬真实亲诚的理念，赓续传统友好，共同讲好中非合作发展的故事，为中非携手推进现代化贡献力量。

　　与会嘉宾认为，中非取得的现代化成就表明，发展中国家有权利也有能力基于自身国情自主探索各具特色的现代化之路。要将现代化置于中非舆论叙事和智库研究的优先议程，深入研究和传播发展中国家的现代化理念与实践，共同探索更高质量、更有韧性、更加包容普惠的发展繁荣之道，为"全球南方"国家破解现代化发展难题提供智力和舆论支持。

　　论坛以"携手同行现代化之路"为主题，由国务院新闻办指导，国家广播电视总局、中国社会科学院、北京市人民政府联合非洲广播联盟主办。论坛期间，中非有关部门机构签署6项广电视听协议，发布20项合作项目，举办"友谊·合作"成果展等活动。来自中国和40多个非洲国家的政府部门、媒体、智库及国际组织的500余名代表与会。

1　新闻稿来源：https://wb.beijing.gov.cn。

第三节　政策类新闻的编译

编译案例

◎ 新闻稿

再扩大！中国 144 小时过境免签政策适用口岸增至 37 个 [1]

2024-07-15　10:42　来源：中国政府网

国家移民管理局今天发布公告，即日起，在河南郑州航空口岸实施 144 小时过境免签政策，停留范围为河南省行政区域；将云南省 144 小时过境免签政策停留范围由昆明市扩大至昆明、丽江、玉溪、普洱、楚雄、大理、西双版纳、红河、文山等 9 个市（州）行政区域。新增郑州新郑国际机场、丽江三义国际机场和磨憨铁路口岸等 3 个口岸为 144 小时过境免签政策适用口岸。

据了解，截至目前，国家移民管理局已在北京、天津、河北石家庄、秦皇岛、辽宁沈阳、大连、上海、江苏南京、连云港、浙江杭州、宁波、温州、舟山、河南郑州、广东广州、深圳、揭阳、山东青岛、重庆、四川成都、陕西西安、福建厦门、湖北武汉、云南昆明、丽江、西双版纳等地的 37 个口岸实施 144 小时过境免签政策。美国、加拿大、英国等 54 国公民持有效国际旅行证件和 144 小时内确定日期及座位的联程客票从上述口岸过境前往第三国（地区），可免办签证在规定区域内停留不超过 144 小时，停留期间可从事旅游、商务、访问、探亲等短期活动（符合与我国签署互免签证协定或我国单方面免签政策的，可从其规定）。

据国家移民管理局相关负责人介绍，中国自 2013 年 1 月实施 72/144 小时过境免签政策以来，过境免签政策在服务国家高水平对外开放、便利中外人员往来、促进对外交流合作方面发挥了重要作用。此次在两省扩大实施 144 小时过境免签政策为外籍人员来华旅游、商贸提供了更多选择。下一步，国家移民管理局将不断改进优化过境免签政策，持续深入推进移民管理制度型开放，以更加开放的姿态欢迎外籍人员来华，全力服务促进高水平开放高质量发展。

编译稿

China's 144-hour visa-free transit policy extended to cover three more entry ports, bringing total number to 37

By Global Times　Published: Jul 15, 2024 11:41 AM

China's National Immigration Administration (NIA) announced on Monday that the

---

[1] 新闻稿来源：https://www.gov.cn。

country's 144-hour visa-free transit policy has been expanded to three more entry ports, taking the number of Chinese ports covered by the policy to 37.

The move marks the ramped-up effort by Chinese government to facilitate international travel and opening-up with more convenient visa policy.

The three new ports are Zhengzhou Xinzheng International Airport in Central China's Henan Province, Lijiang Sanyi International Airport in Southwest China's Yunnan Province, and the Mohan railway port in Yunnan, the administration said in a statement.

Starting from Monday, the 144-hour visa-free transit policy at the Zhengzhou airport will allow visitors to travel within the administrative region of Henan. Additionally, the specific area covered by the 144-hour visa-free policy in Yunnan Province will be expanded from Kunming city to include eight other cities and regions within the province.

With the new addition of entry ports, the NIA has implemented the 144-hour visa-free transit policy in a total of 37 ports in China.

Foreign citizens from 54 countries including the US, Canada, and the UK who enter China through the designated entry ports and hold valid international travel documents and connecting tickets to a third country within 144 hours, will be allowed to stay in designated areas for tourism, business, and visiting relatives visa-free for 144 hours.

The NIA said that the 72/144-hour transit visa-free policies, implemented since January 2013, has played a crucial role in supporting the nation's high-level opening up and facilitating international travel and exchanges.

The expansion of the visa-free transit policy in Henan and Yunnan provinces will offer foreign citizens more options when traveling to China for tourism and business.

According to NIA, the total number of visa-free entries made by eligible foreigners exceeded 8.54 million in the first six months this year, accounting for 52 percent of the inbound trips during the first half year and representing a year-on-year growth of 190.1 percent.

案例分析

原新闻稿中的信息是递进式逐步展开的。全文总共三段，第一段说明新增的适用免签政策的口岸，第二段对该政策进行说明，第三段是实施该政策的背景信息。编译稿的结构与原新闻稿稍有不同，采用了典型的英语新闻报道方式，前两段是导语，点明新闻事实，与标题内容完全一致。从第三段开始说明新增口岸、涉及地区、政策实施的背景等信息。相较于原新闻稿，编译稿包含了较多的小段，符合英语新闻的报道习惯。

> 编译以下汉语新闻稿，编译时考虑对外传播的五个基本要素。
>
> ## 中央发布的"延迟退休"消息来了！[1]
>
> 编辑于 2024-07-23　14:39　发布于：湖北省
>
> 新华社北京 7 月 21 日电，《中共中央关于进一步全面深化改革 推进中国式现代化的决定》中指出了延迟退休相关内容：
>
> 积极应对人口老龄化，完善发展养老事业和养老产业政策机制。发展银发经济，创造适合老年人的多样化、个性化就业岗位。按照自愿、弹性原则，稳妥有序推进渐进式延迟法定退休年龄改革。优化基本养老服务供给，培育社区养老服务机构，健全公办养老机构运营机制，鼓励和引导企业等社会力量积极参与，推进互助性养老服务，促进医养结合。加快补齐农村养老服务短板。改善对孤寡、残障失能等特殊困难老年人的服务，加快建立长期护理保险制度。

第四节　文化类新闻的编译

编译案例

◎ 新闻稿

音乐剧《芝加哥》将于 10 月开启全国巡演 展现原汁原味的百老汇味道[2]

2024-08-24　15:10　发布于：北京市

凭借跌宕起伏的剧情、极致性感的舞姿、经典的爵士乐，音乐剧《芝加哥》成为音乐剧史上的里程碑之作。时隔六年，该剧将再度登上中国的舞台。据环球网 8 月 23 日消息，百老汇英文原版音乐剧《芝加哥》在京宣布即将于 10 月开启全国巡演。

《芝加哥》自 1975 年在百老汇上演至今，长演不衰已近 50 年，它是百老汇和伦敦西区历史上演出时间最长的美国音乐剧，也是目前在演的百老汇演出时间最长的剧目。该剧曾荣获六项托尼奖、五项美国戏剧桌奖、两项奥利弗奖和一项格莱美奖，以其独树一帜的性感风格和黑色幽默，占据着世界音乐剧的重要位置。

早在 2018 年，四海一家就作为"联合运营方"，将芝加哥带到北京、广州、杭州等 5 个城市，赢得了口碑、票房的双丰收，让观众们看到了音乐剧的更多可能性。

---

[1] 新闻稿来源：https://www.sohu.com。
[2] 新闻稿来源：https://cul.sohu.com。

随着海外资源的不断拓展，今年四海一家作为"联合出品方"及"全国巡演运营方"，10月起将携音乐剧《芝加哥》去到至少11个城市，为观众带来74场"爵味儿"十足的演出。北京四海一家文化传播有限责任公司副总经理杨鸿娅表示，"《芝加哥》不仅仅是一场演出，更是一次充满激情与创意的艺术旅程。如此大规模的巡演，对四海一家来说是机遇也是挑战，希望更多人能在家门口感受到地道正宗的百老汇文化。"

谈及此次中国巡演的情况，国际巡演项目负责人蒂姆·里德透露，"这次我们是一个非常国际化的团队，《芝加哥》这部剧不管是从剧情还是编舞等各种层面来说，都是一个非常经典的标杆式的剧目，我们也是很开心能够延续下来这一份经典。"作为一部几十年前创作出来的作品，《芝加哥》一直在"更新迭代"，蒂姆·里德表示，"在做这个剧的时候，我们会用最新的技术设备来保证高品质的灯光和音响效果，与此同时，保持住剧目本身原汁原味的风格，这是我们不断面临的新挑战。"

活动现场，演员们首先演唱了歌曲《My Own Best Friend》（《我最好的朋友》），剧中罗克西·哈特的扮演者莎拉·索塔特和维尔玛·凯利的扮演者米歇尔·安特罗伯斯声音浑厚，极富表现力，传递着来自友情的温暖与力量。曲毕，欢快的音乐响起，深情的女演员瞬间变成光芒四射的女明星，为大家带来《芝加哥》中最著名的双人舞《Hot Honey Rag》（《狂热吊带舞》）。两人性感却不失可爱，力量中又带点娇柔，将原汁原味的百老汇味道展现得淋漓尽致。

金秋十月，音乐剧《芝加哥》全国巡演将于深圳启航，随后前往郑州、佛山、北京、杭州、苏州、宁波、成都、西安、南昌、重庆等城市演出。11月14日至24日将登台北京世纪剧院连演14场。

编译稿

Culture Beat: Broadway sensation 'Chicago' set to tour 11 cities with 74 performances

By Global Times Published: Aug 25, 2024 10:06 PM

The launch ceremony for the nationwide tour of the original Broadway musical *Chicago* was held on Friday at the Century Theater in Beijing. The two female leads, dressed in iconic black outfits, performed two of the most representative songs and dances from the show, instantly immersing the audience in the rich jazz flavor of Broadway.

At the event, the actors first performed the song "My Own Best Friend." Afterward, they showcased Chicago's most famous duet, "Hot Honey Rag."

Starting in October, the musical will tour at least 11 cities across China, and bring 74 performances to audiences. From November 14 to 24, the show will come to Beijing's Century Theater for a 14-performance run.

Since its Broadway debut in 1975, Chicago has enjoyed nearly 50 years of continuous performances. The musical has won six Tony Awards, two Olivier Awards, and one Grammy Award.

案例分析

原新闻稿采用汉语新闻报道模式，开头一句作为引子进入新闻的主题，之后按照时间顺序从过去到现在说明该音乐剧的成功和影响力、与中国的交流、此次巡演的计划、启动仪式现场的情况，最后说明巡演信息。编译稿比较简洁，采用典型的英语新闻报道结构，一共四小段，前两段是导语，点明新闻事实，几乎包含了全部新闻要素，说明了巡演活动启动仪式的情况，第三段是巡演计划，最后介绍相关背景。

编译以下汉语新闻稿，编译时考虑对外传播的五个基本要素。

文化中国行｜山西太原：台湾同胞体验非遗技艺[1]

中国日报网　2024-08-22　09:04

中国日报网太原8月21日电（记者 朱兴鑫）8月21日，2024年"台商台青走晋来"活动在山西省太原市开幕。当天下午，来自台湾妇女联合会台北妇女会和山西省女企业家协会的两岸妇女代表30余人参加"晋台妇女山西非遗项目体验"特色交流活动，她们参观了山西老陈醋集团、太原古县城的太原县衙和文庙。

据悉，本次活动通过组织晋台两地妇女代表体验非遗技艺、品尝非遗美食、观赏古建遗存，让两地妇女共同感受中华传统文化的魅力，增强文化认同，坚定文化自信，促进妇女同胞的交流交往，增进两地妇女的姐妹情谊。

---

1 新闻稿来源：https://baijiahao.baidu.com。

第五节　社会类新闻的编译

编译案例

◎ 新闻稿

与亲人再次"相见"　器官捐献者刁攀娅将爱"说"出口[1]

2024-03-29　20:14:27　来源：央广网

3月28日，重庆市人体器官捐献纪念园，在"生命·礼赞"2024遗体和人体器官捐献缅怀纪念活动中，重庆市第一位器官捐献"数字人"刁攀娅与自己的家人再一次"相见"。

2023年6月7日，48岁的江津区医生刁攀娅医生带着对医学事业的无限热爱和对患者的无限牵挂，永远停止了心跳。而她捐赠的双肾和肝脏被用于挽救3名患者的生命，让他们重获"新生"。

今年，重庆市遗体器官捐献管理中心和西郊福寿园提前筹划，通过AI技术将刁攀娅的形象重现在大屏幕上。来到现场的刁攀娅的母亲钟志先和女儿黄靖雅看着刁攀娅熟悉的脸庞，听着她依旧亲昵的呼唤，忍不住泪流满面，现场群众也无不动容。

重庆市红十字会相关负责人介绍，今年的集中缅怀纪念活动将自3月28日起至4月4日止，持续1周时间。期间将持续在遗体器官捐献纪念园内为来园祭扫群众提供缅怀纪念仪式和静默徒步等追思主题活动。

近年来，重庆参与支持捐献工作的社会新风尚正在形成。截至2024年3月25日，我市登记遗体（角膜）捐献志愿者16.4万余人，实施遗体（角膜）捐献8600余例，已让6300余位眼疾患者重见光明。截至目前，登记人体器官捐献志愿者14.5万余人，累计成功捐献1164例，捐献3200余个大器官，挽救3070余名器官衰竭患者的生命。

---

[1] 新闻稿来源：https://cq.cnr.cn。

编译稿

AI enables digital reunion of organ donor and family

By Tan Yingzi and Deng Rui in Chongqing | China Daily | Updated: 2024-03-29 09:33

Ahead of next week's Tomb Sweeping Day, a new way to commemorate loved ones using artificial intelligence to create digital representations of the deceased has emerged in Southwest China's Chongqing.

On Thursday, the first digital human was presented at a body and organ donation memorial event held at Chongqing Organ Donation Memorial Park.

"Although separated in two different worlds, we will always love each other," a digital representation of Diao Panya said. "This love will let us overcome any obstacle and hardship. And we must embrace tomorrow—with every day filled with happiness. I love you all forever."

Her young daughter, Huang Jingya, burst into tears after hearing her mother's words at the event.

Diao, a gastroenterologist at Chongqing University Jiangjin Hospital, died of a sudden illness in June at the age of 48. Her donated kidneys and liver later saved three people's lives.

On the opening day of this year's memorial week for body and organ donors, Diao's mother and daughter visited the memorial park in Chongqing's Bishan district and "met" with her via AI.

"Although my mother's death was a huge blow to me, she knows from heaven that I will move on and try to live a wonderful life," Jingya said.

Wang Li, general manager of Fu Shou Yuan International Group (Chongqing), which came up with the AI idea, said: "We wanted to offer a new way to commemorate the deceased and to compensate for the many likely regrets of their families."

Last month, after obtaining the consent of Diao's family members, technicians collected a large amount of audio and video recordings that they used to create the AI video.

Fu Shou Yuan has been integrating innovative technologies in recent years to create a new digital "remembrance space" for the funeral industry.

China made voluntary donations the only legitimate source of organ donations after it banned the use of organs from executed prisoners in January 2015.

According to the Chongqing branch of the Red Cross Society of China, more than 164,000 volunteers in the municipality have registered for corneal donation, with over 8,600 donations bringing sight to more than 6,300 patients with eye diseases.

The city has also registered more than 145,000 organ donors, with 1,164 having donated over 3,200 major organs, saving the lives of 3,070 patients with organ failure.

According to the Red Cross Society of China, more than 820,000 people nationwide registered as organ donors last year.

The number of registered organ donors across the country now exceeds 6.65 million, with over 50,000 cases of donation and more than 153,000 donated organs.

案例分析

原新闻稿的标题点明了故事的主人公，但并未直接说明事件，制造了悬念，具有吸引力。报道共有五段，第一段是导语，呈现核心新闻事实，几乎包含了新闻的所有基本要素，后面四段分别介绍了故事主人公的事迹、本次活动的策划、今年活动的安排以及有关遗体捐献的情况等。编译稿的标题更为直接明了，报道结构与原稿一致，第一段为导语，点明新闻主题，后面部分为正文，介绍与当天纪念活动相关的情况，包括故事主人公、本次活动的策划、今年纪念活动周的安排及遗体捐献开展情况等。与原稿不同的是，编译稿提供了更多的细节描写，补充了背景信息，用直接引证的方式引用了事件当事人以及活动负责单位负责人的话，增加了新闻的真实性和现场感。编译稿的段落比较多，但是不太长，符合英语新闻报道的方式。

编译以下汉语新闻稿，编译时考虑对外传播的五个基本要素。

我国人均预期寿命达到 78.6 岁[1]

中国经济网　2024-08-30　06:19

新华社北京 8 月 29 日电　国家卫生健康委 29 日发布的《2023 年我国卫生健康事业发展统计公报》显示，我国人均预期寿命达到 78.6 岁，孕产妇死亡率下降到 15.1/10 万，婴儿死亡率下降到 4.5%，均为历史最好水平。

公报同时显示，我国卫生资源总量持续稳步增长。2023 年末，全国医疗卫

---

[1] 新闻稿来源：https://baijiahao.baidu.com。

生机构总数 1070785 个，比上年增加 37867 个，其中医院 38355 个，比上年增加 1379 个。全国床位 1017.4 万张，比上年增加 42.4 万张。全国卫生人员总数 1523.7 万人，比上年增加 82.7 万人。

根据公报，我国医疗服务提供量和效率同步提升。2023 年，全国医疗卫生机构总诊疗人次 95.5 亿，比上年增加 11.3 亿人次，居民平均到医疗卫生机构就诊 6.8 次。

公报还表明，我国次均医疗费用控制略有成效。2023 年，医院次均住院费用 10315.8 元，按可比价格下降 5.2%；次均门诊费用 361.6 元，按可比价格上涨 5.3%。

2023 年全国卫生总费用初步核算为 90575.8 亿元，其中政府卫生支出占 26.7%，社会卫生支出占 46.0%，个人卫生支出占 27.3%。人均卫生总费用 6425.3 元，卫生总费用占 GDP 的比例为 7.2%。

第六节　经济类新闻的编译

编译案例

◎ 新闻稿

仅 13% 的年轻人没有负债　年轻人的钱花哪去了[1]

中国新闻网　2021-10-26　07:45:45

近日，中银消费金融联合时代数据发布的《当代青年消费报告》（下称"报告"）显示，90 后与 00 后逐渐成为这个时代的消费主力，当下，他们正值 18-32 岁，其中 90 后开始成为社会中坚力量、具有稳定收入，00 后逐步走向职场，由他们组成的新生代消费群体，展现出巨大的消费力。

报告指出，从社交通讯、网络购物、影视娱乐到移动支付，互联网在方方面面塑造着新一代年轻人的消费习惯与生活方式。成长于优渥的环境让他们有着比上一代更强的消费欲望，2021 年，35 岁以下的年轻消费者将创造 65% 的消费增长，是当之无愧的消费主力军，超前消费成为他们的日常。

报告显示，消费贷年龄分布上，90 后几乎占据半壁江山，占比为 49.3%；其次是 80 后，占比为 31.5%。一组数字显示，全国有 1.75 亿名 90 后，其中只有 13.4%

1　新闻稿来源：http://zjnews.china.com.cn。

的年轻人没有负债，而86.6%的90后都接触过信贷产品。

报告认为，除了消费方式上的差异，在最基本的生活需求满足后，90后也有着与上一辈截然不同的消费观念。在他们看来，消费是为了更好的体验，追求更有品质感的生活。他们愿意在自己喜爱的领域投入更多的资金。而互联网金融产品的诞生与繁荣让年轻人的消费少了很多约束。除还房贷外，60%以上的90后将消费贷用于提高生活品质和休闲。

那么，年轻人的钱花哪去了？报告从懒人经济、宠物经济、养生热潮、颜值经济和娱乐产业等五个方面介绍了当代年轻人消费的趋势。

懒人经济方面，数据显示，近三年线上消费者为"偷懒"花费的金额逐年提升，2020年规模超千亿。2020年11月"懒人神器"的搜索频次超过30万次，较去年增长近200%。其中，90、95后的年轻消费者线上"偷懒花费"增长最快。年轻一代热门搜索的懒人神器包括洗鞋机、早餐机、煮蛋器等。

宠物经济方面，数据显示，在中国的宠物猫狗主人中，几乎有一半是90后。近一年线上宠物市场中，90后、95后消费占比超过四成。95后的线上宠物消费，更是连续三年呈倍数级增长。

养生热潮方面，报告指出，生活的压力逐渐呈现在身体病症之上，身体健康成为人们心中的一根刺。年轻人们也开始养生了。在2021年的消费预期中，旅游、保健养生和教育培训位列18–25岁年轻人消费榜单的前三名。据预计，年轻人2021年在保健养生上消费的比例，比去年上涨了7.5%。

颜值经济方面，报告介绍，小红书上52%美妆内容消费女性用户小于22岁。在所有年轻用户中，18岁及以下的人群对于美妆相关的内容兴趣尤其浓厚，正在全方位地关注美妆话题。同比2019年上半年，细分品类的护肤和个人护理的内容消费涨幅更是高达241%和239%，将成为未来主要的购买力。值得注意的是，兼具性价比与质量的国货彩妆开始抢占一部分国际品牌在年轻用户中的内容消费份额。

娱乐产业方面，报告显示，今年，新顶流娱乐方式是剧本杀，预计国内市场规模将超过150亿元，消费者规模或达941万，而其中超7成的用户为30岁以下的年轻人。此外，将购买过程变成趣味体验的盲盒，也被年轻人买成了百亿市场。

编译稿

Report finds only 13 percent of young consumers in China are not in debt

A report on the consumption behavior of young people in China has found that the younger generation of Chinese consumers, primarily people aged between 18 and 32 years old, has jumped forcefully onto the consumption wagon.

By the end of 2021, consumers under the age of 35 are expected to contribute 65 percent to the overall consumption growth in China. Buying now and paying later has become a way of life for young consumers, according to a report jointly released by Bank of China Consumer Finance and Datagoo, a data platform under Time Media Group, based in Guangzhou.

Nearly half of all young consumers who are in debt were born in the 1990s, while 31.5 percent of young consumers in debt were born in the 1980s. The statistics also suggest that only 13.4 percent of the 175 million people born in the 1990s are not currently in debt.

The report also found that in addition to having different consumption behavior, the younger generation is more willing to spend so that they get a better consumer experience and live a high-quality life with better products.

So, how are members of the younger generation spending their money? According to the report, young people are opting to spend lavishly on the following products and services.

Over the past three years, the amount of money spent by young consumers on time-saving and labor-saving products and services, such as shoe washing machines, breakfast makers, and egg boilers, increased year by year. In November 2020, a peak season for shopping in China, such products were searched for 300,000 times on e-commerce platforms, an increase of 200 percent from the same period in the previous year.

People born during the 1990s account for half of all pet owners in China, statistics show. Over the past year, consumers born after 1990, and after 1995, contributed 40 percent to pet-related spending. The amount of money spent by pet owners born after 1995 grew exponentially for three years in a row.

As young people are becoming increasingly health-conscious, they opt to spend more money on healthcare products. It is estimated that in 2021, young people are likely to spend 7.5 percent more on products that help them to maintain their health. In addition, young people are also interested in, and frequently buy beauty products and entertainment products.

案例分析

原新闻稿的标题采用两段式，包含两层意思，说明仅少量年轻人没有负债，进而提出年轻人的钱花到何处的思考。报道的结构层次分明，前四段对应标题的前半部分，后面的段落与标题第二层意思相关。报道开头第一段为总述，说明现在的年轻人是消费主力。编译稿的结构和内容安排与原新闻稿一致，第一段为总述，后面分两个部分分别对主题进行说明。编译稿的标题与原标题稍有不同，只包含原题的第一层意思。

编译以下汉语新闻稿，编译时考虑对外传播的五个基本要素。

马骏：中国绿色金融何以"弯道超车"？[1]

来源：中国日报网　2024-06-07　08:51

中国日报网6月7日电（记者周兰序、刘子峥、闫星周、马清）北京绿色金融与可持续发展研究院、中国金融学会绿色金融专业委员会主任马骏在接受中国日报专访时表示，中国的绿色贷款和绿色债券市场在几年时间内发展为全球规模最大的市场，意味着中国在绿色金融某些领域实现了"一无所有"（zero）向"全球最大"（hero）的弯道超车。

马骏表示，这一快速发展得益于"自上而下"推进方法，这为许多其他新兴经济体和发展中国家提供了有益的借鉴。展望未来，中国的绿色金融行业仍有巨大的发展潜力。钢铁、水泥和石化等难以减排的行业低碳转型需要大量金融支持，而在ESG（环境、社会和公司治理）产品方面中国仍有很大追赶发达经济体的空间。

与此同时，中国正在与欧盟和新加坡合作制定新版本的《共同分类目录》，这将使这项中欧双边绿色金融合作升级为多边项目，进一步促进国际绿色资本流动。简单来说，《共同分类目录》是中欧所共同认可的绿色经济活动清单，使得双方的借款人更容易在对方的资本市场上获得绿色融资。

---

[1] 新闻稿来源：http://cn.chinadaily.com.cn。

第七节　科技类新闻的编译

编译案例

◎ 新闻稿

越星河，携月壤，嫦娥六号逐梦归[1]

新华社北京6月25日电　2024年6月25日14时07分，嫦娥六号返回器准确着陆于内蒙古自治区四子王旗预定区域，工作正常，标志着探月工程嫦娥六号任务取得圆满成功，实现世界首次月球背面采样返回。

嫦娥六号任务自发射后历经53天、11个飞行阶段，突破了月球逆行轨道设计与控制、月背智能快速采样、月背起飞上升等关键技术，首次获取月背的月球样品，这是我国建设航天强国、科技强国取得的又一标志性成果。

模拟上千万条飞行路线，确保顺利"太空打水漂"式返回

在先后完成发射、落月、采样封装、月面起飞、月球轨道交会对接、上升器与轨道器和返回器组合体分离等环节后，嫦娥六号开始准备返回地球。

嫦娥六号回家之路怎么走？

6月25日13时20分许，北京航天飞行控制中心通过地面测控站向嫦娥六号轨道器和返回器组合体注入高精度导航参数。此后，轨道器与返回器在距南大西洋海平面高约5000公里处正常解锁分离，轨道器按计划完成轨道规避机动。

13时41分许，嫦娥六号返回器在距地面高度约120公里处，以接近第二宇宙速度高速在大约大西洋上空第一次进入地球大气层，实施初次气动减速。下降至预定高度后，返回器在大约印度洋上空向上跳出大气层，到达最高点后开始滑行下降。之后，返回器再次进入大气层，实施二次气动减速。这一过程俗称"太空打水漂"，标准术语为"半弹道跳跃式返回"。

为何要"太空打水漂"式返回？中国航天科技集团五院科研人员介绍，嫦娥六号返回器从月球飞向地球速度非常快，返回过程必须减速。这样设计，目的是利用数千公里大气层的阻力和与大气摩擦产生的热量快速消耗返回器的能量，使其再次穿出大气层时速度已经降到第一宇宙速度以下，不再具备环绕地球飞行的条件而第二次进入大气层。

科研人员介绍，"太空打水漂"依靠全数字全系数自适应预测校正制导技术。为

---

[1] 新闻稿来源：https://imgs.xinhuanet.com。

了验证该项技术，2014年，我国专门发射了月地高速再入返回飞行试验器并取得了圆满成功，这是该项技术的首秀。嫦娥五号任务是第二次采用该项技术，嫦娥六号月背自主采样返回任务的成功，再次验证了该项技术的强适应性、高精准度和高稳定性。

"太空打水漂"过程中，既要让返回器减速适中，还要在固定的位置穿出大气层，为实现这一目标，科研人员在制导导航和控制系统的研制过程中开展了大量模拟飞行试验，并模拟了上千万条飞行路线，确保过程的顺利和返回的高精度。

此外，嫦娥六号返回器在返回大气层时速度高达每秒7公里到11公里，因高速剧烈摩擦，返回器表面形成高温等离子气体层，并对电磁波造成屏蔽形成"黑障"，导致通信中断，返回器暂时失去联系。中国电子科技集团有限公司技术专家介绍，应对挑战，中国电科自主研制的多部测量雷达担负了返回区首点截获、"黑障"区连续跟踪等任务，精准"看"到返回器在太空中的飞行轨迹，助力返回器成功穿越"黑障"区。

穿上"贴心防热衣"，降落伞帮助完成两级减速

除了减速，嫦娥六号顺利回家还要克服高温的影响。

中国航天科技集团五院科研人员介绍，嫦娥六号返回器虽然个头小，但是由于再入大气层速度快，高温烧灼不可避免。为保证返回器既防热又抗烧蚀，嫦娥六号返回器充分借鉴了嫦娥五号返回任务的经验，根据不同部位耐烧灼和隔热的具体需求与指标，制备了一件量身定制的"贴心防热衣"，保障其安全顺利返回地球。

此外，嫦娥六号返回器金属壳体科技含量也很高。科研人员介绍，由于返回器结构小，各类舱体焊接类零件在与薄蒙皮进行焊接时，均为壁薄、弱刚度大悬空区域结构，控制不好会造成研制过程中应力变形，影响舱体焊接后的轮廓度。针对返回器球段法兰的焊接结构特点，研制团队设计了分体式法兰焊接工装，大幅提高了舱体球段法兰的焊缝质量和焊接变形控制的效果，最终满足苛刻的整器外形面轮廓度要求。

在降至距地面约20公里高度时，返回器转入开伞姿态。距地面约10公里高度时，嫦娥六号返回器打开降落伞，完成最后减速并保持姿态稳定，随后准确在预定区域平稳着陆。

为确保返回器安全着陆于预定地点，降落伞以两级减速的方式，绽放两次"红白伞花"。其中，第一级降落伞是一朵只有2平方米的"小花"，即减速伞，它负责"踩一脚刹车"，对返回器进行初级减速，并在踩完刹车后分离拉出主伞。第二级降落伞是一朵约为 50 平方米的"大花"，即主伞，负责把返回器速度由数百公里每小时降低到不超过 50 公里每小时。

科研人员介绍，除了降落伞，回收系统中回收控制器、压力高度控制器、弹射器等也不可或缺。

其中，回收控制器是回收系统的"大脑"，控制着每一个关键动作。在返回器距离地球数千公里时，它便"苏醒"进入预备状态。返回器进入大气层后，回收系统的另一位成员——压力高度控制器如"耳朵"一般，时刻聆听着外面的"风声"，通过"耳膜"感受压力，以计算出返回器所处的高度。当高度达到预定的距地面 10 公里附近时，它会发出一个信号给回收系统的"大脑"，"大脑"随即发出弹伞舱盖的点火命令。

择机交接月壤，后续开展样品储存、分析和研究相关工作

嫦娥六号返回器着陆后，负责搜索回收任务的发射场工作人员与回收系统技术人员，根据北京航天飞行控制中心通报的落点位置信息，规划行动路径，开展返回器搜索，及时发现目标，确认返回器状态正常，有序开展回收工作。

为实现返回舱落地后第一时间到现场，今年 5 月开始，嫦娥六号返回器搜索回收任务分队第一批参试力量便进驻四子王旗着陆场进行准备。地面分队组织了 10 多次雨天、暗夜和复杂地形驾驶训练，对着陆区域先后进行了 10 多次勘查，累计出车 50 余台次，行驶里程近 4 万公里，实现了着陆区一手资料全覆盖。

按计划，回收后的嫦娥六号返回器在完成必要的地面处理工作后，将空运至北京开舱，取出样品容器及搭载物。国家航天局将择机举行交接仪式，正式向地面应用系统移交月球样品，后续开展样品储存、分析和研究相关工作。

2020 年 12 月 17 日，嫦娥五号从月球带回 1731 克月壤样品，这是人类首次获得的月表年轻火山岩区样品，也是中国科学家第一次拥有属于自己的地外天体返回样品。截至目前，国家航天局已向国内 131 个研究团队发放 7 批次共 85.48 克科研样品，产出科技论文 100 多篇，取得了许多有价值的科研成果。比如，通过测定月壤样品形成年份，将月球火山活动结束时间推迟约 8 亿年，还发现了月球第六种新矿物"嫦娥石"等。

对嫦娥五号月壤的研究，推动了我国行星科学的发展，培养了行星科学研究的人才队伍，初步形成科学、技术、工程融合创新发展。"有了嫦娥五号月壤研究的积累，我们对嫦娥六号样品研究充满期待，也满怀信心。"中国科学院地质与地球物理研究所研究员贺怀宇说。

在圆满完成嫦娥六号任务后，鹊桥二号中继星将择机开展科学探测任务，其携带的极紫外相机、阵列中性原子成像仪和地月甚长基线干涉测量试验系统，将收集来自月球和深空的科学数据。

嫦娥六号"国际范儿"满满。本次任务搭载了欧空局月表负离子分析仪、法国氡气探测仪、意大利激光角反射器、巴基斯坦立方星等4个国际载荷，务实高效的国际合作受到国际社会广泛关注和好评。

"探索浩瀚宇宙是全人类的共同梦想，唯有开放合作才是正道。中国航天将坚持在平等互利、和平利用、包容发展的基础上，继续敞开胸怀、打开大门，不断拓宽国际合作渠道，组织实施好后续重大工程任务，为拓展人类认知、增进人类福祉而努力前行。"国家航天局局长张克俭表示。

编译稿

China's Chang'e-6 brings back first samples from moon's far side to Earth

Source: Xinhua Editor: huaxia 2024-06-25 14:30:30

BEIJING, June 25 (Xinhua)—The returner of the Chang'e-6 probe touched down on Earth on Tuesday, bringing back the world's first samples collected from the moon's far side.

The return capsule landed precisely in the designated area in Siziwang Banner, north China's Inner Mongolia Autonomous Region, and the mission is a complete success, according to the China National Space Administration (CNSA).

Chang'e-6 is one of the most complex and challenging missions in China's space exploration efforts to date. Consisting of an orbiter, a returner, a lander and an ascender, it was launched on May 3 this year, and has gone through various stages such as Earth-moon transfer, near-moon braking, lunar orbiting and separation of the lander-ascender combination and the orbiter-returner combination.

Supported by the Queqiao-2 relay satellite, the lander-ascender combination landed at the designated landing area in the South Pole-Aitken (SPA) Basin on the far side of the moon on June 2 and carried out sampling work.

On June 4, the ascender took off from the moon with samples and entered the lunar orbit. On June 6, it completed rendezvous and docking with the orbiter-returner combination and transferred samples to the returner. The ascender then separated from the combination and landed on the moon under ground control to avoid becoming space junk.

The orbiter-returner combination spent 13 days in lunar orbit, awaiting the right opportunity to return to Earth. After completing two moon-Earth transfer maneuvers and one orbital correction, the returner separated from the orbiter and delivered the samples to Earth.

"The Chang'e-6 mission represents a significant milestone in the history of human lunar exploration, and it will contribute to a more comprehensive understanding of lunar evolution," said Yang Wei, a researcher at the Institute of Geology and Geophysics of the Chinese Academy of Sciences.

"New samples will inevitably lead to new discoveries. Fascination with the moon is rooted in Chinese culture down the ages, as evidenced by the mythological narrative of Chang'e, a lady who journeyed to and resided on the moon. Now, Chinese scientists are eagerly anticipating the opportunity to contribute to lunar science," Yang added.

案例分析

原新闻稿的标题非常文艺，带有中国文字的浪漫色彩。正文结构明晰，前两段为导语，包含了核心新闻事实，导语之后通过三个小标题，说明了此次月背采样任务在轨道设计、月背采样、月背起飞、返回降落等关键技术的突破以及月壤储存和研究方面的内容，结构清晰、层次分明。编译稿的标题比较平实，客观陈述新闻事实。报道采用了典型的英语新闻报道的结构，前两段为导语，说明核心新闻事实，后面的段落分别说明了此次任务面临的挑战、在技术上的突破、整个任务的几个关键节点以及任务的意义。总体来说，编译稿更加简洁，这也符合英语新闻稿的写作习惯。

编译以下汉语新闻稿，编译时考虑对外传播的五个基本要素。

浙江大学首次实现汉字书写脑机接口 "意念写字"成现实[1]

2024年04月23日 22:20 来源：中国新闻网

中新网杭州4月23日电（郭天奇）23日，浙江大学脑机接口团队的最新研究成果在浙江大学医学院附属第二医院（下称浙大二院）发布。据悉，其最新研究首次实现汉字书写脑机接口，成功实现了侵入式脑机接口控制机械臂书写汉字，科幻电影中才能见到的"意念写字"照进了现实。

---

1 新闻稿来源：http://www.chinanews.com.cn。

浙江大学脑机接口团队自2006年起就开展脑机接口前沿交叉研究，2012年完成国内首例猴子大脑运动皮层植入电极解码勾、抓、捏、握等精确手势；2014年完成国内首例临床病人颅内植入电极、成功解码石头剪刀布等动作；2020年实现国内首例、国际高龄首次临床志愿者侵入式脑控机械手完成喝水、进食、握手等动作。

目前，该团队最新的研究主要集中在脑控汉字书写，依靠这一技术，患者只需想象正常的书写过程，该过程就可以被运动区的神经元活动反映出来，通过对运动区神经信号的解析，可以获得其所想象的书写轨迹，并控制机械臂进行书写。

发布现场，研究团队依靠前期在患者张大伯使用过程中提取的脑电信号，操控机械臂流畅地写下"浙江大学""脑机接口"。

"部分中风、渐冻症的患者失去书写功能，也不能说话，但通过提取脑电信号，控制外部的机械设备，写出他想要的字，就可以实现与外界沟通联系，这就是一个主要的突破。"浙江大学脑机调控临床转化研究中心神经疾病分中心主任、浙大二院神经外科主任张建民说。

实际上，脑控汉字书写在实践研究过程中遇到诸多难点。首先，传统脑机接口中对于机械臂伸抓的控制原理是大关节运动的解析，而汉字书写的过程是一种精细运动。此外，与英文相比，汉字是象形字，有复杂结构，同时笔画更多、分类更难、字数更多，解码难度也就更高。

"我们都知道汉字的书写在偏旁、部首、笔顺等方面有很多讲究，甚至笔画长一点或是短一点，也有可能完全是两个字，而且国外也不会有团队研究汉字，我们没有参照，所以此次对于汉字的成功解码是非常重要的一环，也是脑机接口研究的一个非常关键的突破。"张建民说。

目前，浙江大学脑机接口团队突破了汉字书写的特殊编码机制，在此基础上发展了汉字书写轨迹解码新技术，在离线状态下100个常用汉字的分类正确率达到了91.3%，在语言模型辅助下，在线正确率可提高至96.2%。

如今，侵入式脑机接口控制机械臂书写汉字已经实现，脑机接口的发展也取得了新的突破，未来，如何让该技术更好地服务于患者的日常生活，还需要研究来进一步优化。

"脑机接口未来的路还很长，当其硬件变得更小、创伤更小，并且实现'无线'的时候，我们就可以对部分截瘫患者、渐冻患者进行植入，让他们完成以前不能执行的功能，例如可以控制外骨骼行走，或是控制机械臂协助日常的生活。"浙大二院神经外科副主任、功能神经外科组组长朱君明说。（完）

第八节　教育类新闻的编译

编译案例

◎新闻稿

南京大学将开通全国高校首家 AI 课程　面向 3700 名新生[1]

CNMO 手机中国　2024-02-27　15:17

【CNMO 科技消息】2月27日，CNMO 注意到，南京大学宣布推出全国高校首家针对 3700 余名新生的"1+X+Y"三层次人工智能通识核心课总体方案。这一创新性的课程体系旨在为学生提供全面而深入的人工智能教育，从基础知识到前沿应用，实现跨学科融合学习。

该方案的核心组成部分包括一门必修的人工智能通识核心课，这门课程将从 2024 年起面向全体本科新生开设。此外，还有 X 门人工智能素养课，这些课程旨在培养学生的基本素养和综合能力，帮助他们更好地理解和应用人工智能技术。最后，Y 门与各学科深度融合的人工智能前沿拓展课，将为学生提供与各个学科领域相结合的前沿知识和实践机会。

南京大学此举旨在通过这一独特的课程体系，为学生提供更加系统、全面的人工智能教育，培养具备跨学科知识和实践能力的优秀人才。这一方案不仅有助于提升学生对人工智能技术的理解和应用能力，也将为他们在未来的职业生涯中打下坚实的基础。

目前，人工智能技术正在飞速发展，并且逐渐渗透进智能手机、个人电脑、电动汽车、短视频等多个领域。有调研机构指出，2024 年将是 AI PC 元年，人工智能将帮助 PC 行业走出低谷。同时，预计 2024 年 AI 手机出货量将达 6000 万部，2027 年达 6 亿部。

◎编译稿

Nanjing University pioneers AI education system

By CANG WEI in Nanjing | China Daily | Updated: 2024-03-20 09:22

Nanjing University in Jiangsu province is breaking new ground in Chinese higher

---

[1] 新闻稿来源：https://baijiahao.baidu.com。

education as it prepares to roll out a pioneering "core curriculum system in artificial intelligence literacy" for incoming students this September.

The initiative aims to foster highly adaptable talent, marking a significant first among universities in China. More than 3,700 new students will have access to this AI literacy program, which follows a "1+X+Y" framework.

The framework includes a mandatory core AI literacy course (1), additional AI literacy courses (X), and interdisciplinary courses (Y) that integrate various fields with artificial intelligence. The educational approach will encompass knowledge, skills, values and ethics.

Students who meet certain conditions can obtain a certificate for studying artificial intelligence alongside their majors.

Wang Jun, executive vice-dean of Nanjing University's undergraduate school, said that after conducting comprehensive research and consultation with experts, teachers and students from diverse fields since the latter half of 2023, the university is moving forward with the development of a general education curriculum in AI.

"We believe that promoting general education in artificial intelligence is both timely and urgent," he said, adding that the university has established interdisciplinary teaching and research efforts to address the content, scope, course design and teaching methods for the framework.

Tan Tieniu, a member of the Chinese Academy of Sciences and the Party chief of Nanjing University, emphasized the challenges of providing comprehensive education in AI for students from diverse academic backgrounds.

"We have constructed a curriculum system that balances unity and diversity," he said. "While meeting the basic requirements of core literacy, we also take into account the personalized needs of different students, gradually enhancing their literacy and skills to better adapt to the development of the AI era," he said.

He noted that Nanjing University is encouraging the development of advanced practical courses to support students in applying AI technology for interdisciplinary exploration, ultimately nurturing highly skilled and adaptable talent.

"Artificial intelligence is increasingly becoming an essential and integral part of people's lives and work," Tan said. "As AI rapidly advances, public perceptions have diversified, leading to a sense of cognitive confusion and anxiety. This has sparked an urgent need for the incorporation of general education in AI. In the age of intelligence, every college student should possess fundamental AI literacy."

Tan added that the core general education curriculum system has garnered widespread praise, prompting several universities to inquire about related training programs. Undergraduate students in their second and third years at Nanjing University have also expressed strong interest in studying AI.

The university will collaborate with enterprises to provide students with opportunities to engage in cutting-edge scientific research projects, participate in practical application scenarios, and develop innovative capabilities to address complex challenges across various disciplines in the future intelligent era.

In 2018, Nanjing University took the lead in establishing the School of Artificial Intelligence and released the "Talent Training Program for AI", creating the first comprehensive undergraduate professional AI education system in China.

In 2022, the university expanded its efforts by establishing the Intelligent Science and Technology School and the Intelligent Software and Engineering School at its Suzhou campus with the goal of nurturing skilled professionals to meet the needs of emerging industries.

The university has also initiated interdisciplinary programs such as "AI for Science" and "AI for HASS" (Humanities, Arts and Social Sciences), offering over 50 specialized courses that apply AI technology across various fields.

案例分析

原新闻稿由四个段落组成，第一段是导语，说明开设 AI 课程的计划和宗旨。后面三段是正文，分别介绍了开课的相关信息、开课的目的和开课的背景。编译稿在结构上与原稿一致，前两段为导语，点明新闻主题，后面部分为正文，介绍与开课相关的信息。与原稿不同的是，编译稿提供了更多的细节，正文中还引用了学校相关部门负责人的话，采用直接引语或间接引语的方式，增加了新闻的真实性和对信息解读的权威性，可以帮助目标读者更好地了解课程相关情况、理解课程设置的意图。这个例子也说明，对外报道中的新闻编译有时更像是相对独立的对外新闻写作，根据需要可以增加和补充相关信息，以取得更好的传播效果。

编译以下汉语新闻稿，编译时考虑对外传播的五个基本要素。

教育部部署各地各高校集中开展大规模校园招聘活动[1]

2024-05-27　来源：教育部

为推动高校与重点领域企业开展人才供需对接，助力高校毕业生高质量充分就业，2024届高校毕业生就业促进周系列活动期间，教育部部署各地各高校集中开展大规模校园招聘活动，帮助一批有就业意愿但尚未落实就业去向的毕业生实现就业，加力加速推进高校毕业生就业工作。

5月28日，教育部、工业和信息化部将在北京交通大学联合举办"优企进校 招才引智"专场招聘活动，共有122家专精特新中小企业和重点领域用人单位参加招聘会，涉及信息技术、金融、制造、建筑、医药、交通运输等多个行业，提供岗位400余个，招聘需求近3000人。活动现场将同步开展校企供需对接，提供就业政策宣讲、AI模拟面试、简历门诊、法律咨询等"一站式"服务。

同时，各地各高校将集中组织开展行业性、区域性、联盟性的大规模招聘活动，共同汇聚就业资源，为毕业生提供更多岗位信息。预计将组织开展校园招聘会175场，参会企业近1.7万家。

第九节　体育类新闻的编译

编译案例

◎新闻稿

中国"快递小哥"跑进巴黎奥运会[2]

参考消息 2024-06-29　11:27

新华社6月29日报道，距离2024年巴黎奥运会还有近一个月的时间。许多运动员已经获得了参加这场重大赛事的资格，并准备在巴黎全力以赴。其中有一位非常特殊的参赛者：栾玉帅。这位中国的"快递小哥"赢得了参加巴黎奥运会大众组马拉松赛的资格。

1　新闻稿来源：http://www.moe.gov.cn。
2　新闻稿来源：https://baijiahao.baidu.com。

报道称，栾玉帅是京东物流公司的一名送货员，现年39岁，他将与世界上最好的马拉松选手同场竞技。他每天都在为比赛作准备。在中国首都，他被称为"跑得最快的快递员"。在2021年的北京半程马拉松比赛中，栾玉帅取得了1小时10分31秒的优异成绩，如今他希望能在此基础上更上一层楼。

为了达到国际田联的选拔要求，栾玉帅已经作了最充分的准备。根据规定，报名选手需要绑定运动软件，在2023年底之前通过徒步、跑步、骑车、游泳、滑雪等运动完成10万积分。

编译稿

Chinese delivery man to chase Olympic dream

China Daily, June 24, 2024

A Chinese delivery man will race on the route of his dreams, but not on a mission of sending packages.

Luan Yushuai, known virtually as China's fastest delivery man working for JD Delivery, was picked as one of the amateur runners to race at Paris Olympics' marathon event in August, when amateur competitors will be for the first time invited to run with processional runners on the Olympic stage.

The chance was not won only by luck. Luan, 39 and a nine-year delivery employee, is an old hand runner who managed to collect the requited points by the organizers from his daily exercises before the Paris marathon lottery.

He finished his debut 42.195 kilometers at the 2017 Beijing Marathon and won the amateur group at the 2021 Beijing Half Marathon race. His personal full marathon best is 2 hours, 25 minutes and 55 seconds.

Luan practices his running skills through his daily routines—skipping elevators and using stairs with weight bags on his legs when delivering even heavy packages. In the preparation for the Olympics, he is keeping a distance of 300–400 kilometers worth of exercise monthly.

National May 1st Labor Medal winner of 2023 and torch bearer of the 2022 Beijing Winter Olympics, Luan believes that one may distinguish himself in any trade. He tops in delivery outputs among his near counterparts, managing to deliver as many as 600 packages daily during a "double eleven" online shopping peak. One of his frequent customers was amazed by Luan's speed: He could manage to finish the delivery between ringing at the ground entrance guard to the receiver's appearance at the door on the third level.

A total of 40,048 lucky amateur runners out of 800,000 global applicants will race on the Paris Olympics route on August 10.

案例分析

原新闻稿的标题很亮眼，"跑"字一语双关，使"快递小哥"与奥运产生联系，制造了悬念，能够引起读者兴趣。正文由三个段落组成，第一段是导语，直接点题，后面两段主要介绍了新闻报道的主角以及他为奥运所作的准备。编译稿的标题处理方式与原文稍有不同，却有异曲同工的效果。正文包含较多段落，第一段为导语，简单说明主题，但留下了很大的悬念。导语之后，报道以叙述故事的方式按照时间顺序逐渐展开，将更多细节呈现给目标读者，充满趣味性和可读性。

编译以下汉语新闻稿，编译时考虑对外传播的五个基本要素。

（巴黎残奥会）第17届夏季残奥会在巴黎开幕[1]

北青网　2024-08-29　14:35

中新社巴黎8月29日电　当地时间28日晚，第17届夏季残疾人奥林匹克运动会开幕式在巴黎举行，法国总统马克龙宣布巴黎残奥会正式开幕。

巴黎残奥会共设22个大项，549个小项，共有来自逾160个国家和地区的约4400名运动员参赛。中国体育代表团的284名运动员将参加19个大项、302个小项的角逐，其中126名男运动员，158名女运动员，这是中国体育代表团第11次参加夏季残奥会。

巴黎残奥会开幕式于当地时间28日晚8时开始，各代表团成员从巴黎著名的香榭丽舍大街出发，抵达开幕式的主会场巴黎协和广场。这是残奥会历史上首个离开传统体育场馆的开幕式。

身穿红色上衣、手持五星红旗的中国体育代表团在两名旗手——女子轮椅击剑运动员辜海燕和男子举重运动员齐勇凯的引导下入场，亮丽的"中国红"在协和广场的灯光和晚霞辉映下分外耀眼。

1　新闻稿来源：https://baijiahao.baidu.com。

巴黎奥组委主席托尼·埃斯坦盖在致辞中称,残奥会就是让世界变得更美好的力量,"不仅感动我们,更能改变我们"。

国际残奥委会主席安德鲁·帕森斯表示,残奥运动员的韧性和决心将给人们带来力量,"他们的团结精神将激励我们"。

在火炬传递环节,法国奥运代表团开幕式旗手马诺杜手持火炬进场,将火炬传递给残奥选手,象征着巴黎奥运会和残奥会的完美交接。

随后,作为巴黎奥运会主火炬塔的热气球再次出现,5名火炬手一起点燃了巴黎残奥会的主火炬。

巴黎残奥会的比赛将于当地时间8月29日至9月8日进行,赛会首金将于当地时间29日下午在自行车赛场产生。

参考文献

白润生，1998. 中国新闻通史纲要 [M]. 北京：新华出版社.

程维，2013."再叙事"视阈下的英汉新闻编译 [J]. 中国翻译, (5): 100–103.

郭影平，2017. 新闻英语阅读与翻译 [M]. 上海：上海交通大学出版社.

刘其中，2009. 汉英新闻编译 [M]. 北京：清华大学出版社.

刘其中，2009. 英汉新闻翻译 [M]. 北京：清华大学出版社.

尚京华，李新宇，2016. 国际新闻编译 [M]. 北京：中国传媒大学出版社.

许明武，2003. 新闻英语与翻译 [M]. 北京：中国对外翻译出版公司.

张健，2016. 新闻英语文体与范文评析 [M]. 上海：上海外语教育出版社.